MARY STEWART VAN LEEUWEN

GENDER & GRACE

LOVE,
WORK &
PARENTING
in a Changing
World

INTERVARSITY PRESS
DOWNERS GROVE, ILLINOIS 60515

InterVarsity Press is the book-publishing division of InterVarsity Christian Fellowship, a student movement active on campus at hundreds of universities, colleges and schools of nursing in the United States of America, and a member movement of the International Fellowship of Evangelical Students. For information about local and regional activities, write Public Relations Dept., InterVarsity Christian Fellowship, 6400 Schroeder Rd., P.O. Box 7895, Madison, WI 53707-7895.

Distributed in Canada through InterVarsity Press, 860 Denison St., Unit 3, Markham, Ontario L3R 4H1, Canada.

The Scripture quotations contained herein are from the Revised Standard Version of the Bible copyrighted 1946, 1952, 1971 by the Division of Christian Education of the National Council of the Churches of Christ in the U.S.A. and are used by permission. All rights reserved.

Illustrations: Jerry Tiritilli

ISBN 0-8308-1297-0

Printed in the United States of America ∞

Library of Congress Cataloging-in-Publication Data

Van Leeuwen, Mary Stewart, 1943-
    Gender and grace: Love, work, and parenting in a changing world/
Mary Stewart Van Leeuwen.
       p.   cm.
    Includes bibliographical references.
    ISBN 0-8308-1297-0
    1. Sex role—Religious aspects—Christianity.   2. Parenting-
-Religious aspects—Christianity.   I. Title.
BT708.V35 1990
261.8'343—dc20

89-49770
CIP

16	15	14	13	12	11	10	9	8	7	6	5	4	3	2
99	98	97	96	95	94	93	92	91	90					

To
Dirk and Neil Van Leeuwen
and to their cousins
Christena, Edward and Sarah Stewart

Thanks for the memories—especially the ones
that found their way into this book.

Preface

The idea behind this book has a rather long history, both in my own mind and that of the book's editors. It began in the mid-1970s, at a time when "Christian feminism" was regarded as a contradiction in terms by many Christians as well as by most feminists. Nevertheless, despite such pronouncements many women and not a few men who considered themselves biblical Christians also began to identify themselves as biblical feminists. At the same time, some people who had found a real but limited vision of hope in the neo-feminism of the late sixties went on to find a more comprehensive one in the call of Jesus Christ. As a newly hatched assistant professor of psychology, I was one of those people.

Because I was familiar with the growing literature on sex and gender I was asked by Jim Sire, then the editor of InterVarsity Press, to consider writing a book from the perspective of a Christian social scientist on the changing roles of women. I duly submitted an outline and a contract was drawn up. Upon reflection however, I realized that to do justice to the project I needed some time to become more theologically literate, both in general biblical theology and, more specifically, in terms of the biblical meaning of personhood, gender and community. My editors were most kind in releasing me from the contract to pursue those studies—although I doubt if they realized it would be almost fifteen years before their book finally saw the light of day!

Nevertheless, both they and I feel that the wait has been worthwhile. Many attempts to come to theological grips with the feminist movement have ended up making only slight adjustments to traditional, male-centered ways of thinking—what one critic has called the "add women and stir" approach. Others have taken secular feminism as their implicit starting point and filtered it through a less than completely biblical world-view—for example, one which may lean heavily on the goodness of creation but places too little emphasis on human fallenness and the need for personal redemption in women and men alike. To do justice to the legitimate criticisms of feminists and to the burgeoning literature in gender studies, while at the same time subjecting both feminism and received theology to a fresh reading of Scripture is not an easy task. I hope that I have succeeded in making at least a modest contribution to that goal.

In aiming for that goal I have benefitted from two sources of help which would have been absent had I written the book when originally planned. First of all, the literature which has accumulated in gender studies over the past fifteen years is both enormous and increasingly sophisticated. My own college library's collection has gained more than 2,000 titles in gender studies over the past four years alone. Furthermore, what began in the 1970s as "women's studies" has slowly branched out to become women's and men's studies. It used to be a feminist truism that all disciplines were concerned with men's studies—for example, with "history" rather than "herstory"—and that was why women's studies were so desperately needed to balance the account. Now we realize that so-called androcentric scholarship has short-changed men as well. It has concentrated on the public activities of elite, powerful males, effectively ignoring all other groups as well as life in the semi-public and private realms. A visiting Martian anthropologist doing research in our earthly libraries would hardly guess that human males did other things besides wage wars, draft treaties, or make advances in art, business, science and technology.

That they also played, worshiped, married, parented, joined service clubs or had identity crises has hardly been acknowledged outside of the writings of novelists and playwrights. It is the goal of the best gender-studies scholars—and this book as well—to fill in some of these gaps, in addition to those which bear on women's lives.

My second source of help has been the riches of the Reformed theological and intellectual tradition, particularly in its neo-Calvinist expression. Its refusal to see some parts of life as sacred and others as secular (and therefore less worthy of Christian inquiry) has provided a base for my attempt to look at gender in terms of a fresh biblical perspective. A further dualism which Calvinism rejects is one which sees the body as less valuable or "spiritual" than the mind or the soul. Its thoroughly incarnational view of Christ and of those Christ came to save, and its conviction that we will be resurrected as glorified *bodies* is what lies behind my careful but qualified attention to the biology of male and female in this volume. Finally, Calvinism's commitment to the principle *semper reformanda* ("always reforming") has allowed me to take a critical look at what Christians thought was a correct reading of gender, in keeping with the Calvinist conviction that human sin and finitude require us always to be re-evaluating our own limited readings of Scripture. The fact that Calvinist scholars have done so little work on gender issues (other than mostly to shore up the status quo in gender roles and relations) shows that these worthy principles are sometimes honored more in the breach than in the observance. And that inconsistency was in part what motivated the writing of this book in the first place!

Having said all this, I also need to say that although this book is an interdisciplinary examination of gender—combining psychology with some theology, history, biology and sociology—it remains in the end primarily the book of a trained psychologist who is at best an amateur in other disciplines. If I seem to have gone beyond my theological, historical or sociological depth in some places (or, conversely, if I have remained too narrowly psychological in others), I hope that readers will forgive me and perhaps be motivated to produce other books and articles on gender from their own disciplinary and Christian perspectives. Certainly the church at large can use as many fresh insights as possible on this important and controversial topic.

In addition, although I am aware that the topic of gender intersects with topics such as race, class and ethnicity, it was not possible for me to consider these topics more than fleetingly in a book of this length. Also, despite having had more than an average amount of cross-cultural experience (some of which I share in the book), I am painfully aware of the limitations of my perspective as a white, middle-class professional woman blessed with a stable marriage and two apparently normal children. I hope that my identity and activity as a Christian has chastened me somewhat, for the body of Christ cuts across race, class and ethnic divisions, and it would be an irresponsible Christian who did not listen to her sisters and brothers in other parts of the church universal. Still, I am in my daily life a professor at a Christian liberal arts college in a medium-sized, conservative midwestern city, and this is bound to limit my vision in some ways. So again, when readers experience these limits I hope that some will be encouraged to add their voices and expertise to the conversation.

Finally, some acknowledgments. As readers will discover, my husband, my two sons and various other family members have been the source of case studies as well as constant encouragement. Students in my psychology of women courses in places as far apart as Michigan, Vancouver and Toronto have given me valuable feedback as they have read parts of the manuscript in progress. Colleagues at Calvin College, particularly those in the philosophy department, have offered constructive criticisms of various chapter drafts, forcing me to clarify my arguments and often my style. My fellow researchers at the Calvin Center for Christian Scholarship on the 1989-1990 "gender roles" team took the time to read and comment in writing on the entire manuscript, submitting analyses of such detail that I'm sure my editors had second thoughts about recruiting them as evaluators in the first place. And as I have tried out various chapters on the lecture circuit, I have received much appreciated feedback from fellow Christians of both sexes and of many backgrounds and levels of education. In particular I want to thank members of the Christian Reformed

Church of Brandon, Manitoba, for their hospitality during the year 1987-1988. When my husband was their interim pastor, I took advantage of a leave of absence to complete much of this manuscript while lodged in their parsonage.

Any errors and overstatements that remain are certainly my own responsibility. I hope, in spite of them, that the book will be a helpful addition to the ongoing dialog on gender and perhaps a guide to personal change in the lives of some of its readers.

Grand Rapids, Michigan
Thanksgiving 1989

PART 1

Understanding the Issues

1 Why Read This Book?

My husband and I are the parents of two boys, ages eight and ten. Not surprisingly, we sometimes have to deal with sibling rivalry between these two who are so close in age. When I recently had to stop a fight, I tried to distract the antagonists by wondering aloud if I'd have less trouble if I traded them in for a couple of girls. The ploy worked; it distracted them from their fight. But my younger son's reactions also initiated a new set of hostilities.

"Oh, no. You don't want girls!" he announced with loud indignation. "They're tattletales! They're always going to the teacher and saying, 'Blab-blab-blab! He did this! He did that!' " My son raised his voice half an octave, enhancing the effect so convincingly that I knew this must be the voice of recent experience speaking.

"Besides," he continued, "most of them only want to play with wimpy toys like Barbie dolls!" I countered his second point by saying that his father and I had no more use for Barbie dolls than we had for toy guns and would hesitate to buy either for any child we happened to be rearing. As for girls being tattletales, I said, putting on my best professional psychologist's demeanor, he had to remember that most girls couldn't fight physically as well as boys could, so it made sense for them to defend themselves with words.

A Complex Issue

This particular round in the battle between the sexes ended in a draw; my son grudgingly held his peace and went off to some other activity. But it serves to introduce the terms and issues surrounding this book. My son had noted (and passed judgment on) a different pattern of behavior between boys and girls. I, while refusing to take sides on the issue, had not denied the general accuracy of his observations. Neither of us went on to discuss the deeper and more vexing question: namely, if differences in behavior and temperament do seem to separate boys from girls, where do they originate? Are they rooted in biology? In childrearing practices? In a mixture of the two? Or in something else instead or as well?

If our answer is some combination of nature and nurture, or biology and culture, we have merely multiplied our difficulties. For when we consider the apparent differences between males and females, how are we to determine just how much is contributed by nature and how much by nurture? How, indeed, could we even separate out the contributions of each? Princeton psychologist Leon Kamin has captured this dilemma in the context of a different but related question— that of the relative contributions of heredity and environment to children's I.Q. scores. Kamin writes:

It's certainly true that I.Q. scores tend to run in families. But this by itself does not tell us that I.Q. test performance is genetically determined. Parents who read books tend to have children who read books. Parents who are athletic tend to have children who are athletic. Parents who eat bagels and lox tend to produce children who eat bagels and lox. The point is, that since we pass our *environments* on to our children along with our *genes*, there is no way of saying for sure which of these factors is producing a certain behavior in a certain child, or by how much it outweighs the other factor.[1]

Kamin is right when he says that there is no sure way of weighing the contributions of genes versus learning to the differences we observe between groups of people—certainly not in a way that could apply to all persons in all times and places. To use the standard social scientific jargon, these two factors are almost totally "confounded," or mixed together, in all cultural and racial groups, as well as in both sexes. There are indirect ways of trying to sort out nature and nurture as they concern sex differences, some of which we will discuss later in this book. But the use of such methods still produces results which are almost always capable of more than one interpretation.[2]

But the fact that there is no sure way of separating the contributions of nature and nurture has not stopped the social scientific community from developing conceptual labels for each. It is common in social scientific writing to use the term *sex* when conjecturing about purely biological contributions to male or female behavior: for example, contributions that seem to be made by genes, hormones or brain anatomy. And it is common to use the term *gender* or *gender roles* when talking about what seem more clearly to be learned, or socialized, differences. Among men and women such differences can run the gamut from who wears jewelry to who builds houses, who passes on the family name or who initiates a sexual relationship. These are some of the many behaviors that show a great deal of crosscultural variability with regard to whether they are the domain of men or women, of both, or in some instances, of neither.

In keeping with the above terminology, this book will use the terms *gender* or *gender roles* when talking about what might be learned differences in behavior between males and females, and the terms *sex* or *biological sex* when referring to what seem to be biological givens. But the question as to how much nature or nurture contributes to differences between girls and boys, men and women, is not the only one that thoughtful people ask. In fact, most people are preoccupied with questions that are much less abstract and more personal.

Complicated Questions: Identity and Marriage

One such question has to do with personal identity. People often ask, "What is it that makes me 'normal' or 'adequate' as a male or female?" Usually an answer based on obvious anatomical differences does not satisfy. We want to know whether certain behaviors, thoughts and feelings are part of the normative package, and if so whether we ourselves are behaving, thinking and feeling according to the standard. Or we may ask how far we can stray outside those limits without jeopardizing our status as "true" women or men.

Pinning down an answer to the identity question is made even harder by the fact that the boundary between acceptable female and male behavior is constantly shifting. When typewriters were first invented, they were considered much too complicated for women to operate. Until recently, it was deemed inappropriate for men to be present at the birth of their children. When I was a child, any girl who came to school in slacks or jeans instead of a skirt (no matter what the weather) was promptly sent home to change. And any boy who wanted to take home economics instead of woodworking was considered a prime candidate for whatever rudimentary psychological counseling was available in the school systems of the day. The list could go on and on. Even in our own culture (let alone on a universal basis) defining what is "appropriate" behavior for girls and boys, men and women, is like trying to catch a goldfish with your bare hands—just when you think you've captured it, it swims away from you again.

A second issue that exercises thoughtful people concerns the dynamics of marriage. In Western society people are educated together according to a curriculum that demands basically the same performance from everyone. Each young person (at least in theory) is being prepared to assume the role of literate, self-supporting, well-informed, adult citizen. How much, if at all, should this change when a woman and a man marry? Here too we find that standards can be very changeable.

For example, my own mother trained as an elementary-school teacher at a time when getting married meant that she automatically gave up her job—not just in response to unwritten social custom, but also to standard school-board policy in the city where I was raised. By the time I began school, things had loosened up. It was possible to have a woman teacher who was married, but not one who had started a family. Even being visibly pregnant while teaching was considered inappropriate until sometime around the mid-1950s. At about the same time, however, because the postwar baby boom had created a teacher shortage, my mother's training was hastily updated, and she was welcomed back into the classroom even though she was still very much married, and her youngest child was only eight years old. Now, a generation later, things have changed so much that my younger son can be in a Christian school classroom whose teaching duties are split between two married women, each of whom has young children, and one of whom recently took off only six months to have a third child before returning to her teaching job!

Similar changes have occurred regarding what is acceptable behavior for fathers and husbands. A generation ago, it was unusual to see a grown man pushing a baby carriage. Today one sees young fathers carrying infants in an assortment of body slings and backpacks as if it were the most normal of masculine activities. A generation ago most middle-class men felt somehow emasculated if their wives entered the paid labor force. Today, it is not unusual for wives who *prefer* to stay home to complain that it is their husbands who are pressuring them to enter or stay in the paid work force in order to increase the family income!

These are only a few examples of the shifting social standards for gender role behavior. Christians in particular may wonder how exclusively they should appeal to the Bible for answers to their questions about gender roles, or how much they should appeal to the findings of the biological and social sciences They are especially confused when pastors and theologians equally committed to the authority of Scripture disagree with each other as to what certain passages really mean, or when social scientists present conflicting answers, each supposedly the fruit of objective research. Part of the purpose of this book, particularly its first three chapters, is to provide guidelines for interpreting both kinds of authority: that of science (which is a legitimate part of God's general revelation to humankind) and that of Scripture (which is God's special revelation).

More Complicated Questions: Parenting and Equality

A third area that raises questions about sex and gender is that of parenting. If we find it difficult to pin down what it means to be a woman or man ourselves, how much more complicated it becomes when we take on the task of turning children into adult men and women who are secure in their own gender identities. Here too both the church and the social sciences seem to be giving us mixed messages. I know of one communally organized Christian group where men are discouraged from changing their children's diapers for fear that their sons, observing them doing "women's work," will grow up with an insecure sense of their own manhood. But there are other Christians—many of them well-trained exegetes of Scripture—who insist that, read correctly, the Bible supports not only the equal value of men and women but also the virtual interchangeability of gender roles. We will meet people on both sides of this debate throughout this book and try to weigh the claims of each.

Among psychologists there are some who still side with Freud in maintaining that the dynamics of masculine and feminine identity formation are very different and that any interference with the "normal" course of either will breed pathology in adulthood. There are others, however, who claim that people who identify very strongly with the stereotypes of their own sex are less healthy than those whose personality profiles combine both typically masculine and typically feminine elements. Debates such as these—about gender identity formation and the kind of parenting that facilitates it—will constitute a large portion of this book's third section in chapters seven to nine.

Finally, there is for many people the most sensitive issue of all: the question of equality (or perhaps, more accurately, *justice*) between the sexes and what that means. "A feminist," actor Alan Alda once remarked, "is anyone who believes that women are people." All well and good; by this criterion, every Christian is (or ought to be) a convinced feminist. Yet Christians find themselves disagreeing about just what is implied for family, church and societal life by the truism that "women are people." Many Christians, especially women, feel that if the Bible gives husbands a nonreciprocal authority over their wives or forbids women to hold certain offices in the church, any accompanying talk about "spiritual equality" or "equality in Christ" is at best meaningless, at worst hypocritical. At the same time many social scientists, particularly if they are women, assert that whenever "differences" are postulated between women and men, they almost always turn out to be "deficits" on the part of women. Therefore they believe that differences of any sort should never be acknowledged, let alone studied in any depth.

Others, both Christian and non-Christian, feel quite differently. In America, one of the oddest alliances of recent times is one that has taken place between Phyllis Schlafly, whose Eagle Forum movement opposes the Equal Rights Amendment, and certain prominent feminists who have begun to assert that the minimization of sex differences, however well-intentioned, leads in practice to *less* justice for women. While rejecting Schlafly's conservatism in politics and religion, these feminists agree with her that to be on truly equal terms with men women need not just *equal* but also *preferential* treatment in some areas of their lives.[3] Both agree that the ERA, in its presently proposed form, would actually make women more vulnerable. They believe it would strip away any and all state laws aimed at providing a "safety net" for non-wage-earning wives, new mothers, divorced women and women in the armed services. At the same time, it would add nothing by way of protection from job discrimination that is not already covered by other legislation. Economist Sylvia Hewlitt concludes that if the price of equality is the insistence that women become "clones of men," then it is a dubious equality indeed.[4] Questions about social justice and gender roles are particularly relevant to the waged workplace, and will concern us especially in chapter ten, but also at various other points in the book as well.

No Easy Answers

Can a Christian psychologist, in a book such as this, provide final answers to volatile questions about sex and gender in the areas just mentioned: identity, marriage, parenting and justice between the sexes? Hardly. Considering that these issues have been matters of debate not just for decades, but centuries, and not just among scientists, but among philosophers, theologians and legal scholars as well, they will not be quickly resolved. Moreover, there is a growing recognition among psychologists that theirs is a more profoundly historical enterprise than they once thought. That is, the so-called laws of human behavior that psychologists strive to articulate often turn out to apply only to certain kinds of people at certain points in time.[5]

For example, the social psychological experiments that showed most people to be meek conformists in the 1950s, when repeated detail for detail in the 1970s, were hard pressed to find any "conformers" at all. Similarly, studies that regularly found women to be more easily influenced than men in the fifties and sixties now rarely find them different from men in this regard.[6] Social scientists, like all other scientists, must generalize only tentatively, for it is a difficult business separating out what is constant from what is historically changeable, and doubly difficult to pin down the origin of even those male/female differences that appear, on the average, to be fairly constant.

Because this is the case, I believe that having a Christian world view, shaped and informed by the Bible, can be of great help in sifting and judging the large body of literature on sex and gender. For although the Bible is not a detailed psychology text, it does set forth some basic claims about the nature of women and men. These claims have to do with their ultimate origins, their importance to God, the roots of their inability to be at peace in the world and with each other and the source and scope of their potential healing. It is true that Christians who share an equally high view of scriptural authority often differ about the finer details of this "biblical drama," especially those parts that speak of men and women in their relationship to God and each other. This should not really surprise us. The sin and finitude that are common to all make it impossible for us to read the Bible entirely as it should be read. We must be content, on some issues, to see through a glass darkly and strive to be charitable toward those with whom we disagree.

Nevertheless, in the following chapter I will try to construct a theoretical framework about sex and gender based on the biblical drama of creation, fall, redemption and renewal. That framework in turn will provide a critical backdrop against which to evaluate the social science theory and research that we will explore in later chapters. But before we begin our analysis of the biblical drama and our application of its conclusions to studies of sex and gender, something needs to be said about the relationship of the Bible to social science in general and psychology in particular.

The Bible and Social Science: Can They Be Friends?
One of my sons at age six was playing with his aunt's poodle. (You know—one of those small, clipped poodles whose tails stand straight up and hide nothing.) He stared in fascination at the dog's genitals, then turned to me with an air of great thoughtfulness and asked: "Why don't animals have to wear clothes, like people?" Now, speaking strictly as a psychologist, I could have dodged his question several ways. I could have appealed to biology and said that dogs' fur keeps them warm enough without extra covering. Or I could have turned cultural relativist, and said that it was custom in our society to dress people, but (except in circus acts) not animals. Or I could have just laughed indulgently and remembered what the great Swiss child psychologist Jean Piaget concluded: up to about age seven children ask such questions because they "think artificially"—that is, they think that everything has to have a purpose in some grand, universal design. Only later, said Piaget, do they learn to "think scientifically" and realize that everything either has a natural cause or happens by chance.[7]

But as a Christian parent, I sensed that my son was asking a question that could only be answered by going beyond science and social science to the biblical drama in which we are all players. So I thought carefully for several seconds, then answered, "I think that animals don't need to wear clothes because they didn't disobey God the way Adam and Eve did." I reminded him of the story in Genesis 3, where the first man and woman ate the forbidden fruit, then suddenly realized they were naked and covered themselves with leaves. We remembered that God also noticed their embarrassment about being naked and showed them how to make clothes out of animal skins before sending them out of the garden. Then my son ran off to play some more with the dog. But my answer must have struck home, because a few minutes later I passed him sitting on the floor stroking the dog's head and murmuring, "Nice doggy, good doggy; you didn't eat the forbidden dog biscuit, did you?"

Valuable but Limited
I have mentioned this little incident in order to develop an important point. Earlier in this chapter I said that we need a biblically based world view to help us evaluate the enormous literature on sex and gender that has accumulated in the past two decades.[8] But how are we to do this evaluation? The first thing that needs to be said is this: the realm of psychological explanation is valuable, but limited.

If asked "Why do six-year-olds (like my son) alternate between fascination and embarrassment in their attitude towards genitals?" social scientists might answer the question in one of several ways. Sociobiologists, who stress the biological underpinnings of behavior, might point out that reproducing the human race (with all its pain, inconvenience and lengthy commitment to childrearing) depends on the uniquely powerful pleasure that sexual stimulation offers—pleasure that even young children sense when they explore their bodies. Freudian psychologists would agree that sexual desire is one of the main engines that drive human development. But they would add that children's alternation between fascination and embarrassment comes from the mental conflict that parents and the rest of society set up between the child's natural urge to satisfy those desires and the pressure to delay gratification for the sake of social order. A social-learning theorist would probably avoid the Freudian language of mental conflict, but would agree that social rewards, punishments and role models lead children to avoid sexual talk and exploration in one family or indulge in both more openly in another. And a cognitive psychologist might stress that six-year-olds are mentally struggling to classify events and things in an orderly, reliable way, and thus want to know as much as possible about what makes "boys" different from "girls" and "animals" different from "people."

Must the Christian who regards the Bible as authoritative reject any or all of these explanations? Some Christians would answer yes. Some are even convinced that social sciences in general, and psychology in particular, are unnecessary and perhaps even downright evil. What these disciplines are trying to accomplish in understanding the human condition, they insist, should only be done by Christians using only the Bible as their textbook.[9] But many others point out that because all persons are created in God's image, and because God's purposes can be accomplished through whomever God chooses, truth that is compatible with biblical revelation should be respected regardless of its origin, a theme that we will explore more closely in chapter six.[10] What people think is compatible with biblical revelation depends, of course, on how they believe the Bible should be interpreted and applied. But at the very least the Bible makes it clear that, as well as being created in God's image, human beings' grasp of the truth is limited by their creatureliness and distorted by sin. This means that neither Christians nor non-Christians have a guaranteed "pipeline" to final truth, in biblical interpretation or any other discipline. We must constantly be sifting wheat from chaff in our own thinking and in that of even our favorite thinkers.

So my answer to the question "Can the Bible and social science be friends?" is a qualified yes. But even if we could agree that each of the theories mentioned above contains some truth, and even if we could reliably sift out all remaining distortions according to biblical standards, we would still need to realize that every scientific explanation is limited. For example, psychological theories (like most scientific theories) tend toward specialization. The cognitive psychologist tends to see everything in terms of the development of thinking and pays scant attention to emotion. The psychoanalytic psychologist, by contrast, argues that even the most cool-headed thinking is really driven by our emotions. And some behavioral psychologists have argued that we can simply ignore what goes on in our heads (thinking or feeling) and concentrate only on how outward behavior is regulated by rewards and punishments in the environment.

Furthermore, none of these theories in its purest form gives any place to the possibility of revealed truth or the accountability of human beings to a God who is both Creator and Redeemer. In the same way, theories about sex and gender—no matter how much empirical data support them—are at best limited in scope and at worst (like all human thinking) subject to the distortions of sin. This is a point readers should keep in mind throughout the chapters that follow.

Judging Theories According to Biblical Control Beliefs

Accurate theorizing about sex and gender, I have said, is neither limited to Christians nor guaranteed by the methods of social science. I have rejected the suggestion that a complete understanding of human behavior can be gained from studying Scripture alone. But I have also said that theories about sex and gender need to be tested against biblical revelation.

Now there are Christian social scientists with a high view of Scripture who nonetheless become very uneasy over this latter suggestion. They remember that Galileo was branded a heretic because he insisted that the earth moved around the sun while his accusers asserted that the Bible clearly stated otherwise. They remember those Victorian Christians who dated the creation of the world at exactly 4004 B.C., insisting that a backward count of the "generations" of the Bible pointed to this conclusion and no other. They remember how Anglos in both America and South Africa have used certain parts of the Bible to justify their unfair treatment of blacks and how some males have selectively used other parts of Scripture to justify the lower status of women.

From this perspective, the Bible is not to be used as a science textbook. It tells us nothing about the mechanics or natural history of the world, but only about supernatural or redemptive history. Adherents of this position point out that the entire Old Testament looks forward to Christ's death and resurrection, which are the "midpoint of history" from God's perspective, and the writings of the apostles anticipate the culmination of salvation history with Christ's triumphant return. Now it is quite correct to say that the Bible is about God's cosmic plans and activities—activities that must be viewed through eyes of faith. Indeed, this is the entire theme around which the following chapter, "Male and Female in the Biblical Drama," is organized. But are we justified in saying that this is all the Bible is about, and that to use it to judge scientific theories is simply to misuse it? Persons who hold such a view seem to be at the opposite extreme from those who say that the Bible is the *only* textbook we need. Instead, they insist, the Bible can *never* be used to evaluate theories about the natural and social world because it simply doesn't function on that level of knowledge.

According to this way of dichotomizing revealed, scriptural truth and empirical, scientific truth, it was quite inappropriate for me to answer my sons's question about animals and clothing the way I did because that would be using the Bible to suggest a theory about the human use of clothes, which is not part of the Bible's kind of revelation. Also in this view, Christian scientists and social scientists should indeed be "different" from others in the way they pursue their disciplines, but these differences will affect only the person of the psychologist, and not his or her scientific theories or methods. Thus, for example, Christian psychologists, just by virtue of being Christian, should have a high regard for truth, a confidence that truth can be uncovered and an increased concern and empathy for their clients or their research participants. But beyond this, it is said, Christian psychologists should be "objective" and not let their religious beliefs affect any part of the research or counseling process.[11]

Now I agree wholeheartedly that Christian commitment should affect the person of the psychologist (or other scientist) in the ways suggested above. But in company with a growing number of other Christian scholars, I also believe that the Bible, while not a textbook

in the usual sense of the word, can and should provide us with certain
background assumptions, or "control beliefs," by which we can both
shape and judge scientific theories, including those about sex and
gender.[12] The reason for this is that the Bible is more than an account
of human redemption; it also contains a world view. It tells us about
the ultimate orgin and nature of the universe as God's creation; it tells
us what women and men were meant to be as part of this creation,
how they fell from this state, what consequences followed and how
persons can at least make a start at reversing these when they accept
Christ's sacrificial work on their behalf.

So the Bible is profoundly relevant for social scientific theorizing
because (as we will elaborate in chapter two) men and women are
creatures made in God's image, whom God intended to be his accountable rulers on earth. But we have botched the job badly and
need to know how to get straightened out. And while the Bible does
not give us the answers in all the detail we need for our day-to-day
lives, it does set forth some basic themes to which other, more detailed
answers need to conform. In this sense it is something like the framework of a house that we must build upon. We must use available
materials and our intelligence to add the siding, the floors, the wiring
and so on. We have considerable freedom in the ways we can do this;
and there is nothing wrong with having specialized tasks: some people can concentrate on the floor, others on the roof, others on the
wiring and so on. But if we are to have a house that will endure, we
must work within the given limits of the framework. With regard to
sex and gender (as well as many other topics in social science), the
Bible provides such a framework. Due to our creaturely limitations
and our sinful inclinations, we can probably never reconstruct that
framework with total accuracy. But that does not exempt us from the
responsibility to keep trying.

For all these reasons we can and should look to Scripture as a
source of basic truths about sex and gender. We will certainly have
to go beyond these, and we certainly will not suppose that God has
confined his insights to Christian thinkers alone. But at least we will
have to start with a basic framework of scriptural themes. That is the

task of the following chapter.

Then in chapter three we will tackle in a general way the tricky question noted earlier—namely, the extent to which gendered behavior is due to nature, nurture or neither. Chapters four and five go on to explore certain aspects of the nature/nurture controversy—for example, the relative importance of genes, hormones and brain hemisphericity on gendered behavior.

I believe that these more biologically oriented chapters are important to include in a book like this because many people ascribe either too little or too much to biology when trying to account for male-female differences. These chapters are, however, the most technically challenging in the entire book, and while I have tried to keep my explanations both clear and concrete, readers with little or no background in biology may still find themselves somewhat mystified. Such readers should feel free to skim or even skip chapters three through five and settle in again at chapter six. But before that decision is made, all readers need to know how the book as a whole rests on my biblical world view and its assumptions about personhood, maleness and femaleness. It is to these issues that we now turn.

2
Male & Female in the Biblical Drama

Anyone who reads novels or watches movies knows what
is meant by "flashbacks." These are used by novelists and screen-
writers who start us somewhere in the middle of a story, then pick up
earlier parts of it by "flashing back" to things that occurred before the
events of the opening page or scene. Why do they start in the middle,
then use flashbacks to fill in the earlier parts? Perhaps because what
happens in these first few pages or film frames is terribly important
for the rest of the story, but might easily be missed or underrated if
the story sequence was left in its usual order. Our attention is caught
by telling or portraying these significant events right away.

I am going to do the same thing in my discussion of male and
female in the "acts" of the biblical drama: creation, fall, redemption,

Pentecost and renewal. I am going to start with act four—one that
many people ignore completely—and flash back to acts one through
three from there. Act four, Pentecost, is a very significant event for our
basic understanding of sex and gender.

Act Four: Pentecost as Emancipation Day
Pentecost (from the Greek word meaning "fiftieth") was a Jewish
holiday observed fifty days after Passover. Although originally regarded as a harvest festival, by the end of the Old Testament era
Pentecost had become a feast during which the Jews celebrated God's
giving of the Law to Moses on Mount Sinai. And it was during the
postcrucifixion celebration of Pentecost that act four of the biblical
drama took place.

In the first chapter of Acts we read that Jesus appeared intermit-
tently to his disciples during the forty days after his resurrection. Then
he ascended into heaven after telling them to wait in Jerusalem until
they received power to become his witnesses throughout the world.
Significantly, both women and men waited ten days in prayer for this
promised coming of the Holy Spirit. And it is equally significant that
God chose the feast of Pentecost to pour out the Holy Spirit on the
young church. God seemed to be saying that the era of obedience
under the Law was over, to be replaced by an era of freedom and
empowerment in the Spirit. At Pentecost, the redemptive act of Easter
was completed and the harvest of nations began.

My younger son asked me this past Pentecost why people don't get
as excited about this holiday as they do about Christmas and Easter.
He thinks we should send up fireworks on Pentecost. ("After all, that's
when God sent fire down, isn't it?") I agree. Pentecost is a very exciting
act of the biblical drama. Peter explained it to the bewildered spec-
tators in Jerusalem as a fulfillment of Joel's prophecy:

> And in those last days it shall be, God declares, that I will pour out
> my Spirit upon all flesh, and your sons and your daughters shall
> prophesy, and your young men shall see visions and your old men
> shall dream dreams; yea, and on my manservants and maidser-
> vants in those days I will pour out my spirit; and they shall proph-

esy. (Acts 2:17-18; compare also, Joel 2:28-29)

Pentecost has sometimes been called "women's emancipation day," because of women's inclusion with men in the outpouring of the Spirit. Before, it had been the Jewish custom to recognize only males as full members of the community through the sign of circumcision. After Pentecost, the church baptized men and women alike. Before, it was considered at best unnecessary and at worst scandalous for women to study the Scriptures beside men in the synagogue. Now they broke bread and participated in worship services with the men. Before, women's freedom of movement was rigidly restricted because of the rabbinic assertion that public contact between non-married women and men was bound to produce lust. Now women assumed positions of leadership even in mixed gatherings and were acknowledged and praised by Paul at various points in his letters.[1] And it is important to remember that not only did the barriers between men and women come tumbling down after Pentecost; so did those separating Jews from non-Jews and slaves from free persons. "You are all one in Christ Jesus" is how Paul summarized it in Galatians 3:28.

One student of the history of missions, Kari Malcolm, has pointed out that whenever the church has been in a state of revival—whenever it experiences a "mini-Pentecost"—arguments about which sex should do what seem to recede into the background. At such times, women simply have "no time for silence" (and most men, apparently, could care less about enforcing it).[2] This does not mean that women always do exactly the same things as men or even that they always want or need to. But with the clarified vision of the Holy Spirit, they affirm Christ as their first love, recognize the kingdom-building gifts he has given them and proceed to find new and challenging arenas in which to use these gifts.

At other times (let's admit it) men and women alike seem to regress to a pre-Pentecost anxiety about gender roles and become preoccupied with details concerning headship and submission. The terrible irony of this regression (often rationalized as a "return" to the most important requirements of Scripture) is captured by Malcolm's comment on it: "We have a world to win for Christ. The ship is sinking,

and we [stand] on the shore arguing about who should go to the
rescue, men or women."³ But in fact every Christian is a "sent one"
(the meaning of the Latin word from which *mission* is derived). In light
of Pentecost, they are all called to proclaim the lordship of Christ and
the healing and hope he offers, so that through active witness and
self-sacrificing service their fellow sinners may be drawn to God and
share in the building up of his kingdom. All other callings—whether
as wife or husband, married or single, clergy or laity—are merely
secondary offices within this larger calling that all Christians share.

Pentecost and Gender Justice

Thus a Christian is a saved one who is Spirit-filled in order to become
a sent one. And a Christian feminist (if I may now venture my own
definition) is a person of either sex who sees women and men as
equally saved, *equally* Spirit-filled and *equally* sent. Please note this does
not imply that there are no differences between men and women. The
notion of justice between the sexes does not have to mean that men
and women must always do exactly the same things in exactly the
same way. We can understand this when we think about how parents
treat their children. My children are both boys and close together in
age. But one is socially extroverted, while the other is a shy, somewhat
deep thinker. Last summer we sent them both to day camp for two
weeks. The older one thrived; the younger one was miserable the
entire time. This summer, the older one is back at camp while the
younger one delights in having the whole house to himself and
spends hours constructing a playhouse with his friend across the
street.

You can see my point: to treat them equally, taking into account the
needs and personality of each child, we had to treat them differently.
The same will sometimes hold for men and women. However, there
are limits to the parallel. For one thing, in most families both parents
come to some agreement as to what each child needs to fulfill his or
her potential—and we see this as entirely right. But when it comes to
the treatment of men and women, men have almost always decided
what it is women need (and women, to be fair, have often abdicated

responsibility for recognizing and stating their own needs). Why this is so is something we will consider later. But let me just reiterate for now that justice or equity for women and men (in the sense of all persons getting what they need and deserve) does not require total lack of differentiation. It does require that the voices of both men and women be heard and that neither presume to second-guess the other.

Something else needs to be said here too. In the example about my sons, you may have noticed that we didn't decide that they should do exactly the same thing just because they were both boys. We didn't, for example, decide that learning to rough it at camp was indispensable for becoming a normal male, and that because of this our younger son should go to camp whether he was miserable there or not. Doing so would have been applying a gender role stereotype, an oversimplified conception of what males and females are, or should be, like.[4] Yet—let's again admit it—Christians are often as guilty as other people of using such confining stereotypes.

And let us admit something else: such stereotypes confine women more frequently than they do men. Back in the days when almost everyone lived on farms, people expected both their sons and daughters to assume the traditional roles of farmer and farmer's wife. Men still had more social power in rural society. Even so, the confinement of gender roles applied to men and women to a somewhat more equal degree (as it still does, for example, among groups like the Amish). But as society became more urbanized and industrialized, men began doing a greater variety of jobs away from the home, while "normal" women were expected to become full-time wives and mothers in the home setting. Now, however, they were deprived of the productive economic role they had on the farm, of the support of the rural extended family and of their husbands' presence during the day. This is not to say that the jobs the men went to were always satisfying or glamorous. But they did provide built-in opportunities for adult sociability (something that domesticity does not), and they did confirm the husband's ability to be an economic provider (something that farm-wives share, but urban homemakers do not).

The fact that Christians have bought into this cultural pattern so

unthinkingly exposes another irony. Christians believe in the uniqueness of each individual life—a belief that quite rightly undergirds
their opposition to abortion on demand, for instance. But until recently this was a belief that was regularly qualified the moment a baby girl
was born. When a boy was born, few people presumed to predict what
kind of work he would be doing thirty years down the road. His
options were considered numerous, limited only by his intelligence,
motivation and (ideally) the kind of call God issued. But when it came
to girls, many Christian parents forgot about created uniqueness, and
about Pentecost and its implications. They assumed and even prayed
for a successful career as wife and mother, and nothing else. Indeed,
some still assume that God, by definition, can call their daughters to
nothing else, and that to be single and female (or married, female and
not a full-time homemaker) is somehow to have failed, morally and
spiritually.

How did this inconsistency come about? Is it just a matter of faulty
childrearing practices, which can be reversed with enough effort and
good will, as many feminists claim? Is it just a case of male heavy-
handedness toward women, which can be reversed by enough creative legislation? Do hormones have something to do with it, as the
sociobiologists keep telling us? Or is something even deeper at work—
something that affects men and women equally and for which both
are responsible? To answer this question we need to flash back to acts
one and two of the biblical drama. We need to talk about creation and
the Fall.

Act One: Created in God's Image

In various places throughout the Bible, we are told that all persons
are made "in the image of God" (see Gen 1:26-27; 5:1; 9:6; Jas 3:9).
On closer reading this seems to be a puzzling phrase, because nowhere does the Bible give us an exact list of characteristics that make
us like God. In fact, there are some Christian psychologists who have
concluded that there really is nothing about humans *structurally* that
makes them unique. Their language, their thinking capacity, their
social groupings and so forth differ from those of their closest primate

neighbors only in degree of complexity. According to this interpretation, to be made "in God's image" simply means that we have been chosen for a special relationship to God, at his initiative, a relationship which in no way requires God to have made us discontinuous with the animals.[5]

You can guess why this might be an attractive interpretation. If it is correct, it means that we don't have to look to Scripture as a source of "control beliefs" for evaluating theories produced by social science (see chapter one). If the Bible is really only talking about God's concern for us when it talks about being made in his image, then the degree to which we differ from animals in our capacities is merely an empirical question—one which has to be settled by scientific investigation. And if this is the case, then Christian social scientists don't have to be significantly different from non-Christians—except (as we noted in chapter one) in their own personal conduct. Their research and theorizing about all aspects of human behavior, including sex and gender, needs only to imitate the best models available in their particular discipline.

But I have already affirmed that we should look to Scripture for a framework of control beliefs about sex and gender. So you will not be surprised when I suggest that the image of God in human beings is more than merely a special relationship to God, initiated solely by him. In fact, the longer tradition in theology has always recognized this. People have differed as to what it is that makes us image God. Some have said it is the language and thinking capacities that all human beings share. Others have focused on concretely visible sanctification: the fruits of the Holy Spirit such as love, joy, peace and patience that are promised to those who sincerely follow Jesus.[6] All of these are important aspects of the image of God. But I am going to focus on two that I believe to be of particular importance for our understanding of sex and gender, namely sociability and accountable dominion.

Men and Women Are Inescapably Social
The account of humankind's creation begins in Genesis 1 with the

following words: "Then God said, 'Let us make man in our image, after our own likeness; and let them have dominion over the fish of the sea, and over the birds of the air, and over the cattle, and over all the earth, and over every creeping thing that creeps upon the earth.' So God created man in his own image, in the image of God he created him; male and female he created them" (Gen 1:26-27).

One of the first things that strikes us in this passage is that God refers to himself in the plural. This may simply be a poetic use of the royal "we." But it may also be one of our first biblical hints about the existence of the Trinity—the God/Logos/Spirit through whom all things are created and sustained. God is not (as certain Greek philosophers thought) an abstract "first cause" or a solitary "world governor," devoid of emotion and happy merely to self-contemplate in splendid isolation. God is intrinsically social: Creator, Redeemer and Holy Spirit working in cooperative interdependence throughout the whole of the biblical drama.

Now at first glance, this might seem to be quite irrelevant to a discussion of sex and gender. But it is not, because feminist theologians and psychologists have pointed out that one of the chief features of a feminine perspective on life is a concern for relationships.[7] Whereas male theologians have tended to think of God in terms of hierarchy, rulership and top-down authority, female theologians have pointed out that these images of dominion need to be balanced by an understanding of God in more emotional and relational terms; God as a concerned parent who weeps over wayward children and rejoices when they return, who nurses them and shelters them under his wings like a mother hen (see Num 11:12; Mt 23:37).[8] God is neither male nor female, but incorporates both "masculine" and "feminine" traits into an irreducibly social nature.

And it is not as if God's sociability is given only to women to reflect. If God is a social tri-unity whose image is in all persons, then it comes as no surprise to read in Genesis 2 that it is "not good" for the man to be alone. So God creates the woman. Once they are together, God's clear intention for male and female is equality and interdependence in the context of differing sexuality. Some interpreters have argued for Adam's "headship" over Eve on the basis of his naming her. But the classic Hebrew naming formula (the one used by Adam when he "named" the animals) consists of *calling* a person, an animal or a place *by name*. Upon seeing Eve for the first time, Adam does not "call her by name"—he merely calls or recognizes her as "woman." Writes Old Testament scholar Phyllis Trible: "In calling the woman, the man is not establishing power over her, but rejoicing in their mutuality. . . . The man's poem ('Bone of my bones and flesh of my flesh, this shall be called woman') does not determine who the woman is, but rather delights in what God has already done in creating sexuality."[9]

So, like God, both men and women are intrinsically social. Christians, unlike the philosopher Thomas Hobbes, can never say that people are at root individualists who grudgingly enter into a "social contract" with others merely to advance their own private interests. On the contrary, we are so unshakably created for community that we cannot even develop as full persons unless we grow up in nurturing contact with others. Moreover, the fulfillment of our sociability depends on fellowship with the opposite sex. This does not mean that everyone has to marry in order to be fully human, but it does mean that subcultures of men or women only (whether this is in an enforced prison setting or a freely chosen community) are something less than fully human. There may be tragic but understandable reasons why some people want to shun the opposite sex. But that does not make the practice normative.

Women and Men Have Accountable Dominion under God

A second thing is immediately apparent in Genesis 1:26-27. Not only are both male and female created in God's image as social beings, but both are given dominion over the rest of creation. Some Christians who argue for stereotypical gender roles (and who claim to have a great reverence for the authority of Scripture) have actually argued for male headship on the basis of Genesis 1:26, stating that it gives dominion to Adam.[10] Either they have not read the rest of the chapter or they are deliberately ignoring it. (And, as one author has commented, "I'm not sure which is worse.")[11] *Both* the man and woman are told to fill the earth and subdue it; *both* are told to be fruitful and multiply; *both* are told they have dominion over every other living thing.

Theologians have often referred to this set of commandments as the "cultural mandate." Men and women were commanded by God to "open up" the possibilities latent in the creation. Although sustained by and accountable to God, they were to use the intelligence God gave them to make good and stewardly decisions in all realms of human activity. That is why it is so sad to see Christians abdicating from science, politics, the arts and so forth on the grounds that these are "worldly" pursuits. Our world belongs to God, in all of its variety. There may be points in history where separating into a Christian subculture is unavoidable (during times of persecution, for instance). But that is not God's intended norm.[12]

Nor is there any indication in the creation accounts that the man was to take the lead in this process. Interpreters who have preferred to keep men and women in stereotypical roles used to argue that God's making Eve a "helper fit" for Adam places her in a secondary position. He is to decide how the creation is to be developed (by being the research scientist, the business executive, the doctor and so on) and she is to be his assistant (by being the lab worker, the secretary, the nurse and so on). But this is an argument that biblical scholarship has (ironically!) turned on its head. The Hebrew word for "helper," as used in Genesis 2, is used overwhelmingly in the Old Testament of the person of God. It is the word we use when we speak of God as "our help and deliverer" (Ps 70:5), or affirm that our "help comes from the LORD" (Ps 121:2). Yet we would never dream of suggesting that in referring to God as "our help" we are making him secondary to ourselves. Quite the contrary! Nor does this interpretation argue (as some feminists might hope) for the woman's superiority. She is, in Phyllis Trible's translation, the "helper *corresponding* to the man," one who can walk beside him and work together with him because she is like him in every essential, God-imaging way.[13]

Act Two: Trouble in Paradise
So men and women are equally created in God's image, and a big part

of our "imaging" God lies in our sociability and our dominion over the earth. But both of these capacities were to be exercised within limits set by God alone. God and humans were in a partnership, a covenant, sealed with a condition. They were to have eternal, satisfying fellowship with their Creator in return for a modest behavioral token of their dependence on God. The exact historical details may be debatable, but this much is clear: they were not to use their freedom and dominion to decide the nature of good and evil. The cultural mandate stopped at this point, for the freedom to determine good and evil belonged to God alone.

Nor were they to misuse their "one flesh" sociability to persuade each other to step beyond these bounds. But that is exactly what happened. Led astray by a rebel angel in disguise, the woman abused her dominion by eating of "the tree of the knowledge of good and evil" (Gen 2:17). The man, in turn, abused his sociability by accepting some of the fruit from her even though he knew that their unity as man and woman was not to supersede their obedience to God. From then on, the creation love story, with its intended mutuality and equality, goes sadly awry. Genesis 3 tells us how.

First of all, the woman and man hide from each other. Their differing sexuality is now a source of self-consciousness rather than delight, so they clothe their bodies. Then they hide from God. And when God finds them and questions the man about his disobedience, the man first blames God (for giving him the woman in the first place), then blames the woman (for giving him the fruit). Only then does he reluctantly confess, "and I ate" (Gen 3:12). The woman, on the other hand, tries to pass the buck to the serpent, completely ignoring her influence on her husband in her confession. "By betraying the woman before God," writes Phyllis Trible, "the man opposes himself to her; by ignoring him in her reply to God, the woman separates herself from the man . . . Split apart, one flesh awaits the outcome."[14]

We read in Genesis 3 what the features of that outcome were for both of them. They were banished from the Garden and faced with the prospect of painful labor while reproducing the race and feeding it only to see death at the end of it all—at least until the Redeemer, dimly hinted at in Genesis 3:15, would come to "bruise [the serpent's] head" and begin to reverse the consequences of the Fall. But for our purposes, one particular consequence needs to be understood in greater detail. It is announced by God to Eve in Genesis 3:16, in the words, "I will greatly multiply your pain in childbearing; in pain you shall bring forth children, *yet your desire shall be for your husband, and he shall rule over you.*"[15]

Now the first thing you find out when you try to exegete the final part of this mysterious verse is that the Hebrew word translated as "desire" occurs only three times in the Old Testament. This, of course, makes the business of understanding its meaning somewhat difficult. One biblical scholar, Gilbert Bilezikian, has done a great deal of work comparing the contexts in which this word is used and concludes that in Genesis 3:16 the woman is being warned that she will experience an unreciprocated longing for intimacy with the man.

> [The woman's] desire will be for her husband, so as to perpetuate the intimacy that had characterized their relationship in paradise lost. But her nostalgia for the relation of love and mutuality that existed between them before the fall, when they both desired each other, will not be reciprocated by her husband. Instead of meeting her desire, he will rule over her . . . [In short], the woman wants a mate and she gets a master; she wants a lover and she gets a lord; she wants a husband and she gets a hierarch.[16]

The Man's Abuse: Dominion Becomes Domination

Now let's first be clear about what is *not* being said here. It is not the case that the positive, mutual interdependence that existed between man and woman at creation totally disappeared after the Fall. We are still created in God's image, even though this image is distorted. Moreover, there are many places in the Bible where we are reminded that the worst effects of the Fall are restrained for the sake of social order and in order to accomplish God's purposes through believers and nonbelievers alike. Nor is it the case that being a "master," a "lord" or a "hierarch" is totally against the creation order. For the human abuse of power is possible only because we were originally given that power by God—the power and freedom to exercise accountable dominion over the creation. But what I take God to be saying in Genesis 3:16 is that as a result of the Fall there will be a propensity in men to let their dominion run wild, to impose it in cavalier and illegitimate ways not only on the earth and on other men, but also upon the person who is bone of his bones and flesh of his flesh—upon the helper corresponding to his very self. Legitimate, accountable dominion all too easily becomes male domination.

The results of this have been with us throughout history. British author Anne Atkins writes:

> In the last analysis a man can usually enforce his wishes upon his wife. Even if he never lays a finger on her, he will almost always be capable of bullying her to get what he wants . . . We should simply face up to the fact, on the basis of Genesis 3:16 and empirical evidence, that the fall gives a man a certain power over a woman which he can easily use at her expense. His "strength" can be his wife's enslavement.[17]

Again, this is not to say that all men at all times behave this way toward all women. But it does mean that there is something akin to a congenital flaw in males that makes it all too easy for them to assume that they have a right to dominate women. However, this is not the end of our exegesis of Genesis 3:16. For this is a verse that I suspect is being very evenhanded in its prediction of post-Fall sinfulness in both sexes.

The Woman's Abuse: Sociability Becomes Social Enmeshment

I have just said that it is men's post-Fall tendency to let domination replace dominion, a dominion which in its proper form was originally given to both man and woman by God at creation. So let me now point out that just as there is something creationally legitimate about the man's desire for dominion (even though it is misused against women) so there is also something creationally right about the woman's desire for union and intimacy with the man. It is part of the social mandate given by God to both Adam and Eve. But because of the Fall, Genesis

3:16 warns us, this desire on the part of women for community is also distorted by sin. Indeed, there are two opposite ways we can abuse our God-given exercise of accountable dominion. The first (the man's sin) is to try to exercise dominion without regard for God's original plan for male/female relationships. But the second—the peculiarly female sin—is *to use the preservation of those relationships as an excuse not to exercise accountable dominion in the first place.* In other words, the woman's analogue of the man's congenital flaw, in light of Genesis 3:16, is the temptation to avoid taking risks that might upset relationships. It is the temptation to let creational sociability become fallen "social enmeshment."

Now this is a very seductive temptation indeed, for it so very easily masquerades as virtue. After all, don't Christians see self-sacrificing servanthood and the desire to maintain peace and social unity as fruits of the Holy Spirit? Well, yes and no, depending on the context. If women insist on peace at any price—if they settle for abnormal quietism as a way of avoiding the risk and potential isolation that may result from opposing evil—then they are not exhibiting the fruit of the Spirit. They are sinning just as surely as the man who rides rough-shod over relationships in order to assert his individual freedom. For "peace," in the biblical sense, does not consist of "peace at any price." It is rather the *shalom* in which all things are in their rightful, creationally ordained place. And in light of the Fall the distortion of *shalom*—including that between men and women—calls for a prophetic refusal to say "Peace, peace when there is no peace" (Jer 6:14) and a willingness to make the changes needed to restore true *shalom.*[18]

This is an important point to understand in anticipation of later chapters in this book. For one of the main problems of today's counseling psychologists is accounting for women's constant tendency to avoid developing personal self-sufficiency for the sake of preserving even pathological relationships with the opposite sex. Despite the progressive removal of external, legal barriers to women's achievement, many psychologists have noted with distress that women still seem to have enormous internal barriers to overcome. The titles of books that have been written on this subject are very telling: *Sweet*

Suffering: Woman as Victim, Women Who Love Too Much, Why Do I Think I Am Nothing without a Man?, and perhaps most telling of all, in light of Genesis 3:16, *Men Who Hate Women and the Women Who Love Them.*[19]

The writers of these books all emphasize that women are responding to faulty child-rearing patterns when they become preoccupied with gaining or maintaining relationships with men. And this is very often true, as is the fact that public institutional power is still very male-dominated, despite the legal changes mentioned above. But these do not constitute the entire story. There is an inescapably religious dimension involved, one which goes right back to the Fall. These authors have done a remarkable job of documenting some of the empirical effects of Genesis 3:16, at least on the psychological level. But they share with many other psychologists the error of trying to reduce such problems to the way women have been socialized. They do not realize (or refuse to admit) that something much deeper is at work: something that cannot finally be eradicated by psychotherapy or by institutional change, however important both these may be.

By way of summary, it seems that the effects of Genesis 3:16 reflect the peculiar way in which each party sinned in the Garden. The man and the woman were equally created for sociability and dominion. But in reaching out to take the fruit, the woman overstepped the bounds of accountable dominion. As a consequence, her sociability was mixed with the problem of social enmeshment, which continues to hamper the proper exercise of her dominion in the world at large. By contrast, the man, in accepting the fruit from his wife, overstepped the bounds of human social unity. As a consequence, his legitimate, accountable dominion became laced with the problem of domination, which has been interfering with his relationships—to God, to the creation and to other people, including women—ever since. In each case, the punishment seems to fit the original crime. In chapters six to eleven we will have more to say about the psychological fallout of all this.

In the meantime, the reader may feel tempted to despair over the state of male/female relations in the wake of the Fall. If we can't change these pathological patterns permanently through resocialization, institutional change, gene-splicing or whatever, what hope is there for the human race? Well, it is true that in the wake of the Fall, all our functions are "depraved"—not through and through, but certainly to a disturbing degree. Yet, as Martin Luther once remarked, the doctrine of total depravity is one of the most comforting doctrines of the Christian church. Why? Because it means we don't have to pretend everything is all right anymore. We don't have to pretend that "we" are not affected, even if "our neighbors" are. We don't have to pretend that anything less than a radical solution can change us. And that, of course, brings us to the climax of the biblical drama.

Acts Three to Five: Redemption and Renewal
A religion scholar by the name of Leonard Swidler recently compiled a hefty volume entitled *Biblical Affirmations of Women.*[20] Close to one hundred pages of this book are devoted to all the biblical passages on Jesus' teachings about men and women. Considered together, these passages show clearly that it was Christ's intention, as part of his healing and saving work, to reverse the consequences of Genesis 3:16. Because we take for granted many of the rights and protections women have achieved throughout modern history (however incomplete these may be), it is difficult for us to realize how revolutionary Jesus' teaching on men and women must have sounded to his hearers. But the rabbinic and other extra-biblical Jewish writings of the period show that the Jews of Jesus' time had an overwhelmingly negative attitude toward women—an attitude that the women, moreover, simply seemed to accept, since to do otherwise would have been to risk having no place in the community whatever. Through the whole of the Old Testament period, Genesis 3:16 was working itself out in predictable fashion.

Reversing the Effects of the Fall
Into this setting comes a rabbi who almost never tells a parable using male images and activities without also using a parallel one involving women. To a culture that allowed easy divorce and even polygamy for men, but not women, he insisted on monogamy and the elimination

of divorce by appealing to God's original intentions for both men and women. (His disciples were so stunned by this teaching that they suggested it would be easier not to marry at all!) To a culture that was obsessed with blood ties, and in which barren women were a disgrace, he taught that the family of God was so much more important that it might even divide parents from children. In a culture that refused to recognize women as teachers or as witnesses in court, he allowed women to be the first witnesses of his resurrection and a woman to proclaim that event to his male disciples. The list could go on and on. Over the course of the four gospels, there is a total of 633 verses in which Jesus refers to women, and almost none of these are negative in tone.

Significantly, those that are negative seem mostly to rebuke women who, in the wake of Genesis 3:16, are caught up in the problem of social enmeshment. Jesus tells Martha of Bethany that being busy in the kitchen over food is not as good a choice as sitting at the master's feet learning. He chides his mother for trying to make him place blood ties before kingdom ties. To the woman in the crowd who cries out to him, "Blessed is the womb which bore you, and the breasts which nursed you!" he quickly replies, "Blessed rather are those who hear the word of God and keep it" (Lk 11:27-28). Jesus does not disparage relationships; he affirms the created sociability of persons, and he uses homey illustrations from family and village life in his parables. He also affirms parenthood as an important calling for both men and women and a role that deserves respect from children. But he does not allow these roles to take precedence over the kingdom of God. He does not allow them to be idolized.

So already in his earthly ministry, Jesus is setting men and women up for the "emancipation proclamation" of Pentecost. Christ-following men are no longer to think that "dominion run wild" can bring in the kingdom, as Jesus' Zealot followers believed, hoping to overthrow their Roman occupiers by force of arms. And with regard to their wives, men are to follow Christ's example of servanthood and self-sacrifice. At the same time, Christ-following women are no longer to use relationship-maintenance as an excuse to avoid the risks that will inevitably accompany the promotion of God's kingdom. They are "joint heirs" of Christ's salvation with men and must act accordingly.

This may sometimes mean doing things which the surrounding culture condemns as "unfeminine." When Christians first became involved in the movement to abolish slavery in America, one of their numbers—an orator named Theodore Weld—observed how women came to realize that they were holding back from the fight against slavery by invoking the excuse of feminine modesty. Weld wrote to two fellow abolitionists:

> The very week I was converted, and the first time I ever spoke in a religious meeting, I urged females both to pray and speak if they felt deeply enough to do it, and not to be restrained from it by the fact that they were females. . . . The result was that seven female Christians confessed their sin in being restrained by their sex, and prayed publicly in succession that very evening.[21]

To be a Christ-following woman is not the same as being a shrinking violet.

Between D-day and V-day

But if Christ preached a clear reversal of the effects of Genesis 3:16 and if Pentecost empowered the early church to overcome them, why are there still so many problems and puzzles surrounding gender and sex in the lives of Christians as well as everyone else? We are like batteries whose power is always running down. During times of spiritual revival in history, we seem to get recharged; at such times, as I pointed out at the beginning of this chapter, relationships between men and women seem to conform much more to the intentions of God the Creator, Christ the Savior and the Holy Spirit as energizer. But why the in-between periods? Why do we inevitably and so often regress from Pentecost back to the problems of Genesis 3:16?

Theologian Oscar Cullman put it well. He reminded us that the period between Pentecost and Christ's final return is like the period between D-day and V-day of World War 2. By D-day, everyone knew that the turning point of the war had come; the Allies would win. But between that day and the surrender of the German army, some of the most vicious fighting of the war took place, with many casualties. It was as if Hitler, furious that his defeat was inevitable, wanted to drag the whole of European civilization down with him. The present period in salvation history is like that. Our "ancient foe," the devil, knows he has been defeated by Christ's death and resurrection, but still "seeks to work us woe," in the words of Martin Luther's hymn. And the more Christians can be kept from acting like post-Pentecost men and women, the less effective will be their witness to the world around them and the less likely will others be to respond to God's offer of salvation.[22]

We cannot, in such a situation, always be at our Pentecostal best, in gender relations or any other area. Our full healing awaits the fifth act of the biblical drama, the inauguration of the new heaven and the new earth. But in Francis Schaeffer's words, we are called to set up "pilot plants," or self-conscious attempts to work out the implications of our salvation in every area of life, whether that be science, the arts, politics, technology or relations between women and men.[23] At the same time we are not to get triumphalistic. Christians are not to assume that, because they have accepted God's salvation and are well intentioned, they can get everything figured out once and for all. For this too can be a trick of the devil; it can blind us to the sin that remains, and make us resistant to reforms that may be desperately needed. Still, substantial healing is possible between D-day and V-day, during this time between the times. And, as I noted in chapter one, we can use our biblical control beliefs about men and women to appreciate and interpret the insights that God has allowed to emerge from those who study sex and gender. That is the task of the rest of this book.

3

How to
Think about
Sex and
Gender

In the following section of this book I will be looking at the impact of "nature and nurture"—or biology and learning—on the behavior of women and men. You might think that this really takes us to the heart of the matter. For if *sex* refers to what is biologically given and *gender* to what is learned, and therefore changeable, and if we can assign weights to each, then surely we will be able to say what is "creationally"—non-negotiably, biologically—male or female and design social policy and church practice accordingly. If women, by virtue of their genes or hormones, really are more nurturing than men, then perhaps it is right and natural to give them primary responsibility for childcare. If men's genes or hormones endow them with a better sense of direction and space than women, surely it is only a good use of social resources to favor male admissions to engineering school. And if, as a now-deceased pastor of my own church used to argue, women simply aren't born with the emotional strength to withstand the stresses of church council meetings, then surely it is doing them a favor, as well as being obedient to God's creational purposes, to keep them out.

This kind of thinking is very common. But I am going to argue that even if we were able to make such a neat separation between the effects of nature and nurture, it is the wrong way to think about sex and gender in the first place. To do this I want to make three related points. First, both psychologically and biologically, men and women are more alike than they are different. Second, sex and gender are mutually influential. It is true that nature limits what nurture can accomplish. But nurture also changes nature: environmental and social experiences affect our biology in profound and often irreversible ways. And third, freedom of choice and a sense of gender identity are important aspects of the image of God in all persons. But both are less important than the principal office to which all believers are called—namely, the advancement of God's kingdom on earth.

Because there is so much popular, erroneous thinking about sex and gender (and in current social science a lot of ambiguity about human freedom), I want to develop these three points along with some examples that will prepare readers for more detailed discussions in the chapters to come.

More Alike Than Different

I have a seven-year-old niece who is in her third year of a French-immersion school program in Canada. Since kindergarten, she has heard only French in the classroom, although English is spoken in her home. She is now learning to read and write in French and will only add English as a "second" classroom language when she gets to fourth grade. By now, her French is fluent and almost flawlessly accented. At the same time, her spoken English is as normal as that of her peers in English-language classrooms. She is on her way to becoming fully bilingual.

When her parents first had to decide whether to enroll her in French-immersion kindergarten, they asked me if I thought the stress of learning two languages would be too much for her. I replied that research seemed to show that for some children it could be. However because Sarah, aside from having fairly high intelligence, is a girl, girls' tendency to speak earlier and more fluently than boys made it likely that she could meet the challenge of learning two languages at once. I suggested that they enroll her in the program and judge the wisdom of the decision a year at a time. Throughout her first year, she performed competently and enthusiastically, and at the end of it I was shown her classroom photo. I was not surprised, given my earlier remarks, to find that the girls outnumbered boys almost two to one.

Now this anecdote begs a number of questions: Was Sarah's class typical in its predominance of girls? After all, I didn't check the enrollment breakdown for the other French-immersion classrooms in that school, let alone for the entire school system. Was her easy adjustment due to the fact that she was a girl? Or was it because she scored above average in general, not just verbal, intelligence? Or had it been because of a home environment which was supportive of her progress? Or all three? Just how much credence can we give to the assertion that girls excel over boys in verbal abilities, or boys over girls in spatial abilities, or to popular press accounts of any such differences? How consistent are these differences? How large are they? And, perhaps most touchy of all, what (if anything) do they imply for social policy and the distribution of training, jobs and rewards?

Let us stay with the example of verbal abilities in order to make some points about method and interpretation in psychological research. For without an understanding of these, it is all too easy simply to look for confirmation of pre-existing prejudices. In addition, research on male/female differences in verbal abilities exposes certain data patterns and research problems common to studies of sex differences in achievement, personality and even biology. So what we conclude about this area of psychological functioning will apply in large part to other areas as well.

Differences in Childhood: More Clear-Cut?
A first essential point has to do with differences that appear in small children as opposed to those that are found in young adulthood, when pubertal changes and growth are complete. Studies of sex differences in young children are legion, because many researchers assume that differences found in very young children (before the social environment has had much chance to affect them) must be due to innate, biological factors. But there are some problems with this assumption. For one thing, it ignores what has happened in the fetal environment within the mother. We do not know how (if at all) this environment is systematically different for boys as opposed to girls. But we do know that approximately 140 boys are conceived for every 100 girls. The rate of miscarriage is so much greater for boys that the ratio of live births is only 105 boys to 100 girls, and the greater early mortality rate for boys is such as to make the ratio an even 1:1 by age one. Boys and girls are at different degrees of risk both before and after birth, and it is far from clear how much this is due to specifically sex-linked biology and how much to the interaction of this with the fetal environment. At the very least it means that we should be slow to generalize about any differences found in the cradle, both because a nine-month environment has preceded birth, and because boys are on the average more fragile than girls both before and after birth.[1]

It is also unwise to underestimate the significance of the earliest *social* experiences. Indeed, because so many critical periods occur in infancy and early childhood, the effect of such experiences is much larger than if they had occurred later. A *critical period* in human development is one in which the brain is optimally flexible (in ways that we still barely understand) to create neural connections that are intended to last for life. Language acquisition is a good example; because young Sarah was immersed in French starting in kindergarten, she speaks it with an almost flawless grammar and accent. Her older sister and brother, who began French as a second language in third grade, cannot match her, and would be unlikely to do so even if they began French immersion now and continued it through high school.

In addition, there are a few revealing historical accounts of young children who have been abandoned but managed to survive in the wild until discovered years later. These suggest that without early exposure to an active language community the potential for complex language is lost. The critical period for its emergence has come and gone, and such children are capable of learning only rudimentary communication skills.

When it comes to the social treatment of baby girls and boys, we have a lot of evidence that they are treated in systematically different ways. In fact, because people do no better than chance at guessing a small infant's sex when it is neutrally clothed, psychologists have developed what is called the *Baby X* strategy for looking at these differences. In these studies, adults have been asked to interact with a baby whom they are told is either a boy or a girl. In half the cases the child is the sex it has been labeled; in the other half it is actually of the opposite sex.

The results of such studies are very consistent. The infant is described and treated by most of the adults in terms of stereotypes about its presumed sex. Girl-labeled boys (as well as girl-labeled girls) are described as more friendly, sociable and feminine. They are handed dolls much more frequently than footballs. They are talked to more. They are described as more physically "fragile" and easily upset (an irony in light of the actually greater fragility of infant boys!). The opposite, masculine stereotypes are applied with equal consistency to boy-labeled boys and boy-labeled girls.[2]

So when a popular science article states that "girls talk earlier and more fluently than boys," what are we to make of it? Well, first we need to know that many studies have found no differences, and even when average differences are present (usually in girls' favor) they are often small to the point of statistical insignificance—which means they could have happened simply by chance. Secondly, even the largest average differences between boys and girls are much smaller than the range of scores within either sex. The overlapping curves in Figure 1 (which, incidentally, could be re-labeled to apply to other sex-related differences) will help make this clearer:

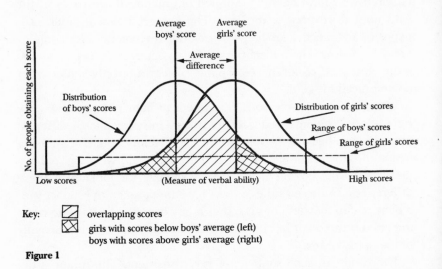

Key: ▨ overlapping scores
      ⊠ girls with scores below boys' average (left)
          boys with scores above girls' average (right)

Figure 1

Notice that the range of vocabulary scores within which each group falls is much greater than the small average difference that separates the two groups. That fact alone renders patently false any talk about rigid polarities between the sexes. Notice also the large number of boys and girls with overlapping scores. They total about a third of each group in this example. (In most studies it is more; in none is it any less.) Notice too that there is even a minority of boys scoring higher than the average girl, and a minority of girls scoring lower than the average boy. And remember, all we know about even the small average difference between groups is that 1) it occurs in *some* (not all) studies, and 2) we cannot say how much of it is due to nature and how much to nurture, because none of these studies have controlled for early differences in the *social* treatment of boys and girls, including the fact that baby girls are talked to more than baby boys.

In the face of this much uncertainty, it would hardly make sense to conclude that more five-year-old girls than boys should be accepted into French-immersion classrooms, no matter how limited the number of spaces. Clearly (to the extent that verbal ability in the mother tongue is relevant) each applicant should be judged according to his or her *actual* verbal ability, and not according to differing male and female quotas.[3] The same logic would apply to math, science and other subjects in which performance is connected, however much or little, with sex-related abilities.

What about Adult Differences?

But I said that we needed to distinguish between studies looking at childhood differences and those that look at adult men and women. This distinction is important because adults have undergone a lot of general physical growth since childhood. But it is also important because some researchers think adolescent changes in hormonal activity, which activate female and male fertility and secondary sex characteristics, affect male and female brains (and hence thinking abilities) differently. There are "hormone hypotheses" that try to explain *both* female verbal superiority and male visual-spatial superiority in just this way. We will learn more about these in chapter five. For now we only need to know that, of some forty studies using the verbal portions of standardized intelligence tests on persons over age sixteen (including tasks measuring vocabulary, verbal problem-solving, verbal fluency and abstract reasoning), more than half have found no differences between men and women. Women did perform better than men in fifteen of the remaining seventeen studies, but the differences, even though statistically significant, were typically quite small.[4]

Nevertheless, it is easy to "lie"—or at least mislead—with such statistics. To announce that a "significant statistical difference" has been found means only that the difference, however large or small, would occur by chance fewer than five times in 1,000 in randomly drawn samples. Thus, in a sample of 100,000 men and 100,000 women, an average difference in a verbal IQ score of .02 points would be "highly statistically significant," in that it would occur only once in 1,000 times by chance. This is because the larger the samples, the smaller the difference needed to yield significance, other things being equal. But statistical significance is not the same as practical significance. To

claim any practical importance for this difference in IQ scores would
be like arguing that a statistically significant difference of 2/100 of a
traffic light per square mile between two cities has stupendous implications for the quality of urban safety!

A more recent statistical procedure tries to go beyond mere statistical significance to assess how meaningful, in reality, is the *size* of
differences over a number of studies. By looking together at all the
samples of men and women, it is able to answer the question about
verbal or other measures: "If the only thing you knew about a par-
ticipant in one of these studies was his or her score on the test used,
how accurately could you guess his or her sex?" Such analysis shows
that, for all intents and purposes, you would do no better than chance
at guessing a person's sex from his or her verbal score. The difference
is that trivial.[5]

This is not to say that it might not be a real difference, or even one
partly dependent on biological factors; such analysis cannot answer
that question. Thus, some theorists continue to highlight female verbal superiority, however minimal, in the studies where it occurs. Others have emphasized the quantity of studies showing no differences.
Each side has to concede that the other might be right. "Given these
data," writes Anne Fausto-Sterling of Brown University, "choosing to
believe in sex-related differences in verbal ability is a judgment call
about which knowledgeable scientists can very legitimately differ."[6]

What about Biology?

We will find in chapters to come that what is true about sex-related
differences in verbal ability is true of other behavioral tendencies as
well. Psychologically, men and women are more alike than they are
different. But when we look at more obviously biological features, are
we not in a totally different ballpark? Freud may have overstated the
matter when he wrote that "anatomy is destiny," but surely anatomy
is the most obvious and stable differentiator between male and female, the one by which we confirm a child's sex in the delivery room.
And aren't those anatomical differences (and the genes and physiology behind them) what make it possible for men and women to as-

sume their different but cooperating roles in reproduction?

On the face of it, yes. But even here there are surprises. For instance, if you were to examine several fetuses miscarried in the third
month of pregnancy, you would not know the males from the females
unless you did a laboratory test to check for a tiny chromosomal body
which characterizes normal female cells but not those of males. Externally, all would have a rectum plus one other rather pronounced
opening, in front of which would be a very small bump of flesh. Inside
the pelvic region of each you would find a pair of undifferentiated
gonads that look neither like ovaries nor testes and which could become either, given the appropriate hormonal environment. You
would also find two sets of primitive tubes, one of which could later
fold over and become a uterus, while the other could become a normal set of male ducts for the production and ejaculation of sperm-
bearing semen. Again, only the correct ratios of hormones at a critical
point in fetal development will cause the primitive female structures
to wither in a male fetus (while the male structures develop) or the
primitive male tubes to wither in a female fetus (while the female
structures mature). Even so, the opposite-sex structures do not completely disappear; they remain present in remnant form on top of
women's ovaries and men's testes.

Thus, being genetically male or female does not automatically lead
to the correct internal or external sexual equipment in any fetus. What
the male or female chromosomes must first do is trigger the release
of appropriate hormone ratios at certain critical periods of fetal development. They do this via yet another set of hormones in the pi-
tuitary gland that control the orchestration of the sex-related hormones. Is this where the real difference lies? Sex-appropriate genes
lead to sex-appropriate hormones; these in turn establish physical and
perhaps psychological differences between the sexes during certain
critical periods, especially during fetal development and at puberty.
Because it respects the complexities of biological development, this
view is closer to the truth than the naive theory that "it's in the genes,
once and for all." But here too there are some surprises. Sex hormones are not uniquely male or female. Both men and women se-

crete androgens (a group of masculinizing hormones) and estrogens (a group of feminizing hormones). *Both* types of hormones (as well as others) are needed for both males and females to achieve sexual maturity; both types are secreted by both ovaries and testes and in smaller amounts by the adrenal cortex that sits on top of the kidneys.[7]

What is crucial to normal sexual differentiation, both internal and external, is not the *absolute* but the *relative* amounts of these hormones at particular points in development. Proportions of androgens and estrogens vary a surprising amount, both in men and women generally and in individuals at different times. If these ratios go beyond a certain range during critical periods prenatally and at puberty, the consequences—at least bodily—can be dramatic, as we will see in the next two chapters. But what is important to grasp now is the surprising degree of similarity between normal female and normal male physiology. In addition, just as one cannot invoke simple genetic explanations for why the sexes are (or should be) different in their behavior, neither can one invoke simple hormonal ones. Many biological reductionists theorize that stereotypical masculinity and femininity are both inevitable and desirable because they directly reflect levels of androgen and estrogen. Hormones are invoked to justify (or at least excuse) behaviors as varied as male dominance (including war, rape and domestic violence), female passivity and flirtatiousness and both the urgency and direction of one's sexual desires.[8] But in human beings no reliable correlations have been found between such things as homosexuality, assertive leadership, aggression or nurturance and either absolute or relative amounts of a given hormone. As one team of scientists has put it:

> We would doubt that we could explain the emergence of a president or a prime minister by measuring the circulating androgen of the contenders for such a post—or even by retrospectively speculating on the levels of these hormones in the days or months following their birth . . . Biologists are unable to predict future Ronald Reagans or Margaret Thatchers from any measurement, however sophisticated, of the biochemistry of today's population of newborn infants.[9]

Men and women are not biologically different enough (or simple enough) to justify the explanation of behavioral differences on the basis of biology alone. There may be other reasons, rooted in value convictions or historical circumstances, for having a degree of gender complementarity, but that is a different story. Moreover, even if physical differences and their behavioral effects were as clear-cut as biological reductionists claim, what Christian could buy the argument that "anatomy is destiny"? For this would be saying, in effect, that "whatever is, is morally right." In other words, because men have always waged war it is always right, or at least always inevitable. Because male promiscuity is historically common, that too is right, or at least excusable. Because female passivity in the face of male abuse is historically common, it is unavoidable and so should not be opposed. No, if we are to explain or justify separate spheres for men or women, however broadly or narrowly defined, we must look more to economic, social, and world view-based explanations. To do less is to say that human beings are nothing but instinct-driven machines.

Nature and Nurture Influence Each Other
Recently my children became the delighted recipients of two tiny kittens whose mother had died in a farm accident. As they fed them milk by hand and watched the kittens develop, the boys learned many introductory psychology lessons. My older son was particularly taken by the kittens' habit of teetering after any pair of moving human feet that came within range of their vision. And even when they were sitting still and resting, the kittens' eyes would follow nearby activities with all the intensity of sports fans watching a tennis match. "They're like babies!" my son concluded. "Babies stare at you like that too!"

Indeed they do—and both kittens and babies do so for very good reasons. For if they are not exposed to a rich variety of visual experience in the first months after birth (another one of those "critical periods" for certain kinds of development), then certain neural connections, essential for normal visual perception, may simply fail to develop properly. In a series of Nobel Prize-winning experiments conducted in the 1960s, kittens were isolated from birth in large, enclosed drums, each with one pattern painted on its interior—either horizontal or vertical black and white stripes. Later, the researchers were able to implant tiny electrodes in individual cells of a part of the visual system between the eyes and the brain and to record the resulting electrical activity when the cats were exposed to various patterns. Normally reared cats, exposed to the complex visual patterns of the everyday world, had cells which were receptive to horizontal and vertical stripes. But the cats exposed only to horizontal stripes had no cells that fired in response to vertical stripes, the experience of which they had missed in early life. The opposite was true for the cats exposed to vertical stripes only.[10]

Similar studies have been done with young rats raised in environments of more versus less visual stimulation. This time, however, what was being examined was the effect on a type of brain cortex cell (called the *pyramidal* cell because of its shape) that is similar in structure in rats and human beings, and on whose thread-like branches tiny "spines" can multiply. We know about the importance of these spines in human beings because of a devastating, genetically based disease called *Tay-Sachs* syndrome. In the course of this disease the pyramidal cells, having produced a normal complement of spines during the first year of life, are progressively stripped of those spines by an enzyme deficiency. The result is a profound form of mental retardation, since loss of the nerve cells' spines means, in effect, the loss of incoming messages to the brain. It also spells inevitable death, usually before age two.

By doing autopsies on young Tay-Sachs victims, researchers have confirmed the importance of these pyramidal spines for the emergence of normal human intelligence. By doing autopsies on young rats raised in various conditions of visual deprivation, other researchers have shown the importance of experience for the multiplication of those spines. Harvard scientist Melvin Konner recalls the first time he looked at photos of stained brain sections and saw for himself the clear correlation of the number of neural spines with the degree of environmental richness during the rats' brief life. "Look, I remember thinking when I first saw the photographs. See for yourself.

Experience changes the brain."[11] Now Konner is no naive environ-mentalist; indeed, the main purpose of his book is to explain the very real constraints that biology imposes on us. The power of these is underlined by the Tay-Sachs example: without the right genetic or-chestration, all the experience in the world will not reverse the dete-rioration of the neural spines produced by this disease. And yet, he concedes, given a normal genetic pattern, "everything from learning ability to brain chemistry has been shown to be changed by experi-ence."[12]

How Nurture Affects Nature in Women

Part of that "everything" encompassed in our experience is, of course, the expression of male and female behavior. Some of the most inter-esting demonstrations of this are crosscultural. Given adequate nutri-tion and normal physiology, most women in the world begin men-struating around age twelve and cease around age forty-eight. But their reactions to both menstruation and menopause vary according to their cultural—and even religious—background. Orthodox Jewish women, who are designated ritually unclean for a full two weeks after the onset of menstruation, tend to associate more pain and inconven-ience with that monthly event than either Catholic or Protestant wom-en. Catholic women whose religious upbringing stresses very tradi-tional gender roles, with little sense of the "priesthood of all believers," report more physical and emotional upset than Protestant women. And the less volatile reactions of some Protestant women may be partly due to their more northern European cultural heritage, which stresses greater emotional reserve in both men and women than is the case in groups of more southern European origin.

This is not to say that the proverbial "stiff upper lip" is always the preferable response to stress—chronic emotional containment can, after all, lead to ulcers. Nor is it to say that all menstrual symptoms are psychosomatic. But it does mean that to a large extent women learn "to sing the menstrual blues."[13] Nurture similarly affects nature at the other end of women's reproductive life when menopause oc-curs. In most Third World cultures, unlike our own, women's social status increases with the onset of middle age, and in such cultures women do not experience menopause as being particularly stressful or depressing—in fact, often quite the opposite. Certainly there are hormonal changes that accompany menopause, and these can lead to inconvenient physical symptoms in some women. But when depression accompanies menopause in our culture, in the words of Harvard psychologist Joanna Rohrbaugh, "It is difficult to say whether children leaving home, a woman's own reentry into the job market, or her view of herself as aging and hence less sexual may be more important than the physical effects of the level of hormones circulating in the body."[14] Hormonal changes are taking place; but social and cultural factors lead to great variety in how women experience and deal with those changes.

How Nurture Affects Nature in Men

The effect of experience on biology can be shown in men as well as women. Although no one has been able to show a reliable connection between levels of androgens (such as testosterone) and aggressive behavior in humans, the opposite relationship is very well established. Under conditions of psychological stress—such as men experience during basic army training, or under threat of attack—levels of testosterone (and several other hormones) plummet. At the same time, levels of adrenalin, cortisone and at least three other hormones go up. It is as if the body in response to stress or emergency is saying "First things first." The sexual arousal associated with testosterone (which is not to be confused with the arousal of aggression) is an unaffordable luxury as long as one's very life is threatened. Needed instead are those chemicals such as adrenalin, which will give the surge of extra energy needed for "fight or flight."[15]

Even then, the effect of such hormones is far from straightforward. In a well-known series of experiments conducted in the 1960s, young men were given injections of adrenalin, then exposed to role models whom they believed had also received the drug. These role models (who were actually accomplices of the researchers) behaved either aggressively, euphorically or passively. The result was that although all the young men had received similar injections, each was most likely to mimic, and to report feeling, the responses of the role model to whom he was exposed. A surge of any hormone will certainly produce physical effects: even the young men exposed to a merely passive role model reported feeling diffusely restless and sometimes nauseous. But social conditions greatly affect how we experience and act on those bodily signals. This must be the case if the same dose of the same hormone can lead to such opposite reactions in oppositely engineered social situations.[16] Biology and experience are mutually influential.

But Where Does Freedom Come In?

Now the discerning reader will sense that something is still missing from this account. I have argued that while biology sets certain limits within which men and women develop, social and other environmental experiences greatly shape what happens within those limits. But to argue either that nurture can override nature or the opposite is still to argue within a mechanistic framework. It is a bit like arguing whether the design of the motor or the design of the body contributes more to a car's speed: either way, the car is at the mercy of inexorable forces about which it has nothing to say. Moreover, if the car does not perform as expected, we may alter its body or its motor, or even throw it on the scrap heap—but we will not hold it morally responsible for its behavior. To hold someone morally responsible for actions performed, we have to be able to say "You could have done otherwise, even given your past and present biology and your past and present social circumstances."[17]

To say that persons have freedom, and therefore moral accountability, is not to say that they are released from all the constraints of biology and socialization. Thus, one of the most valuable contributions of science and social science has been to help show under what circumstances people have reduced responsibility. There was a time when schizophrenic people were burned at the stake as willfully malevolent witches; now we look for medical and environmental interventions that will help them. There was a time when abused women or children trying to escape from their abusive situations were labeled perverse and disobedient. Now we recognize that some social conditions can be so stressful that they generate desperate responses to ensure mere survival.

Nevertheless, it is true that social science still lacks consensus about the nature of human freedom. Research psychology has by and large worked from a mechanistic model of human functioning; some combination of biological and social forces is supposed to be able to explain everything, and it is assumed that the only remaining debate concerns how much of each. Counseling psychology has often been guilty of the opposite error—that of making human beings the authors of their own freedom and encouraging them to "do their own thing" with little regard for either social or biological constraints.

The biblical view of persons cuts right through these two opposite errors. It announces that we are both "dust of the earth" and "made in the image of God." Our creaturehood, with all its biological and social embeddedness, is so good and so inevitable that only by taking on both could the son of God redeem the human race. At the same time, human beings are not "mere products" of nature and nurture; they can partially transcend both, and thus have a hand in shaping themselves. From the biblical point of view, however, this partial autonomy is in relation to nature and nurture only, and not in relation to God, who is the author of both our creaturehood and our autonomy. In the words of philosopher Stephen Evans:

> If persons are transcendent or autonomous, their transcendence is itself a gift from God, not a quality that human beings have achieved on their own. Freedom is limited by God's sovereignty and is only made possible by the mystery in which God "steps back" from his creation and gives to it a limited independence. Though human beings may have something to say about shaping themselves, from a Christian standpoint they play out this role in dialogue, not only with their fellow human beings, but with their creator.[18]

Freedom and Gender Roles
Now nothing I have just said about creaturehood and freedom will

surprise any biblically literate Christian (although it may sound strange, if not downright offensive, to many mainstream social scientists). Where Christians have trouble is in the application of these truths to their lives as women and men. For even if nurture can transcend nature, and even if we can sometimes transcend both by the exercise of our God-given freedom, is this what God wants for us? Does he want an androgynous kingdom in which we work to erase all distinctions between men and women except the basic reproductive ones?

In the previous chapter I argued on scriptural grounds that there are sex-related behavioral tendencies which, being the consequences of the Fall, God does want us to overcome. It is not God's intention that men turn dominion into domination, nor that women turn sociability into social enmeshment, but that both image God by being responsible stewards of creation and mutual servants of each other. I also pointed out that in times of spiritual revival Christians seem to be much less concerned with questions about "proper" gender roles, whether in church- or non-church-related activities. But this is still a far cry from endorsing androgyny. For in spite of the great range of behaviors shown by men and women across time and culture what remains constant (as we will see in chapters six and seven) is the fact of gender-role complementarity. What is considered "proper" for men or women to do varies greatly. But we have yet to find a culture in which there are no gender roles beyond the minimum needed for reproduction. What are we to make of this?

I believe that, at its best and undistorted by sin (and these are of course huge qualifiers) the constant invention and reinvention of gender roles is an expression of our creation-based sense that women and men need each other. Thus we search for ways to symbolize that need. In this sense the practice of gender-role complementarity is very much like a sacrament. In the same way that communion reminds us of Christ's sacrifice, and of our co-membership as living, serving parts of God's body, the observance of gender roles and rituals reminds us that men and women are incomplete without each other. But sacraments, like everything else in life, can be abused; recall Paul's condemnation of some Corinthians for the way they turned the communion feast into a drinking and eating contest that left the poorer church members without any food at all. What was supposed to be an expression of gratitude to God and solidarity with each other had become a power play (1 Cor 11:17-33).

Moreover, the use of sacraments can become legalistic. Instead of being seen as flexible symbols of a deeper relationship that God has already established, they can become vehicles of works-righteousness—activities that we think (or that someone else tells us) we "must" perform to prove our worth or earn favor with God and others. When gender roles take on this distorted function, as they all too often do, then they cease to enhance and instead begin to stifle the God-given personhood of both women and men. How then are we to steer a biblical, middle course? On the one hand I have implied that even if gender roles did not exist, men and women would feel impelled by their God-ordained mutuality to invent some. On the other hand, when they take on too much life of their own, gender roles become cages in which God never intended us to be confined. What are we to do with this paradox?

In trying to answer that question I have found it useful to think of the Christian life as a series of "offices" or vocations that nest inside each other like the progressively smaller boxes of a child's stacking toy. The overriding office of all Christians, whether men or women, is that of the redeemed sinner, committed to building God's kingdom of justice and peace as members of Christ's body. Like the largest box of the stacking toy, this office contains and overrides all others. Within it are nested other smaller "box offices" which are also important, but progressively less so. That we are women and men created to express complementarity and mutuality is important, but not of supreme importance; the goals of the kingdom override it. That God calls some people to marriage is also part of the creation order, an important Christian office within the larger office of gender-complementarity. But again, it is not of supreme importance; the goals of the kingdom override it. That is why Paul can affirm the goodness of marriage, yet praise the office of singleness for the greater freedom it gives for kingdom work (1 Cor 7:25-39).

And even the office of parent is a "box within a box": a marriage is no less a marriage just because it is childless.[19] Nor does our status in Christ's kingdom depend on our "reproductive fitness," as the distortions of sociobiology might tempt us to believe. When Paul announced to the Galatians that in Christ "there is neither Jew nor Greek, slave nor free, male nor female" (Gal 3:28), he was giving examples of his more global proclamation in 2 Corinthians 5:17-20 that *anyone* who is in Christ is a "new creation," reconciled to God and given "the ministry of reconciliation [as an] ambassador for Christ." Again, the office of kingdom builder overrides all others.

Now of course this is an argument that can be used two ways. Recognizing the primacy of kingdom building can lead to a loosening of gender-role stereotypes within the Christian community. But it has also been used as an excuse for maintaining the status quo, as when some Christian feminists are told, "Your campaign for equal rights is surely less important than the goals of God's kingdom—so just keep quiet, for everyone's sake." But such an argument, however well-intentioned, forgets that God's kingdom includes the restoration of creational *shalom* between men and women, as well as the proclamation of God's salvation in Christ. And while Christian anti-feminists are quick to assume that feminist rhetoric will "turn off " potential converts, they are less sensitive to the fact that status quo-oriented sexism also turns away a good many others. Sociologist Elaine Storkey notes that "women students whose [secular] feminist friends have begun to wrestle with the gospel of Christ often ask me: 'Where can we take them, where the sexist attitudes they hate will not be evident?' The question is a real one indeed."[20] It is one indication of the peculiar sinfulness of our age that we have gotten our priorities so mixed up. If the essence of idolatry, as Paul suggests in Romans 1, is the worship of the creation instead of the Creator, then many of us must plead guilty. We have made gender roles, or marriage or parenthood (creationally good things in their proper place) items of such importance that the larger call to preach the gospel and promote kingdom justice is easily lost in the shuffle. As we continue our examination of gender and sex, we will do well to remember which box contains all the others.

PART 2

Nature and Nuture

4

Genes
and
Gender

The first three chapters of this book introduced readers to
the broad issues that affect a Christian understanding of sex and
gender. We learned that God's special revelation in the Bible lays out
the basic human drama of creation, fall, redemption and renewal in
which women and men take part. We also learned that respect for this
special revelation in no way means that we should not learn other
details about sex and gender from God's general revelation, which is
illuminated in part through careful scientific study. But because
scientists are not free from ideology (for example, the ideologies of
materialism and determinism are very common in mainstream
science and social science), we also need to use our understanding
of the Scriptures to judge scientific theories about sex and gender. For

example, theories that deny moral accountability in either men or women, however accurate they may be in other details, are certainly inadequate from the standpoint of a Christian world view.

In the last chapter I also made three points to keep in mind throughout the rest of the book—first, that men and women are more alike than different, both biologically and psychologically; second, that although biology sets limits on what learning can accomplish, learning also affects our biology, including its sex-related aspects; and third, that we cannot appeal to any mechanical combination of nature plus nurture as a way to escape responsibility for our behavior, either as women or men. I also argued that there can be healthy as well as unhealthy gender role complementarity, and that for Christians the standards for the former come from our understanding of what it means to advance the kingdom of God on earth.

Giving Biology Its Due

In this second section of the book we are going to examine in more detail some common controversies surrounding the nature/nurture issue as it applies to women and men. We will examine arguments for the impact of genes, hormones and brain structure, and culture in chapters four, five and six respectively. And although our repeated conclusion will be that nature contributes far less to male and female behavior than is popularly supposed, I want to preface and qualify these three chapters by stating a very important truth: although Christians have often forgotten it, our bodily limits—including our maleness and femaleness—were given to us as the media in which to develop the gift of God's image. They are the forms within which we practice the freedoms of creativity, dominion, sociability, moral choice and the fruits of the Holy Spirit. With the rest of creation, God pronounced those bodily forms "very good." In spite of the Fall, they remain good. And the Bible tells us that in the resurrection life to come, we will not be disembodied, but rather have "glorified" bodies. We are not told in detail just what this means (although I have speculated about it a bit more in chapter eleven); but at the very least it suggests that our bodies, male and female, will again experience "all they were meant to be" at creation, with the distortions of the Fall finally and fully removed.

We have seen that one such distortion is the tendency of men and women to become adversaries. Created social and sexual, we sense that we cannot live without each other. Fallen, and carrying the burden of Genesis 3:16, we too often find that we cannot live peaceably with each other either. As a result, we often turn *differences* into *deficits,* and there follows a grim competition that we think only one side can win. Typically, the traits and habits associated with maleness have been judged "better," or "more human," while what is female has been pronounced "second-best," or "other" or even "not quite human."[1] But lest we think that males have a complete monopoly on such expressions of chauvinism, I should point out that in recent history women have often staked their claim to voting and other rights on the assumption that they are in fact the superior sex. Women, they argued, were less violent than men, or less prone to alcoholism and promiscuity, or more attentive to the welfare of children and old people. And so, they concluded, their involvement in government would tame the barbarian tendencies of those male rulers who, until now, had run society with only questionable success.[2]

Because we so often turn differences into deficits, then enshrine those deficits in our biological theories about men and women, I chose in chapter three to show how biologically similar men and women are, and how much the expression of biological tendencies is shaped by what we learn and by the responsible choices we make. But having done that, I also wish to give biology its due. For while biology does not rigidly determine every detail of our behavior, it is fair to say that in general, and with individual variations, it can nuance that behavior. But before we see how this happens we need a little more clarity about the relationship of biology and learning to human responsibility.

Genes: A Complex Legacy
In debates about the contribution of nature or nurture to human behavior, social reformers usually lean heavily to the nurture side.

Because they see certain social patterns (for example, race prejudice and sexism) as wrong, they want to be able to say that these patterns of behavior are mostly learned, rather than genetically inherited, and can therefore be changed through relearning. The underlying assumption seems to be that behaviors with a strong genetic component somehow "cannot be helped," whereas those which result from learning are easily changeable. But as a Christian who also cares about social reform, I would argue that this is an oversimplified approach.

In the first place, even if a weakness (or a strength) has a genetic base, this does not absolve the holder from responsibility for its management. For example, hemophilia (a deficiency in the body's blood-clotting mechanism) is biologically inherited via a sex-linked gene. But if you are a diagnosed hemophiliac, you have a responsibility to take the appropriate medication, not to play with sharp knives, perhaps to have genetic counseling before considering childbearing, and in general to know as much about this condition as possible. Secondly, it is not the case that what is "learned" is always so easily changeable. Certain behaviors acquired during "critical periods" of development (such as language skills, strong emotional associations or even gender identity) will be very resistant to change thereafter, even if a person sincerely desires such change and sees it as morally right. For example, it is possible that, even as an adult, I could learn to speak and write Chinese. But it is highly unlikely that I could ever speak it like a native, no matter how motivated I might be. (Later on, in chapter eleven, we will see that the same may apply to the acquisition of gender identity.)

So it is important to recognize that human responsibility interacts with nature and nurture in complex ways. But we also need to acknowledge the emotional loading that lies in the very idea of genetic inheritance. Biologist Anne Fausto-Sterling notes that genes have strong ego appeal, because "although my body will someday pass from this earth, part of me will remain, passing itself on to generations yet unborn. And should my children turn out to be brilliant or successful, so much the better. I can claim half the credit, since half their genes came from me."[3] Of course, that argument cuts both ways: if we are going to regard our genes as the bearers of certain virtues, we must also admit that they can incline us toward certain sins! And if we are going to claim male or female distinctives on the basis of our sex-linked genes, here too we will have to take the bad with the good. But above all, we need to recognize that the effect of genes on the behavior of men and women is far too complex to allow simplistic conclusions either about "good versus bad" or "feminine versus masculine."

In genetic studies of sex, two themes get repeated attention. The first has to do with the effects of abnormal numbers of sex chromosomes and the second with the possibility that certain behavioral traits may be sex-linked even in chromosomally normal individuals. Let us look at each of these in turn.

Sex Chromosome Abnormalities

Most readers will remember from their high school biology classes that human beings normally have twenty-three pairs of chromosomes in every bodily cell. Twenty-two pairs are called *autosomes,* because in these each member has the same shape as its mate. The twenty-third pair of chromosomes, being associated with the development of biological sex, are often called the *sex chromosomes.* In females, these appear under the microscope as matched shapes, each looking roughly like the letter X. (Hence they are called the XX chromosomes.) But in males, the pair is unmatched: one chromosome looks like an X and the other something like a Y. (Hence they are called the XY chromosomes.)

The statement that all forty-six chromosomes are in every bodily cell has only one qualifier—when sexual gametes are produced (ova in the female ovaries, sperm in the male testes) the chromosomal pairs split up. You can see why this is necessary. Since an ovum and a sperm combine to make a new individual, there has to be some way of keeping the number of chromosomes from doubling every generation! By having the father's sperm contribute twenty-three single chromosomes, and the mother's ovum likewise, the resulting child, if normal, has the usual total of forty-six, including a pair of sex chromosomes. Moreover, the mixing of chromosomes from unrelated persons generally results in biologically stronger offspring.

The biological sex of the child is determined by the combination of sex chromosomes that happen to be present in the uniting gametes. An ovum, which includes one member of the split-up XX pair, can obviously contain only one or the other of those X chromosomes. But a sperm, which includes one or the other of the split-up XY pair, has an equal chance of carrying an X or a Y sex-chromosome. Thus, if an X-bearing sperm fertilizes an X-bearing ovum, a female child with an XX set of sex chromosomes will result. If a Y-bearing sperm fertilizes the X-bearing ovum, the result will be a male child with an XY set of sex chromosomes.

Too Much of a Good Thing?

All of this is the normal pattern of sex inheritance. But occasionally abnormalities occur: a chromosome can be missing in one of the twenty-three pairs, or oppositely, an extra chromosome will be present, turning one of the pairs into a trio. In Down's syndrome children, for example, there is an extra chromosome with the twenty-first pair. The fact that such persons are both physically and intellectually impaired should dispel any simplistic notion that "extra" chromosomes will automatically mean "extra" doses of whatever skills might be carried on their genes. Among persons with sex chromosome anomalies (called "SCAs" for short) are females with one too many or one too few X chromosomes (XXX or XO) and males with extra X or extra Y chromosomes (XXY or XYY). All such SCA persons are likely to have problems with verbal or spatial skills, although these are mild in comparison to the retardation of Down's syndrome and can often be overcome by extra training. In addition, XO women and XXY men are unable to bear children, since neither the ovaries nor testes develop during the critical prenatal period.

When these anomalies were discovered in 1956, there was much talk about the "hypermasculinity" and "superaggressiveness" of XYY males, and (unsuccessful) attempts to show that they had higher levels of androgens than normal males. Conversely, there were (equally unsuccessful) attempts to link the presence of an extra female chromosome to poorer spatial ability.

The reality, however, is more complicated. In the words of one group of scientists, "the presence of an additional chromosome produces effects that are not merely additive or subtractive to a normal developmental program; rather, such a presence throws the whole program out of kilter."[4] The example of Down's syndrome shows this, as it involves a combination of mental, motor and physical defects, and sometimes even some positive features, such as a sunny, loving disposition. Similarly, boys with either an extra Y or an extra X chromosome tend to be taller, more impulsive and slower to develop self-control than normal males, a finding which certainly contradicts the naive assumption that an "extra dose of masculinity" comes only with an extra male chromosome! In the case of Turner's syndrome (women with only one X chromosome), the results are equally complex. They can include, besides the absence of ovaries, a wide neck, unusually short adult height, incomplete development of secondary sex characteristics, and (despite having only half the usual number of female sex chromosomes) typically feminine interests which result in many becoming successful homemakers and adoptive mothers.[5]

So chromosomal anomalies, sex-linked or otherwise, undeniably affect the body and may make certain behaviors more or less likely. But such effects are too complex to be described in terms of simple gender stereotypes. The fact that some scientists and journalists (and, I regret to say, some Christians) try to force such simple associations is a graphic reminder that what people want to believe colors even what passes for "objective" reporting.

Sex-Linked Genes and Gendered Behavior

So far we have been discussing sex chromosomes and the effects of too few or too many. But each of our forty-six chromosomes contains a wealth of genetic information encoded in large, double-spiralled molecules of deoxyribonucleic acid, or DNA. High school biology courses usually teach us only about the simplest, all-or-nothing kinds of genetic inheritance—the kind associated with eye color, for example. We learn that there are both dominant and recessive states, or *alleles,* for eyecolor and that brown eyes *(B)* are dominant over blue *(b).* Thus, if the father and mother both contribute a *B* allele, the *BB* pairing will produce a brown-eyed child. If one parent contributes a *B,* and the other a *b,* the result will still be brown eyes, since the brown *(B)* state dominates or "masks" the blue *(b)* one. Only if the child inherits a blue *(b)* allele from both parents will the resulting *bb* combination produce a blue-eyed child.

We also learn from this paradigm how two brown-eyed parents can produce a blue-eyed child (as my husband and I did!). If each parent carries a masked, recessive *b* allele for blue eyes along with a dominant *B* for brown, their chromosomally split ova and sperm may carry either the *b* or *B* allele, and there is a one in four chance that a *b* ovum will connect with a *b* sperm, resulting in a blue-eyed child. But genes for eyecolor (and most other traits) are carried on one of the twenty-two chromosome pairs not associated with sex. The twenty-third pair (XX or XY), in addition to determining biological sex, carry a lot of other genetic information, almost all of it on the X chromosomes. And because of the unmatched nature of the male (XY) pair, the transmission of characteristics associated with these genes (called *sex-linked transmission* since the genes involved ride on the sex chromosomes) is different from the simpler case of eyecoloring.

How Sex-Linked Transmission Works

Hemophilia, an uncommon affliction in which the blood fails to clot normally, has just such sex-linked transmission. The crucial, mutated gene resides only in the X chromosome (which, you will remember, is present in both male and female sex chromosome pairs). Because it is recessive in character (let's call it *h* for short, and the normal blood-clotting gene *H*), if it appears only on one chromosome of a female's XX pair—in an *Hh* pattern, that is—it will work just like the *Bb* pattern for eye color. In other words, it won't have any effect at all, and the woman's blood-clotting mechanism will be normal. Only in those rare cases where a woman gets an *h* from her mother's X chromosome and also an *h* from her father's X chromosome will she be hemophiliac.

But a man is not so fortunate. Because the *h* gene can only appear on his X chromosome, and cannot be "masked" or dominated by a corresponding *H* on his Y chromosome, he needs only to inherit an *h* gene on the X chromosome donated by his mother (who could in turn have inherited that X from her mother or her father) in order for the disease to show up. Moreover, the mother is usually an unwitting carrier since she carries the culprit *h* gene comfortably masked by a normal *H* on her other X chromosome, and thus is non-hemophiliac herself. That is why hemophilia shows up in men so much more frequently than in women. It is also why couples with a history of hemophilia in either family are wise to have genetic screening to determine the risks of passing it on to their own children.

Because its effects are so specific and its pattern of transmission so clear, the sex-linked nature of hemophilia is easy to agree about. Other sex-linked conditions, such as color blindness, are equally uncontroversial. But when we come across theories about the sex-linked nature of psychological traits, such as intelligence or spatial ability, the picture becomes more clouded. This is because first, there is so much controversy among psychologists regarding both the exact nature of these traits and the best ways to measure them. Second, from the point of view of geneticists, things like intelligence and spatial ability (in which most psychologists include a sense of direction, a sense of verticality and the ability to take apart and rotate figures mentally to see how they fit together) are so complex that they are unlikely to be governed by a single pair of genes to begin with, let alone genes associated only with the X chromosomes.[6]

An X-Linked Gene for Science?

These problems have not stopped some people from theorizing that certain thinking skills, or aspects of them, are sex-linked in the same way as hemophilia or color blindness and are thus much more likely to show up in men than women (this time, of course, to men's advantage). At the turn of the century, two pioneer American psychologists named Edward Thorndike and James McKeen Cattell noted a seemingly puzzling pattern: a greater number of men than women were diagnosed as mentally defective, but at the same time, a much greater number of men than women became eminent scientists. Now there are plausible social explanations for both these patterns. Rates of mental retardation were often based only on a count of institutionalized persons, and it could be that parents kept retarded daughters at home more than retarded sons, thus biasing the sexual breakdown of retardation figures. As for the dearth of eminent women scientists, there are a host of social factors, from simple discrimination to the demands of unregulated childbearing, which have kept even the brightest women from entering (let alone excelling in) *all* professions until recently.

But McKeen and Cattell, and more recently psychologists Robert Lehrke and Robert Stafford,[7] chose to advance an alternative, biological explanation of the fact that men outnumber women both at the "weak" and the "gifted" ends of the human-accomplishment spectrum. They suggested that there must be X-linkage transmission of the "major intellectual traits" (including logical and spatial ability) that they thought typical of the most gifted and productive scientists. Here is how the explanation works. Recall that the X-linked gene associated with hemophilia exists only in two states, H for the normal clotting mechanism and h for the non-clotting, hemophiliac one. In Lehrke's theory, however, an X-linked gene for "intelligence" (in Stafford's theory it is a gene for somewhat more specific "spatial ability") may exist in as many as six graded states, or alleles, running from low to high. Geneticists agree that if this kind of gradation of a trait occurs on ordinary genes, the gene carried on one chromosome will compromise, or average, with the one carried on the other chromosome of the pair. This, of course, is different from the simple, all-or-nothing transmission of eye color; it is more like what happens when persons of different skin colors marry and produce children whose skin color is intermediate between the father's and the mother's.

According to this theory, a woman who had a gene for high spatial ability on one X chromosome, and one for low ability on the other, would end up, when the two genes averaged, with middle-range spatial skills. But now consider the case of a man. He has only one X chromosome, whose sex-linked gene cannot be masked or averaged with a corresponding gene on his Y chromosome (just as in the case of hemophilia.) So if he has a gene for high spatial ability on his X chromosome, it will show up undiluted—but so will a gene for low spatial ability, if he has that one instead. In other words, because both extremes of ability would require the chance union of two X-linked genes in women ("high-high" or "low-low") whereas the same extremes would result from only one X-linked gene in men, the theory predicts just what we happen to get: more men than women with very high or very low scores and more women than men clustered in the middle range of scores.

Not So Simple
On the face of it, this theory sounds elegant and plausible. But it has a number of serious flaws. The first, which I mentioned above, is that it makes little sense to talk about specific genes for qualities such as intelligence and spatial ability whose definition has always been so non-specific and controversial. In fact, it makes about as much sense as hypothesizing a gene for religion. Whose definition of religion would we use, and why? How would we measure religiosity? What does the person who practices cannibalism as a religious ritual have in common with the person who listens to a three-point sermon every Sunday? And couldn't we "prove" that religiosity was also sex-linked? After all, more women than men are in the intermediate ranks of churchgoers, and more men than women both scoff at religion (one extreme) and rise to high religious offices (the other extreme). Surely, then, religiosity must be sex-linked in the same way that the above-mentioned researchers have claimed for "intellectual capacity" and "spatial ability"! But the weaknesses of hypothesizing X-linked genes for intellectual abilities become obvious when we draw such a parallel.

A second problem with X-linked theories of ability is that even with a behavioral trait about whose definition scientists agree, there is no way to measure its pure, genetic component separate from the effects of environment. Remember the point made in chapter one: because we grow up with the influence of our parents' genes *and simultaneously* with the influence of their training, the net effects of the two are almost impossible to separate.[8]

We can better see the difficulty of separating the effects of heredity from those of environment if we take the less controversial example of obesity. Medical doctors generally agree about the ratio of fat to bone and muscle that is healthiest for men and women of various heights. But when we say about a group of people that "obesity runs in their family," what do we mean? That we believe they share a dominant gene for overeating? Or a gene for undermetabolizing their food? Or do we mean that the parents have learned poor eating habits that they teach to their children, who then end up obese like the parents? Or do we suspect it's some of both—that there may be a genetic predisposition, but that its effects are inflated by learned habits? And if the latter, how could we separate out the percentage contribution of genetic versus socialization factors, since all we have to go on is the end result of both working together?

Even more complex answers are possible. In an extensive follow-up study of children born to women who were pregnant during the severe year of Dutch famine during World War 2, it turned out that starvation of the mother during the first six months of pregnancy may have caused damage to a part of the child's brain (the hypothalamus) concerned with appetite regulation. The children of such mothers (in contrast to those who were starved only during the final third of pregnancy, when hypothalamus development was complete) had a higher-than-average rate of obesity due to overeating. But in this case the cause was an environmental condition—inadequate nutrition of the mother during a critical period of pregnancy—that had irreversible biological effects (but not genetically determined ones!) on the appetite-regulating center of the brain.[9]

My point should be clear by now. If the effects of genes and environment are so hard to separate with regard to more easily defined conditions like obesity, how can we glibly invoke single pairs of sex-linked genes to explain the distribution of something as difficult to pin down as intelligence or spatial ability?

Of Males and Math Genes

These criticisms have generally put X-linkage theories of ability into disrepute in the scientific community. Unfortunately, many science journalists, in search of a dramatic story, are not so carefully critical. Recently I ran across a newspaper story resurrecting the X-linkage theory to explain why so many more boys than girls get recruited into mathematics talent-search contests. But most such studies have controlled neither for the different numbers of math courses taken by boys and girls, nor for the lesser encouragement given to mathematically bright girls compared to boys (itself a well-documented finding). Moreover, the students involved are an atypical sample, since they have usually been handpicked by teachers or entered in the math contest by parents. To even begin to assess genetic heritability, a large, randomly selected sample of the population at large is needed—a much more expensive and complex kind of study. The single existing study of this sort, using a large number of Scottish schoolchildren, found (1) that boys' mathematics scores were indeed more variable than girls' by a small but statistically significant amount, but (2) that most of this difference was due to an excess of males with very low scores, not very high ones![10]

Looking at spatial-ability scores, it turns out (as with the example of verbal ability discussed in chapter three) that only a small amount—about five per cent—of their variability can be accounted for by sex. This small difference does seem to favor boys. So let us assume, for the sake of argument and despite all previous qualifiers, that, small though this difference is, it is both sex-linked and socially significant. After all, it is apt to be the very people scoring in the top five per cent who become the most creative, highly paid engineers, mathematicians and so on. Arguing from just such an X-linkage theory, one researcher has calculated that males should outnumber females by a ratio of about two to one in engineering fields. But currently in the United States only three in a hundred engineers is female—which is a far cry from one in three. One reviewer of the literature summarizes:

If one did believe that the only thing standing in the way of an engineering career for women was their immutable, sex-linked, inferior spatial ability, one would still expect to find women in about one-third of all engineering jobs. In short, differences between men and women in this respect remain too small to account for the tiny number of women who become professional mathematicians, architects, and engineers.[11]

Something else must be at work, and the answer which springs to most minds is "socialization." Just as women learn to some extent to "sing the menstrual blues" (see chapter three), so they learn to avoid mathematics courses. Perhaps it is because they consider them unfeminine, because so few of their women friends take them, because they get little encouragement from parents and teachers, or because they know that their mathematical gifts will still go undercompensated in the male-dominated fields to which they might aspire. But alternative biological theories persist. Some theorists now argue that behavioral tendencies which are not under direct genetic control are still indirectly controlled by genes via their effect on sex-related hormones. These hormones, in turn, are said to affect men's and women's brains (and hence their behavior) in different ways. Alternately, without invoking hormones, some theorists simply argue that differences in the structure and functioning of male and female brains lead to differing, gender-stereotyped behaviors. We will look at these two kinds of arguments in the following chapter.

5 Hormones and Hemispheres

I can still recall my annoyance over an incident that occurred during my graduate-school days in the early 1970s. The personal physician of a U.S. vice president went into print in the *New York Times* to answer a Congresswoman's complaint that the administration was dragging its heels about placing women in higher-level government positions. The doctor's reply went in part as follows:

> Even a Congresswoman must defer to scientific truths . . . there just are physical and psychological inhibitants that limit a female's potential. . . . I would still rather have a male John F. Kennedy make the Cuban missile crisis decisions than a female of the same age who could possibly be subject to the raging hormones and curious mental aberrations of that age group.[1]

Since then, we have seen women heads of state function quite cred-
ibly in countries as culturally varied as Iceland, India, Israel, Pakistan,
the Philippines and Great Britain. In fact, Britain's prime minister,
Margaret Thatcher, was recently returned to power for her third con-
secutive term, thus surpassing the election record of every other
(male) British prime minister in this century. But during the 1970s,
statements like the one quoted above prompted predictable, tit-for-tat
responses from women journalists. Columnist Ellen Goodman wrote
that once again women were being forced to prove that they could
do certain jobs despite their "hormonal flaws"; in other words, they
were presumed guilty until proven innocent. Men, on the other hand,
were "allowed to labor on as if they were normal." In fact, she continued, tongue in cheek, males suffered from a much more severe
problem, that of "testosterone poisoning," which led them to be violent and competitive.

This was a particularly cruel disorder, she stated, "because its sufferers usually don't know they have it. They even give each other
medals for exhibiting the most advanced symptoms of the illness."
Goodman also entered the debate about whether women police officers could safely leave the confines of precinct desk jobs to join men
on patrol duty. "The truth is that the vast majority of police situations
call for tact, flexibility, and the ability to read a touchy situation," she
wrote. "Testosterone sufferers are more likely to produce or to esca-
late violence. . . . Women, however, blessed with estrogen, may [as
police studies had already suggested] have greater success in cooling
down violent situations." She concluded that, far from questioning the
wisdom of women on patrol, cities needed to reconsider whether
patrol duty should ever have been monopolized by men with "this
raging hormonal imbalance. . . . Certainly we shouldn't let them stalk
the streets alone, or in pairs. They must each be assigned a partner
who isn't born with the disease and can't catch it. Perhaps someone
with just the right level of estrogen."[2]

Hormones and Sociobiology
Amusing though such sparring may be, it should remind us again of

the foolishness of trying to prove either sex superior, whether in seriousness or in jest. For one thing, as I pointed out in chapter three, there appears to be no consistent relationship between testosterone levels and violent behavior in human beings. Nor, as we will see later in this chapter, do women's hormonal fluctuations result in mass cognitive incapacities during certain times of the month. Most importantly, Christians need to recall their confession that "*all* have sinned, and fallen short of the glory of God" and that salvation rests in neither our biological sex nor our gender roles, but only in "God's grace through the redemption that comes from Jesus Christ" (Rom 3:23-24).

But the popular press is not yet done with sex hormones. Nowadays the argument is supposedly no longer about the superiority of one sex, but about the "survival relevance" for the entire human race of separate kinds of behavior in men and women. The leading spokespersons of this position are a recent breed of scholars called sociobiologists, who theorize that the genes controlling male and female hormone patterns evolved over thousands of years of adaptation to the hunter/gatherer lifestyle practiced by our earliest human ancestors. According to such theories, men were hormonally "primed" for aggression and vigorous movement by the demands of hunting, and women were equally primed for staying home and nurturing by the demands of pregnancy and nursing, which made extended hunting trips impossible for them.

Because the genetic selections corresponding to such survival strategies took so long to emerge, sociobiologists insist that they are still with us, not having "caught up," as it were, with the changes in lifestyle brought about by urbanization and advanced technology. Translated into modern terms, this means the inevitability, if not the desirability, of men being leaders and women, followers. In the most extreme version, advanced by sociologist Steven Goldberg, men's and women's behaviors are so rigidly dictated by past survival adaptations that it is pointless to try to de-stereotype them. Patriarchy—in the home, the marketplace, government, academy and elsewhere—is inevitable, because "the inexorable pull of sexual and familial biological forces" eventually overrides all visions of a more just society, whether these visions are "nationalistic, religious, ideological or psychological."[3] In the slightly less mechanistic version of Harvard's Edward O. Wilson we do have enough freedom and flexibility to teach new roles to men and women. However this would be at the cost of considerable social inefficiency and personal stress since we would always implement such changes in resistance to our deeper "biological program."[4]

Many sociobiologists also argue for the biological inevitability of a double standard in human sexual behavior. They argue that the males of any species will maximize the survival of their own genes by copulating with as many females as possible. By contrast, once a female is impregnated, further copulations are pointless for the increase of her genes' survival. In addition, since she so heavily "invests" in carrying only a few infants to term, it is in her genes' survival interests for her to play "coy" and "hard to get" until the genetically strongest male wins "copulatory rights" with her by defeating all male rivals. Translated into modern human terms, this means that there is really not much point in trying to change patterns such as male promiscuity or female sexual subterfuge. Our genetic program, mediated by our sex-linked hormones, turns both into the biological equivalent of a religious ritual against which mere religious conviction is quite helpless. Thus, it is important to realize that Christians who argue for "traditional" gender roles by appealing to the natural revelation of sociobiology will get more than they bargained for. They will get nothing less than the swallowing up of moral accountability, in both men and women, by the mechanics of biological determinism.[5]

Hormones in Humans

Sociobiology is a sweeping, conjectural theory that explains even the most complex human behavior by appealing to past evolutionary adaptations for genetic survival and environmental fitness. Besides being biologically reductionistic and ignoring vast cultural and historical variations in human sexual behavior, its evidence comes almost entirely from animal studies using methodologies that many responsible biologists find defective. In addition, sociobiological explanations are all offered after the fact. They begin with an observation (for example, about the greater aggressiveness of males as compared to females) and work backwards to conjure up an explanation which, being buried in history, cannot be tested in any way. With this kind of hindsight, explanations can become infinitely malleable. If it happened to be the case that females rather than males were the more aggressive sex, sociobiologists would have no trouble working the finding into their theory. "Obviously" females are genetically programmed for greater aggression so that they can protect their offspring and hence the survival of their own genes! When a theory is thus rendered untestable—when its proponents refuse to specify *any* kind of evidence that would lead them to revise it—it ceases to be scientific, no matter how erudite and complex it may sound.[6]

So let us ask instead, what do we find when we examine sex-related hormonal patterns in human beings? You will recall from chapter three that it is misleading to speak of strictly "male" and "female" sex hormones since all such hormones are secreted by both women and men. What is crucial to the production of a male or female body are the relative, not the absolute, amounts of various sex-related hormones, especially during certain critical periods of development. Most of these occur before birth, as the internal and external sex organs are developing in sequential fashion However, adolescence is another such critical period, when secondary sex characteristics (such as voice tone, distribution of body hair, breast development) as well as fertility start to emerge.

From shortly after birth until shortly before puberty, sex-hormone production barely occurs in either boys and girls. Because of this, theories about the effects of hormones on gender-related behavior must take one of two forms. First, they may suggest that hormone ratio differences in boys and girls during prenatal development so affect their developing brains (in addition to their sex organs) that the consequences are set for life. Or secondly, they may propose that boys' and girls' differing hormone ratios at puberty start to inflate behavioral differences that were minimal up until then. Let us look at each of these theories in turn.

The Effect of Prenatal Hormones

The most fascinating tests of the first kind of theory have been done with children who might be called "unplanned experiments." Of course, no one is deliberately going to inject extra hormones into pregnant mothers to see what effect they have on their male or female children. But during the 1950s and 1960s, some women with a history of miscarriages took a synthetic hormone (Progestin) during subsequent pregnancies because it reduced the risk of yet another miscarriage. Unfortunately, it turned out that this drug acted like progesterone (a "female" hormone) in its ability to prevent miscarriage, but in other ways like testosterone (the hormone among "male" androgens which causes male sex organs to form in a fetus, regardless of its genetic sex).[7] This did not cause any bodily changes in genetic male (XY) babies; but it did cause some genetic female (XX) babies to have external genitals that looked more or less masculine (depending on when and for how long during pregnancy their mothers took the drug). This problem by itself was not as terrible as it seems at first glance; for one thing, the baby girls' internal sex organs were perfectly female, thus assuring normal fertility when they grew up. In addition, surgery early in life was able to "refeminize" their external genitals, making them look and function normally.[8]

But the question remains: what effects did those extra, androgen-like substances during pregnancy have on the behavior of the girls as they grew up? None of significance when it came to various measures of verbal or spatial ability. But the first follow-up studies of these "fetally androgenized" girls showed that they tended to have "tomboyish" personalities. Most enjoyed contact sports, were rather uninterested in doll-play and valued having a career over marriage (even though they were thoroughly heterosexual in orientation).

Critics rightly pointed out that parental bias might have helped produce these effects. After all, the parents knew in the delivery room that their baby girls had masculinized genitals, so even after surgical correction they might have been expecting tomboyish behavior and thus subtly reinforced it in their daughters. Moreover, the psychologists judging the girls' later behavior also knew that they had been fetally androgenized, and thus may have attributed more "boyishness" to their behavior than was in fact present. What was needed was a "double blind" study—that is, a study in which neither the childrens' parents nor the researchers later judging their behavior knew what had "gone wrong" prenatally.

Psychologist June Reinisch designed such a study in the 1970s.[9] To begin with, she chose fetally androgenized girls who had *not* been born with masculinized genitals and whose parents thus knew nothing about the potential side-effects of the drug the mother had taken. Consequently, they could not have had any tomboyish expectations about their daughters. She also studied fetally androgenized boys, on the assumption that even though they all had normal sexual anatomy, their overdose of prenatal androgens might make certain behaviors more likely. (These boys also came from families who knew nothing about the risks their children had been exposed to.) Finally, as a control group she chose same-sex siblings close in age to each of these boys and girls; this way she had pairs of children matched for family environment, only one of which had been fetally exposed to extra androgens. The crucial question was, how did the fetally androgenized children differ behaviorally from their same-sex siblings?

Reinisch concentrated on one particular kind of behavior—namely, how aggressively the children reported they would act in various childhood-conflict situations (such as arguments over the rules of a game). She found that both the boys and the girls exposed to prenatal androgens were more likely than their same-sex siblings to say they would use physical force in such situations. But two features of these findings are of particular interest. First, the differences between unexposed girls, exposed girls and unexposed boys were very small, even though statistically significant. The children were asked to respond to eighteen imaginary conflict situations. Of these, the normal girls said they would respond with physical aggression in about three; their fetally androgenized sisters averaged four, and the normal boys av eraged almost five physical-aggression answers out of a possible eight een. Again, we need to ask ourselves, how much practical difference does this make? (It certainly isn't enough of a difference to make biology the major explanation for why over ninety per cent of violent crimes are committed by men!)

Secondly, the most surprising finding was the scores of the fetally androgenized boys. They preferred physically aggressive responses twice as often as the normal boys—that is, in ten, as opposed to five, of the eighteen situations. This was surprising because research with animals seemed to show that testosterone had a "ceiling effect"; that is to say, "more" above a certain proportion made no difference to either male anatomy or behavior. However, we need to remember that this study, although elegantly controlled in most ways, was not a test of the effects of pure testosterone. It tested a synthetic hormone which turned out to function in some ways like a "female" hormone and in other ways like a "male" hormone. Consequently, it is still unwise to compare from the children in this study to those who have had a normal hormonal environment prenatally.

We also need to remember that the study was not measuring actual physical violence, but only fantasized acts by children who might very well show more self-control in the actual event. And even if we ignore the ambiguous nature of Progestin, unless we are to assume that all violent males have been fetally over-androgenized (which is unlikely) we cannot conclude that hormones "make" certain sex differences in behavior inevitable. At most, they may tilt our inclinations one way or another; but by far the greater contribution to such differences comes from our learning and choice-making histories.

Hormone Levels in Adulthood

I have described June Reinisch's study in some detail because it shows the kind of painstaking, expensive research design needed even to begin separating the effects of nature from those of nurture on gendered behavior. I cannot stress strongly enough that this kind of study is extremely rare, both because of its costs in time and money, and because the kind of "unplanned experiment" represented by the boys and girls involved is, of course, very uncommon. What this means is that most studies claiming to "settle" the nature/nurture controversy have methodological limitations that make their results capable of more than one interpretation. Indeed, even Reinisch's results are not completely clear-cut, since she was not testing the effects of pure, naturally secreted testosterone. Consequently, the interpretation that one chooses, whether it be "traditionalist" or "egalitarian," usually comes as much from the researcher's prescientific attitudes about men or women as it does from a dispassionate interpretation of the data.

We should also note that it is precisely the designers of the most careful studies who are least likely to make sweeping, one-sided claims about the origins (and implications) of sex differences. Although she is a psychobiologist who firmly resists the notion that "learning accounts for everything," Reinisch's research has convinced her that differences between men and women in perception, thinking and personality are built on a foundation of very small biological differences that are highly magnified by our personal and social histories and by the immediate demands of situations in which we find ourselves. Unfortunately, others who go into print are not so cautious. This is certainly the case with a second kind of hormone theory—one which claims to explain sex differences on the basis of adult, rather than prenatal, levels of hormones.

The "Thinking" Hormones?

Toward the end of childhood, sex hormones in men and women begin to follow very different patterns. In childhood, both androgens and estrogens are almost undetectable in the urine samples of either boys or girls. But around age ten, androgens increase sharply in both sexes, whereas estrogens increase only in girls. And from puberty on, women's hormone ratios change according to the phase of the menstrual cycle, whereas men's remain relatively constant. Some theorists have claimed that there is a causal relationship between these male/female hormone differences and the pattern of greater male achievement in academic and professional fields, in contrast to the greater number of women in "adjunct" roles such as clerks, secretaries and bookkeepers.

According to this theory, the increase of adult hormones in both

sexes activates the brain in a way that helps the performance of simple, habitual tasks (such as typing, filing and doing routine calculations.) At the same time, sex-related hormones are said to interfere
with the performance of more sophisticated tasks—the kind that require us to "stop and think" (like scientists, doctors and engineers)
rather than just go with our first impulse or our familiar habits. The
theory then goes on to suggest that estrogens inflate this effect more
than androgens. Hence we should not be surprised to find just what
we do find: more men in highly paid professional roles that require
much original thought and more women in lower-paid "routine activity" positions. (There is also, as in sociobiological theories, the
strong suggestion that if this job distribution is based on biology, there
is nothing we can do about it.)[10]

But as it turns out there is no support even for the initial assumption
that sex hormones do help or hinder task performance in the ways
suggested. For one thing, if true, it would make women's performance
of "routine tasks" best in the middle of their menstrual cycle when
estrogens are at their highest level. It would also make women's performance of tasks requiring "higher level thinking" best just before
and after menstruation, when estrogens are at their lowest level. Yet
research involving as many as thirteen cognitive tasks given to women
at all phases of the menstrual cycle has found no such fluctuations.
Some women do report emotional fluctuations—feeling more buoy-
ant and self-confident at mid-cycle and more gloomy premenstrually.
But these changes apparently are not significant enough to influence
either kind of task performance. (In fact, study after study has shown
that it is men, not women, who have the highest rates of job absen-
teeism, despite the greater stability of their hormones!)[11]

The "Sexy" Hormone?
Aside from certain mood fluctuations in women (and we still don't
know either how or how much these are hormonally caused), do
hormone differences in men and women affect any other behavior?
Surprising as it may seem, the most interesting difference is also a
similarity. It appears that testosterone is connected with sexual arousal

in both men and women. Loss of testosterone in males, whether from physical castration or chemical interference, generally leads to a progressive decrease in sexual arousal and in the capacity for erection and ejaculation. But when women suffer estrogen deficiency (for example, after removal of the ovaries), it is mostly lubrication of the vagina that decreases and not so much sexual arousal or orgasmic capacity.

John Money, who has done a great deal of research on the relationship of sexual biology to behavior, finally concluded that the testosterone-like substance produced by women's adrenal glands (which rest on top of the kidneys) is responsible for much of their sexual arousal. In women who have lost adrenal glands as treatment for certain forms of cancer, sexual arousability, activity and orgasmic capacity all decline. By contrast, women who have had injections of testosterone for the treatment of breast cancer often report an increase in sex drive (although the testosterone may also produce masculinization in terms of increased body hair, deepening of the voice, and the like).[12] It is true that men's adrenal cortex also produces small amounts of the androgen-like substance, so that in normal males this "double source" of androgen (a lot from the testicles plus a little from the adrenal glands) may help explain why most men are more easily sexually aroused than most women. But after the loss of testicular androgen, the ratios of a man's androgens to estrogens—and recall that it is ratios, not absolute amounts, that are crucial in both sexes—may be so altered as to make the adrenal cortex androgen of little help.

And even here we have unexpected surprises. Although androgen replacement therapy usually helps to restore sexual potency in men, the relationship is not a simple one. As I write this chapter during a leave of absence on the Canadian prairies, the Fifteenth Winter Olympic Games have begun in nearby Calgary, Alberta. Among the features of the Olympic site is a sophisticated laboratory for detecting traces of over 400 banned drugs in the athletes' post-performance urine. Chief among the suspects are steroids, synthetic androgens which help to build muscle if taken over a period of months. Their prohibition at the games is not based just on the fact that they give their users an unfair advantage in competition, but also on the medical problems they can provoke after long-term use—including impotence in men! To the extent that these steroids function like natural androgens, "more" is not always "better"![13]

It is even the case that "less" is not always "worse." Sexual arousability, like all human behavior, is greatly affected by learning, as witnessed by the fact that some adult castrates, and even paraplegics who lack genital sensation, continue active sexual lives. As psychologist Joanna Rohrbaugh puts it:

> Sexually mature adults have already accumulated memories of sexual sensation and the feelings accompanying arousal, orgasm, and ejaculation, as well as a network of habitual sexual responses. The drastic reduction of sex hormones does not eradicate these memories and habits . . . Eroticism can continue—in imagery and behavior.[14]

A Hormonal Summary: The "Juke Box Theory"

So as in our overview of genes and gender, we must conclude that although sex-related hormones affect behavior, they do not do so in ways that conform to simple stereotypes about men and women. The chemistry of our bodies is extremely complex. Moreover, it is subject to what psychologist George Mandler called "the juke box effect." In the experiment with adrenalin injections mentioned in chapter three, you will recall that this same hormone, in the same dosage, affected different groups of people in different ways, depending on the social situation they were in. All could "feel" the effects of the drug; but how they acted on those feelings was very variable. Like the quarter in the juke box, which is necessary for getting a tune but does not determine which tune gets selected, so our hormones—sex-related and otherwise—produce certain tangible, physiological effects but do not "make" us act in rigidly prescribed ways.[15] Another researcher aptly expressed it as follows:

> Hormones alone, including the differing hormonal profiles of human males and females, do not explain anything. For hormones alone do not exist. Hormonal events merge with brain events and

social events, and causation works like a blender, or at least like a casserole, in which no single ingredient determines the end result. Hormones do not rage, they insinuate.[16]

Thus hormones cannot be used to excuse violent, incompetent or sexually licentious behavior in either men or women. Nor can we responsibly invoke them to argue for the inevitability of patriarchy (or, for that matter, matriarchy). They are part of our creational package; how we choose to live with them will reflect the accountability that is part of God's image in all of us.

Sex and the Brain

There is one other research tradition that tries to assess the effect of biology on men's and women's behavior. This is the field of neuroscience, or brain science, which studies the development, structure and functioning of the brain. In one sense it is a very old field: ever since human beings have made war on each other (and even more so now that they drive cars and motorcycles), doctors have been able to study people who have survived assaults on their brains, but been left with physical or psychological impairments. Brain damage can also result from strokes, which may deprive a brain area of oxygen long enough to cause temporary or permanent changes in its functions. By studying persons' behavior after these traumas, and sometimes by studying their brains after they die, we have gradually "mapped" the gross functions of the brain—the areas associated with vision, smell, hearing, language skills and so on. More recently, we have begun to learn other things by recording the brain's electrical activity in both normal and clinical groups of people, and by tracking the brain's blood flow using injections of radioactive isotopes.[17]

If you looked at a human brain minus its protective skull covering, you might be reminded of a giant, shelled walnut. You would see two wrinkled handfuls of soft, pinkish-grey matter, separated by a deep, long groove but joined together by a bridge of connective tissue across the lower middle part. On the surface, the two halves look very much alike; but we have known for some time that the two sides, or "hemispheres," of the brain are somewhat specialized for different kinds of thinking. In virtually all right-handed people, and the majority of left-handed ones, the left hemisphere is more specialized for language, logical analysis, mathematics and other "sequential" activities—that is, those that proceed a step at a time in an orderly fashion. The right hemisphere, by contrast, is more specialized for artistic and spatial abilities, and for an emotional, non-analytic, non-verbal approach to reality.

It is important to understand that hemispheric specialization is not an all-or-nothing affair; it merely means that one side may be more proficient than the other in its ability to handle certain kinds of tasks. Nor does such specialization mean that the two sides of the brain have trouble communicating or coordinating their activities. Normally such communication is guaranteed by the thick band of nerve fibers that connects the two halves, as well as by some smaller connections. Finally, unlike our sexual anatomy, hemispheric specialization is not fixed either prenatally or early in childhood. In children who have had considerable brain damage to only one hemisphere, the undamaged hemisphere can take over and eventually carry out all the activities of a normal brain—something which cannot happen in adults. Because of this early "plasticity" of the brain, it is possible that childhood experience, both social and physical, helps to shape adult hemispheric patterns in the same way that we saw experience altering nerve-cell structures in both cats and humans in chapter three. This is an important point to bear in mind as we talk about possible sex differences in hemispheric functioning. Just because such differences seem to be common in adults does not mean that they are based solely, or even mostly, in biology. Too little work has been done on the relationship of experience to the brain hemispheres to warrant such a conclusion.[18]

Brain Lateralization in Women and Men
All major theories about sex differences in brain organization begin with two observations already familiar to us. When sex differences in verbal abilities are found, they are more likely to favor women; when differences in spatial abilities are found, they are more likely to favor

men. Moreover, as we have just noted, these same verbal and spatial abilities tend to be concentrated in different hemispheres of the adult brain. Thus, "given that the types of abilities that differ by hemisphere are the same ones that differ by sex, it seemed to many psychologists only a short leap to suggest that the sexes differ in the way their hemispheres specialize these abilities."[19] Please note that this is a much more modest proposal than the popular view that "men are more left-brained" and "women are more right-brained." Such generalizations hide nonsensical inconsistencies, since the left brain is specialized both for language (a supposedly female strength) and mathematics (a stereotypically male strength). Similarly, the right brain is specialized both for spatial ability (a supposedly male strength) and intuitive, holistic thinking (a stereotypically female strength).

What is being proposed is that men's and women's brains are in some ways "differently lateralized"—in other words, that the extent of hemispheric specialization may differ between the sexes and that somehow this accounts for the modest differences we find in ability patterns. Just what these different patterns of lateralization are, and how they might relate to sex differences in thinking styles, is the subject of much controversy, with many contradictory findings. There is, however, some evidence for the first step in this debate—that is, for the theory that men's brain hemispheres are more strongly specialized, or "lateralized," for their respective functions than women's.

Psychological tasks involving both hearing and seeing seem to bear this out. In the hearing tasks, for example, persons put on a headset and hear conflicting messages in each ear—for example, two different sets of number sequences. Later they are asked to recall as many of the numbers as they can. In general, women tend to remember the input to each ear fairly equally, whereas men tend to remember their right-ear input better than their left. Since the right ear is mostly connected to the left brain hemisphere (and vice-versa), this suggests that men's left hemispheres are more specialized to handle verbal materials than women's.[20]

Of course, men's greater left-brain specialization for language gives them no particular advantage, since if anything it is women who do better on verbal tasks. What complicates the matter is that when visual-spatial tasks are used (those which draw on right-hemisphere special-ization), most men are still more lateralized than most women, this time in the right hemisphere and this time to their advantage! What some theorists are now trying to do is find a way to explain why women benefit from having their language processing more "spread out" between the two halves of the brain, while at the same time men benefit from having their spatial abilities more localized in the right hemisphere![21] The debate is such a tortured one that many psychol-ogists—especially those who are unconvinced about the biological origin of cognitive sex differences to begin with—question whether it should consume so much energy.

I agree with this position, not because I belittle the importance of researching the biological basis of behavior, but because the idea of right brain/left brain dichotomy is one which easily gets blown out of proportion. In fact, the popular media have made so much of it that more cautious neuroscientists even have a name for the craze: they call it "dichotomania." Neuroscientist Roger Sperry, who won a Nobel Prize for his work on hemispheric specialization, has publicly criti-cized the tendency to over-connect certain abilities to each side of the brain. Other divisions, such as front versus back and top versus bot-tom, may be equally fundamental; most importantly, Sperry pointed out, the brain works as a closely integrated whole in ways that we have barely begun to understand, and too much emphasis on its different parts may lead us to neglect this most fascinating puzzle of all.[22]

Ironically, some of the most interesting findings of the "brain local-ists" have demonstrated this very point—that the brain works as a whole and finds ways to overcome the limits of its different parts. For even those studies which show men to be more right-brained than women on spatial tasks often end up finding no sex differences in overall scores. Most reviewers take this to indicate that women often resort to verbal strategies to solve nonverbal problems having to do with spatial relations.[23] I find this a most interesting conclusion, be-cause it reflects my own experience. I am one of those people who easily gets "turned around" in strange places—so much so that I always drive with a compass on the car's dashboard and warn my children not to distract me as I navigate my way around unfamiliar cities. Yet I seldom get lost and have always scored higher than average on measures of spatial relations. At the same time, I am aware that my methods for solving spatial problems involve very verbal, step-by-step conversations with myself ("Turn south onto this freeway, then east onto that one," and so on). They are, in other words, very "left brain" strategies.

By contrast, I know other people who always seem to know which direction they're facing, no matter how many turns they've taken and even if they're in a place several stories underground. When I asked one of them how he managed this, he replied, "I guess I must constantly be processing information about direction on some unconscious level, because I really can't explain how it happens!" In a way, his reply was not surprising, because if he used primarily right-brain strategies, then of course he wouldn't be able to explain how he did it, since the right hemisphere is the nonverbal one. But his reply was also amusing, because it was a fine example of "male intuition," in contrast to my own "female rationality," which always breaks spatial tasks down into logical steps!

Conclusion

So once again, the complexity of human functioning eludes simple stereotypes about what men and women "are" or "should be" like. In these past two chapters I have been careful to give attention to biology as a possible explanation for sex differences in behavior. Yet in all three areas we have examined—genes, hormones and hemispheres—we have found that the differences, when they occur, are both smaller and more complex than we thought. In most cases they are impossible to separate from the effects of learning. Moreover, we cannot invoke biology to excuse our moral failures as men or women. Our lives are permeated with a God-ordained freedom and accountability that works through, but at the same time transcends, our biological assets and liabilities. And, as we will see in the next chapter, this leads both to crosscultural similarities and crosscultural differences in the way that human beings think about sex and gender.

6

Nature, Culture and Common Grace

When I graduated from college at twenty-two years of age, I had never been out of Canada except for an afternoon visit to the Detroit Zoo, a few hours drive from my family home in Ontario. I had never been in an airplane except for a quick spin in a four-seater above the farms and forests lining the southeastern shore of Lake Huron. I could count on my fingers the number of black people, aside from international students, that I had ever met. Yet a scant three months after receiving a degree in psychology and biology, I was sitting in a Canadian Air Force transport plane on my way to a destination halfway around the world, under a two-year contract to teach English and French to African high school students in the newly independent republic of Zambia.

It sounds like an unbeatable recipe for culture shock, doesn't it? But in fact neither my decision to teach in Africa nor my preparation for going there were undertaken hastily. My sponsoring agency, a Canadian analog to the Peace Corps, put its applicants through a rigorous and lengthy screening process. Once accepted, I spent the three months between graduation and departure getting intensive teacher training and cultural orientation with about a hundred other volunteers of various ages and backgrounds from all over Canada. And after my arrival in Zambia, where I was posted to a large, rural secondary school run by the Salvation Army, my cultural adjustment and teaching progress were monitored by officials both from the Canadian agency and the Zambian Ministry of Education.

By the time I had finished my two-year teaching stint, I was ready to begin graduate training back in North America—but with a difference. As a result of my African experience, I chose to do graduate work in the embryonic field of crosscultural psychology. In addition, I was accepted by a university with an African Studies program in which I could also take courses. And within a year or two I became interested in the newly reborn women's movement and the impact it was beginning to have on social and crosscultural psychology. All of this eventually led to my returning to Zambia to do my doctoral research on the influence of both culture and gender on visual perception.[1] Along the way, also in Africa, I became a Christian, partly through the influence of a British family who convinced me that being a Christian need not be synonymous with being anti-intellectual. Their example, combined with the practical love and activism of my earlier teaching colleagues from the Salvation Army, catapulted me into the kingdom once and for all.

Needed: A Theology of Culture
In previous chapters I outlined a biblical approach to the topics of sex and gender and used it to evaluate some of the burgeoning, Western world literature on the psychobiology of men and women. But we have already seen, even in studies confined to our own Western culture, that biology is both augmented and reshaped by learning. We

know that learning experiences vary not just across individuals, but across sex and social class as well. How much more variety will we encounter when we step outside North America and the rest of the Western world? And how is a Christian to react to such diversity, in gender-related and other behavior?

In past chapters I have taken a consistent stand against the idea that "mechanics replaces ethics"—the idea that we can appeal to the mechanisms of either biology or learning to bypass responsibility in women or men. But my own crosscultural experience, to which I have added other field trips since my graduate-school days,[2] has left me very skeptical of the notion that America is at root a model "Christian" nation whose political, economic and social organization (or some past version of these) should simply be copied by everyone else. Does this make me a cultural relativist at heart—one who holds that beliefs about what is true or false, right or wrong, are solely determined by differing cultural experiences and hence cannot be judged according to any absolute standards? Obviously, such a position would not square with my insistence that mechanics cannot replace ethics.[3] Nor would it square with my belief, as a Christian, that we have "an eternal Gospel to proclaim . . . to every nation, tribe, tongue, and people" (Rev 14:6).

Culture is the crucible in which all human development takes place. But before we sample the crosscultural literature on gender roles, we need some biblically based principles to guide us. To steer a fine line between total cultural relativism and rigid ethnocentrism (the belief that one's own culture should be the standard for all others), we need first of all a theology of culture.

Creation, Fall or Both?

Let us look more closely at Genesis 1—11, which deals with salvation history up to the time of Abraham. Genesis 1—3 speaks of the creation and fall of woman and man as gendered, interdependent individuals. It is only after their expulsion from the Garden that they begin to create more complex cultures. This has led some people to conclude that cultural diversity is a result of the Fall, and hence something we should only regretfully tolerate, or even replace, as far as possible, with a single, totally "Christian" culture (one whose blueprint usually turns out to look remarkably like the home culture of the would-be Christianizer). This point of view is frequently supported by appealing to the Genesis 11 account of the Tower of Babel. Here we are told that humankind, having assembled in one place with one language, decided to "build a city, and a tower with its top in the heavens, and . . . make a name for [themselves] (Gen 11:4). God, correctly seeing this as another bid to replace him (this time due to an entire culture's arrogance, rather than that of one couple), decides to divide and conquer. He proceeds to diversify their languages so that groups cannot understand each other, and to "scatter them abroad over the face of the earth" (Gen 11:9).

No doubt that this account portrays the most basic roots of cultural chauvinism and competitiveness, with all the ethnocentrism, warfare and mutual exploitation that we see throughout history. But is this the same as saying that all aspects of cultural diversity are due to the Fall? If we back up a bit to the chapters prior to Genesis 11, we find that things are really more complex than this point of view suggests. Recall from chapter three that at creation, God issues a "cultural mandate" to the man and woman: they should create families, fill the earth, subdue it and have dominion over every living thing. There is "freedom within form" here: being made in God's image, the woman and man have latitude for creativity and variety. But being creatures accountable to God, they are to exercise dominion within the norms set down by him. Yet even after their expulsion from the Garden, this cultural mandate is not withdrawn. In the words of theologian Herman Bavinck:

> Their punishment does not follow immediately nor in full force. They do not die on the self-same day they have sinned, but remain alive; they are not sent to hell, but instead find themselves entrusted with a task on earth. In short, a condition now sets in which has a very special character. It is one in which wrath and grace, punishment and blessing, judgment and longsuffering are mingled with each other. It is the condition which still exists in nature and

among men, and one which comprehends the sharpest contrasts within itself.[4]

Thus, although post-Fall culture is a mixed blessing (just as post-Fall men and women are), it still bears the stamp of God's protection and approval as the vehicle through which the image of God in human beings expresses itself. Moreover, even though human wickedness led to the flood of Genesis 6—8, with only "righteous Noah" and his family surviving, God repeats the cultural mandate and even expands it at the beginning of chapter 9, when the flood is over. Right away, of course, we see the mixed character of human culture. Noah becomes "the first tiller of the soil . . . [and plants] a vineyard" (Gen 9:20), but also gets drunk with the wine he makes from its fruit, embarrassing his sons with his nakedness. Nevertheless, God covenants not send another catastrophe to judge human wickedness, but instead promises a faithful rotation of the seasons and the preservation of "every living creature of all flesh that is upon the earth" (Gen 9:17). This "covenant of nature," as it is sometimes called, ensures a regularity to earthly life which makes human cultural activity even more possible than before the flood. Bavinck again expresses it well:

The tremendous catastrophes which formerly shook the cosmos gave way to a regular course of events. The span of human life was shortened, man's [sic] strength was diminished, his nature was mellowed, he was chastened to the requirements of a society and placed under the discipline of government. . . . There were dams and dikes now to hold back the stream of iniquities. Order, measure, and number came to be the characterizing earmark of creation. God curbs the wild animal in man and so gives him opportunity to develop his gifts and energies in art and science, in state and society, in work and calling. Thus God fulfills the conditions which make history possible.[5]

When the Kings Come Marching In

Again, this is not to say that any culture (including our own) is exempt from the effects of the Fall. But there is wheat mixed with the chaff: all women and men, whether they explicitly acknowledge God or not, are able to do cultural work which has God's blessing, including the work of crafting various human roles which make for an orderly and just society. This is part of what theologians have called "common grace." In a famous passage near the end of Isaiah God is pictured at the close of history as follows: "Your gates shall be open continually; day and night they shall not be shut; that men may bring to you the wealth of nations, with their kings led in procession" (Is 60:11). Throughout this chapter, Isaiah sees God gladly receiving the best that human cultural efforts have achieved. And at the end of the New Testament the apostle John affirms Isaiah's vision: kings will bring the "glory and honor of nations" into the new Jerusalem (Rev 21:26).

Many of those results will first need purifying, for as John also writes, "Nothing unclean shall enter [the city]" (Rev 21: 27). Swords will have to be beaten into plowshares; some cultures will no doubt have to account for their men's misuse of dominion, or their women's misuse of sociability (recall chapter two here). Still, there is no doubt that from a biblical point of view cultures other than our own are worthy of study and respect and not just evangelization accompanied by reflex "Americanization." Indeed, we cannot properly evangelize other cultures unless we have first studied them with respect and been prepared to learn things we may have missed or suppressed that God, in his grace, has revealed to other groups.[6] And this is as true of the study of gender roles as it is of any other topic.

Culture and Gender
Cultural anthropologists have a challenging but unenviable task. Social scientists working in their home cultures can take for granted that they understand the meaning of much that they observe. But the visitor to another culture must learn a whole new set of (largely unspoken) rules—rules about what is considered polite or rude, rules about how different generations and social classes should interact, rules about how tragedy and prosperity are to be interpreted and, of course, beliefs about the nature and proper behavior of women and men. In fact, there is one school of social psychology that holds the most basic characteristic of all human beings is their self-conscious

production and enforcement of social rules. Cultures and individuals may adhere to different world views and hence justify their behavior by appealing to different sets of complex rules. But what unites them all, on this account, is a concern to be perceived as "doing the right thing" in the eyes of the group to which they belong or would like to belong.[7]

But anthropologists are not just concerned with cultural diversity. As they collect data from more and more cultures—especially cultures practicing the more basic subsistence styles of our earliest human ancestors—they begin to ask if there are common threads running through the behavior and thinking of *all* such cultures, and if so, what might account for these. Anthropologist Sherry Ortner states that "much of the creativity of anthropology derives from the tension between two sets of demands: that we explain human universals, and that we explain cultural particulars."[8] A certain behavior pattern, such as warfare, may be universal or nearly so. But its universality does not necessarily mean that it is biologically programmed (otherwise we would expect all cultures to be equally warlike at all points in history). Nor does its universality make it morally virtuous (although we might argue that it is morally permissible as the lesser of two evils in some circumstances). It is such cultural "themes and variations" that anthropologists wish to explain and often (despite claims about value neutrality) to judge.

The Universally "Second Sex"

One such human universal is the lower social status of women as compared to men. Now even in simple subsistence societies there are almost no activities that are universally the domain of only women or men. The few exceptions center around childbearing and nursing activities, which are biologically restricted to women, and activities such as making war, acquiring raw materials and dealing with large animals, most of which require male strength. What is universal is the higher status of whatever is considered "men's work." If in one culture it is men who build houses and women who make baskets, then that culture will see house building as more important than basket weaving. In another culture, perhaps right next door, where women construct houses and men make baskets, basket-weaving will have higher social status than house-building. (This example comes from my own field work in West Africa.) In fact, such differences may even become a basis for cultural chauvinism: "they" cannot possibly be normal human beings like "us," because their men do women's work, and they let their women do men's work!

It is important to understand that this thesis about the universally higher status of men's activities is not just a prejudice based on the skewed observations of male anthropologists. It is something about which feminist women anthropologists also agree. In the words of two of these:

> Whereas [all anthropologists] agree that there are societies in which women have achieved considerable social recognition and power, none has observed a society in which women have publicly recognized power and authority surpassing that of men. Everywhere we find that women are excluded from certain crucial economic or political activities, that their roles as wives and mothers are associated with fewer powers and prerogatives than the roles of men. It seems fair to say then, that all contemporary societies are to some extent male-dominated, and although the degree and expression of female subordination vary greatly, sexual asymmetry is presently a universal fact of human life.[9]

In the past, however, male anthropologists have generally regarded this finding as unproblematic or unworthy of further exploration. (Note the implicit value judgment!) By contrast, more recently trained women anthropologists, and some men too, have begun to ask further questions about this universal theme. Why do women, in our own society and elsewhere, accept their subordinate status so willingly? What common factors unite those cultures in which men's and women's status is more equal? Are women really as powerless as they appear to be in both public and private life, or do they in fact exercise a considerable amount of covert influence while paying lip-service to the cultural norm of male supremacy?

Cultural anthropologists, both male and female, generally agree that it is not enough to appeal to biology for an explanation of male dominance. On the average, men do have greater physical strength, and women's mobility is certainly constrained at times by childbearing and nursing. But these biological differences acquire differing values only within the framework of human culture. Indeed, since only women give birth to new human beings, there is no inherent reason why they should not be valued more than men rather than less. Yet in most cultures, ironically, less social recognition is given to the women who produce new life than to male warriors who risk their own lives in the process of destroying the lives of others.

I have argued on biblical grounds that male domination, and female acceptance of it via social enmeshment, are ultimately traceable to the results of the Fall (see chapter two). But given the freedom human beings have to shape culture, we should not be surprised to find that these fallen tendencies get expressed and rationalized in a variety of ways—sometimes tending more, sometimes less, toward proper justice between women and men. Anthropologists have suggested at least three different theories to account for the universality of male dominance and female subordination. One of these I will deal with in the balance of this chapter. The other two, because they have such rich psychological implications for both sexes, will be outlined and applied in the following chapter.

Nature versus Culture
One explanation of women's subordination begins with the thesis that in all cultures women are seen as closer to nature than men, whereas men are seen as more involved with culture than women. Furthermore, since the cultural is universally valued more than the merely natural, it follows that women, being closer to nature, are devalued by their association with it. Now in order to unpack this explanation, we first need to understand how the words *culture* and *nature* are being used. Sherry Ortner, who has developed this theory quite fully, shares the common anthropological understanding that culture

is the process of generating and sustaining meaningful forms (symbols, artifacts, etc.) by means of which humanity transcends the givens of natural existence, bends them to its purposes, controls them in its interest. We may thus broadly equate culture with the notion of human consciousness, or the products of human consciousness (i.e., technology and systems of thought), by means of which humanity tries to assert its control over nature.[10]

Why should women be considered closer to nature than men? First of all, because their bodies are necessarily more involved with what Ortner calls "species life": menstruation, pregnancy and nursing are reproductive functions women share closely with non-human female mammals. Furthermore, reproductive functions take up proportionately more of women's adult life than men's, especially in cultures that lack birth control and in which each child may be breast-fed for two or three years after birth. Reproduction may even drastically shorten women's lives, given the risks of childbirth in most cultures throughout history. By contrast, men's role in reproduction involves very little time, energy or bodily risk. Thus they have more freedom and energy to invest in technology, trade, games, art, politics and religion. All of these cultural activities separate human beings from mere animals, and so they (and the people who get to practice them most) are somehow seen as "superior."

Of course it is quite clear that women also practice culture. In most societies they are the ones who transform food from raw to cooked; they are the main socializers of young children, the makers of many artifacts and even (common wisdom to the contrary) the chief suppliers of food from farming or gathering.[11] But due to the constraints of reproduction, much more of their cultural work takes place in or near the household unit and is combined with the care of young children. And young children themselves are easily regarded as part of "prehuman" nature. They are born incontinent and largely unsocialized; like animals, they cannot walk upright, talk intelligibly or take social responsibility. And so women are seen as relatively less cultural, or more connected to nature, not just because of their involvement in reproduction, but because of their subsequent care of "unacculturated" children. Indeed, women are often seen as "childlike" themselves, because of their greater restriction to the home base and their constant association with children in that setting.

This idea that women are less cultural and more childlike is almost universally accepted by both women and men. And yet it is a view fraught with contradiction. In the first place, the socialization of children obviously requires a very detailed knowledge of the culture as a whole. One cannot be unacculturated and do a very good job of acculturating the next generation! Secondly, if we accept Ortner's idea that culture can be equated with human consciousness, then woman's cultural consciousness is seen in the very fact that "she has followed out the logic of the culture's arguments and has reached culture's conclusions along with the men [about her own status]."[12] In other words, she understands, accepts and offers the same reasons as men do for the differing status of the sexes. This is hardly what one would expect from people who somehow lack cultural consciousness to much the same degree that children do. Something else must be at work.

A Biblical Critique
Recall that from a biblical standpoint wheat and chaff—good and evil—are intermingled in all cultures. Recall too that in wake of the Fall both sexes tend to accept men's transformation of dominion into domination and women's transformation of sociability into social enmeshment. Thus, the "nature versus culture" reason, universally accepted to explain the lower status of women, is more likely to be an unconscious rationalization for the fallen state of both. This is all the more plausible when we realize that Christians too, for the most part, have participated in this ideology and offered the same arguments for it throughout history.[13] Yet ironically, the chief New Testament metaphors for being a Christian are not drawn from male-dominated activities such as warfare, politics, international trade, or even high art. They are mainly metaphors concerned with giving birth (witnessing so that others can be "born again"), nurturing (patiently discipling others), caring for the body (of interdependent believers) and taking the lower status of a servant—all activities taken as the more "natural"

domain of women! Christians are also reminded that they must become "like children": they must not assume that their acculturation
or worldly power can save them, but instead adopt the receptive status
of a learner.[14]

That the wisdom of this world should be so turned upside down was
a shock to many of Jesus' disciples. One of them even felt justified in
betraying him for his failure to bring in the kingdom by force of arms,
as a proper male Messiah would be expected to do. And to this day,
I suspect, it is hard for many men to accept that becoming a Christian
means being more like a woman or a child in the eyes of the world.
The very idea—so foreign and low status in the thinking of almost
every culture—is a stumbling block that prevents many from even
considering the claims of the Gospel.[15] And even among men who
become professing Christians, I suspect that there are still some who
feel conflicted about becoming culturally "feminized" in the process.
After all, wasn't it Freud who said that the domains of women were
Kinder, Küche und Kirche (children, cooking and church)? The obvious
implication is that real men will not be caught even dabbling in any
of these areas!

I have often wondered how Christian men handle such conflicts.
It is difficult to ask most of them directly, because self-esteem is so
closely tied to gender identity that any threats to the latter are often
denied on the conscious level and dealt with only by unconscious
defense mechanisms. But I do have some hypotheses about their
coping behavior. One of the ways that men can soften the conflict
between their cultural masculinity and their "feminization" as Christians is to turn churches and other Christian agencies into thoroughly
hierarchical institutions, with women kept as low in the hierarchy as
possible. By so distancing themselves from women who are their fellow believers men may feel correspondingly less feminized themselves.

More specifically, men may delegate the interpersonal, nurturing
tasks of the church—from care of children and the sick to the preparation and serving of food—largely to women. (In the process, ironically, they are undertraining future male pastors in the social skills

and sensitivity that are essential to their job!) The more formal, visible and well-paid tasks—theologizing, preaching, the making of important administrative decisions—are then concentrated in male hands. In addition, when a special vocabulary and training (available only to men) are required to be an administrator, pastor or theologian, then the "safety gap" between Christian women and Christian men (who are afraid of appearing unmasculine) is made even more secure.[16]

Another way males can cope with the cultural view that Christians are "effeminate" is to become quite authoritarian as husbands and fathers. Although in the cultural chain of command a man may have low status as a "namby-pamby Christian," he can still assert his manhood by being very controlling on the home front. "A man's home is his castle" is a proverb that even Christian men seem to accept without hesitation. And in his own castle, a man can often exercise power as if he were king. For example, I would like very much to be able to say that the statistics for wife abuse and father/daughter incest are dramatically lowered when church affiliation is taken into account—but the facts are otherwise.[17] Of course, merely being associated with a church is no guarantee of a deep, intrinsically motivated faith in a man. But it is still a shock to discover how little difference it makes in the likelihood of such behavior (see also chapters eleven and twelve). Again, something else must be at work, and part of that "something" may be a defensive masculinity, in this case taken to pathological extremes.

Finally, men may handle their fear of being feminized as Christians by establishing a tradition of "muscular Christianity," in which the model Christian man (with God's help, of course) ends up being not less, but more masculine in physical strength and skill than his anti-Christian critics.[18] This desire for a thoroughly "muscularized" Christianity may lead preachers and theologians to underemphasize or even ignore feminine biblical metaphors for the Christian life, such as the ones I mentioned earlier. Which of us has not heard several sermons on "the whole armor of God" metaphor that Paul uses in Ephesians 6, or his image in 1 Corinthians 9 of the disciplined racer competing for first place? By contrast, how often have we heard ser-

mons using the many metaphors of childbirth to describe God's struggle to overcome sin and bring about his final kingdom through his
Son and his church, as in Micah 5 or Revelation 12? These are images
which many male exegetes seem to find unimportant or even repugnant.

Why Do Women Take It?
Of course, if my analysis of the Fall is correct, then women are often
as responsible as men for letting these kinds of situations continue.
By valuing the preservation of relationships (however unhealthy)
more than the pursuit of biblical justice—and sometimes even more
than the dignity of God's image in themselves—are they not contributing to the very circumstances which devalue them? And isn't the fact
that women outnumber men in most churches just another confirmation of their tendency to be meek followers of men, even when the
latter are in a minority?

No doubt both these accusations apply to many Christian women—
perhaps even to all Christian women some of the time. (I certainly
can't exempt myself from them.) But women's attraction to Christianity cannot be written off merely as meek conformity. When women
read their Bibles closely, they find in it a message of hope for themselves. For as it progresses from Genesis to Revelation, the biblical
drama is the story of increasing inclusiveness in the kingdom of God
(see also chapter twelve.) It is true that women prophets and judges
were rare in the Old Testament—but then, so was the incorporation
of Gentiles into the Jewish people. Yet when we read Jesus' genealogy
and see the names of Gentiles like Ruth and Rahab, we rightly conclude that this is a taste of things to come. God is getting ready to open
the doors of the kingdom beyond the confines of the Jewish nation.
If the rarity of women leaders in the Old Testament meant something
radically different—that they were raised up only to shame the men
into shouldering their responsibility, for example—then we would
certainly expect Jesus to have made it clear that women were to "stay
in their place." Yet he did no such thing. And, not surprisingly, women flocked to him. In Dorothy Sayers's memorable words:

Perhaps it is no wonder that the women were first at the cradle and last at the cross. They had never known a man like this Man—there never has been such another. A prophet and teacher who never nagged at them, never flattered or coaxed or patronized; who never made arch jokes about them, never treated them as "The women, God help us!" or "The ladies, God bless them!"; who rebuked without querulousness and praised without condescension; who took their questions and arguments seriously; who never mapped out their sphere for them, never urged them to be feminine or jeered at them for being female; who had no axe to grind and no uneasy male dignity to defend; who took them as he found them and was completely unself-conscious. . . . Nobody could possibly guess from the words and deeds of Jesus that there was anything "funny" about women's nature.[19]

But in speaking about men's fear of being feminized, and about women's reluctance to compromise relationships, I have anticipated themes I wish to develop more fully in the following chapter. Earlier I pointed out that anthropologists have two other theories besides the nature/culture one for explaining the universality of male dominance and female subordination. So let us look more closely at these two theories now.

PART 3

Parents and Partners

7 The Persistence of Patriarchy

Whenever I attend a church other than my own, I try to take a look in the nursery before the service starts. If I can't find where the babies and toddlers are cared for, I at least glance at the nursery-duty roster. My reason for doing these things is not just that I like to watch babies at play (though that's an added attraction!). I'm mainly interested in finding out who is actually looking after these children. And in the course of visiting churches, I've found that the rules for nursery duty seem to have shifted over the past ten years or so. Until recently, most churches simply took it for granted that childcare was the responsibility of women. So women of all ages added their names to the nursery-duty roster, and young girls considered it a badge of "being grown up" when allowed to join them. In a pinch, if a woman from the duty list failed to show up and no other woman could step in, a father might occasionally be recruited—though with due apologies.

But in many churches nowadays the pattern seems to be like this: care of the youngest babies is done mainly by adults of both sexes who have had experience with infants (quite sensibly, considering the special needs of such young human beings). By contrast, toddlers are supervised not just by mothers and fathers, but by older children and teen-agers of both sexes. The only apparent restriction (also quite sensible) is that there must be an experienced adult—perhaps two, depending on the volume of toddler traffic—to supervise the younger workers. My own sons are willing volunteers for toddler nursery duty, and while I suspect that the chance to avoid sitting through the sermon is part of their motivation, it's clear that other forces are at work too. My older son is close to the age where he can legally start baby-sitting, which he much prefers over lawnmowing or snow shoveling as a way to earn money. He figures that a long record of successful nursery duty will look good on his résumé. My younger son is convinced that the nursery routine would degenerate into chaos without the help of bigger boys like himself. More than once, with a touch of superiority in his voice, he has told me, "Those girls and adults—they just can't keep up with frisky little kids!"

At its best the church is an extended family and a public institution, both of which God has called into being.[1] And although parental role models are undoubtedly our first and most influential ones, in the Christian life parents were never meant to function in isolation. Because of the excessive individualism of our age, and because of the split between private domesticity and public wage-earning, this confession of interdependence is often honored more in the breach than in the observance. But it is still the biblical norm; and where it is practiced effectively—even in the church nursery—it modifies the effects on children of some negative social and psychological forces I will be describing in this chapter.

In the last chapter we learned that one way to justify power and status differences between the sexes is to highlight the superiority of human culture over "raw" nature, then to associate men more with culture and women more with nature. We also learned that this is fairly easy to do in most societies, since women's cultural activities are limited by bearing and nursing young children. And since children themselves are born unacculturated, the women who care for them somehow seem less acculturated by association with them.

Anthropologists who have advanced this theory are quick to point out that it is not biologically reductionist. It does not justify the conclusion that "anatomy is destiny" or that biology decrees only a limited, never-changing set of roles for men or women. The biology of reproduction does make certain divisions of labor more efficient and hence more likely, especially in subsistence cultures that rely on manual labor and do not store or preserve large quantities of food. But even simple subsistence societies organize gender roles in a great variety of ways, despite the constancy of biological differences between men and women. This fact alone argues against a rigid "anatomy is destiny" position. In addition, as we learned in chapter six, the fact that all societies have some kind of gendered division of labor which indirectly reflects biology cannot account for the fact that it is men's activities that are universally more highly valued.

Beyond Sociobiology

Now some sociobiologists have tried to argue that there is a biological basis for the higher status of men's work, one which reflects the subsistence lifestyle of our earliest hunter-gatherer ancestors and is still enshrined in our genes. Their argument goes something like this: Men are physically stronger and more mobile than women. Therefore, they supply more food for the group, especially the essential protein that comes from hunting. Without this food the group would starve and eventually die out. Therefore, the higher status of men's work flows naturally from their historically greater importance as food suppliers. In addition, persons of both sexes whose genetic makeup inclines them to value men more will be more likely to survive because of the encouragement they give men to carry out the hard work of hunting. So it is no surprise that these "male-valuing" genes have persisted to this day and little likelihood that they will pass out of human makeup soon.

But like most sociobiological theories, this one does not stand up to empirical scrutiny. When anthropologists look more closely at the eating habits of hunter-gatherers, they find that hunting is actually a sporadic, irregular activity. Most of the group's nourishment (protein as well as other foods) comes from the day-to-day gathering efforts of women. So on a purely sociobiological account, human evolution should favor the higher social value of females, not males.[2] As we will see later in this chapter, the status of women is much closer to men's in hunter-gatherer groups than in others—but not simply because of their role in supplying food. In fact, when groups begin to farm rather than hunt and gather, women on the average do more of the manual labor than men do (and this despite their lesser strength and the constraints of reproduction). Yet the more they do, the lower their social status tends to be; in the same way that slaves do not gain status from their harder work in the fields, neither do women. It is simply rationalized as "natural" (or supernaturally decreed) that women or slaves should relieve the socially dominant men of the need to worry about food production.[3] So something other than food contribution must be at the root of status differences between men and women.

Domestic versus Public

The biblical metaphor of the church as a body tells us that no part, however humble or invisible, has greater importance than any other. "If one member suffers, all suffer together; if one member is honored, all rejoice together" (1 Cor 12:26; see also Rom 12). In recent years some Christians have appealed to this teaching to defend the usual division of labor between men and women. As a Christian, they point out, no woman is "just a housewife." No Christian man should put on airs just because he is the more visible family breadwinner. And since Protestantism stresses the priesthood of all believers, no pastor should consider himself superior in God's eyes, but like Christ, "humble himself and take the form of a servant" (for example, Phil 2:3-11). All of this is biblical truth; but it is not always what Christians have practiced.

For Christians cannot deny that they are affected by wider cultural influences; when they do, or when they deny the impact of the Fall on male/female relations, then certain problems are not dealt with. They simply "go underground" and make many men and women feel unhappy yet guilty about their discontent over "a problem that has no name."[4]

So what is that problem? This brings us to a second theory which tries to explain the universal devaluation of women as compared to men. The theory begins by contrasting the private or domestic sphere of human life with the public. To understand this theory and its implications we need to know how the terms *domestic* and *public* are being used. Anthropologist Michelle Rosaldo states that, in its most universal sense, domestic refers to "those minimal institutions and modes of activity that are immediately organized around one or more mothers and their children."[5] She adopts this definition not to downplay the importance of fathers but because it is mothers, much more than fathers, whose mobility and range of activity are limited by childbearing and nursing activities. And she speaks of "one or more mothers" because of the existence of polygamy through much of human history and in many present day, non-Western cultures.

As we have already seen, the fact that women bear and nurse children does not inevitably force them to keep their cultural activities close to a permanent home base. In nomadic hunter-gatherer groups like the Bushmen and the Pygmies, everyone moves camp whenever the group has picked one area clean of game and edible wild plants. Furthermore, a woman's food-gathering activities often take her quite far from home base. If she has an infant, she slings it on her back; older children either come along to help or stay behind in the camp with other adults. Even so, the reproductive activities of women provide a focus for the simplest human division of labor: women, more than men, are apt to do tasks that are easily combined with childcare. And these, as it turns out, are often tasks that are close to home and centered around intimate relationships with a few people. In our culture those people are usually a woman's children; in other cultures they may include co-wives and their children and sometimes their own mothers or mothers-in-law.

By contrast, *public* refers to "activities, institutions and forms of association that link, rank, organize or subsume particular mother-child groups."[6] In other words, if the mother-child unit is the most domestic, and the most potent in its intimacy, then it is larger and more impersonal public structures—political, economic, military, religious—which join these units together to transcend biological and other family ties. By "reproductive default," as it were, such activities are dominated by men. In Rosaldo's words:

> Put quite simply, men have no single commitment as enduring, time-consuming, and emotionally compelling—as close to seeming necessary and natural—as the relation of a woman to her infant child. And so men are free to form those broader associations that we call "society:" universalistic systems of order, meaning, and commitment that link particular mother-child groups.[7]

The Ambiguity of Domesticity

It is these public, formal and male-dominated activities that almost always have more cultural respect than the domestic, less visible and more socially intimate activities of women. Perhaps this happens because public activities seem to transcend nature more than domestic tasks do and hence seem more uniquely human or culture creating. And the higher status of "the public" is another reason why women's heavy contribution to food production does not automatically raise their status. For if women's farming or gathering activities take place in small, isolated family groups, and if women have little or no control over the more public activities of food distribution, marketing and ritual feasting, then their food production activities will gain them little social value.

Again, there is no necessary, biological reason why this should be so. And again, there is great cultural variety in the degree to which the public sphere is valued over the private: in general, the gap is least in small, nomadic hunter-gatherer groups (which are largely monogamous) and greatest in larger, permanent, farming cultures (which are more likely to be polygamous). We will explore why this is so presently. But for now we should note that our own culture gives its people a mixed message. In theory, we place high value on domestic and marital intimacy, as well as on the task of parenting. In practice, however, we do very little to support these activities, since the norm until recently has been a largely absentee father who works away from the home in the public sphere, and a largely domestic mother who lacks the daily support not just of a husband, but of a mother, a mother-in-law or even a co-wife!

So this is "the problem that has no name" in our culture, one which affects Christians almost as much as non-Christians. Despite the high value we place on marriage and parenting, most of us are bound by economic changes that emerged only at the time of the Industrial Revolution. The advent of factories and mass production forced men to start commuting to the workplace, whereas for centuries before they had farmed or practiced their trades close to home. As a result of the same economic forces, women more and more worked at home alone with their children. And while Christians confess that the (largely male) public realm is no more important than the (largely female) domestic one, it is not easy to resist the universal tendency to value the male-dominated, public domain more. Indeed, if men already feel ambivalent about being "feminized" as Christians (see chapter six), they may be all the more tempted to value and protect their masculine public sphere as a way of compensating for this feminization in the eyes of the dominant, secular society.

But even more profound psychological consequences flow from this public/private split—consequences that affect children and adults of both sexes. I wish to explain these by looking at a third and final theory that tries to account for the differing social status of men and women. In the process I believe we will come to understand an important psychological mechanism—working in tandem with human willfulness and resistant social structures—by which fallen relationships between the sexes perpetuate themselves.

Object Relations and Family Life
Let me begin with an anecdote which may help bring this third theory

to life. A few years ago, after speaking at a Christian conference on gender roles, I was approached by an attractive, well-dressed woman who wanted to talk to me about my presentation. She began by saying it helped her to understand a pattern of behavior in her family that had puzzled and distressed her for some time. This woman, the wife of a medical doctor, had two sons in their early twenties. What puzzled and distressed her, she said, was that from the time these young men had begun dating, they had regularly expressed a superior and even contemptuous attitude toward women—including the women they dated. They came from a Christian family; she herself had taught them, by word and example, to respect women; she respected herself and liked other women. Why then, should her sons turn out to be such male chauvinists? (It was she who used that label!)

She had thought that if sons have a mother who respects herself and other women, they will do likewise. What she realized from my talk was that her example to her sons had to be considered in light of their father's behavior. It was not that their father was particularly hostile toward women. But, like the average American medical doctor, he was at home irregularly and seldom. As an economic provider, he was beyond reproach; in all other respects, however, she had raised the sons virtually as a single parent. The gist of my talk had been that the physical and psychological absence of fathers from their growing sons was often an important cause of men's continuing devaluation of women—regardless of how well the mother has filled the gap. Furthermore, this process can become a vicious spiral that continues down the generations. For the more men devalue women and the activities associated with them, the less likely they are to share the "women's work" of nurturing children. Thus, their own sons are apt to grow up underfathered, contemptuous of women and wanting to distance themselves from "women's work," just like their fathers before them.

Critical Periods Revisited

Now obviously the above summary of my argument has some steps missing. *Why* should the relative absence of fathers from their sons produce devaluation of women, even in families where the mother is a conscientious parent and has a healthy sense of self-esteem? And what evidence is there that this process actually takes place? To answer these questions, we need to continue our review of work done by cultural anthropologists. In addition, we need to learn something about "object relations theory," a variant on classical psychoanalysis which stresses the child's earliest social, emotional and cognitive relationships with the people and other "objects" of attachment.[8]

In their first few years, children face an awesome array of emotional tasks, and the way they handle these strongly colors their later lives as adults. The newborn infant is totally dependent on others for the satisfaction of bodily needs. She was literally "one flesh" with the mother for nine months prior to birth; and although after birth, the baby can breathe, feed and excrete without an umbilical cord, he is still at the mercy of the primary caretaker—almost universally the mother—for food, comfort and bodily care. Of course, it is impossible to know exactly what goes on in the mind of a tiny infant. But clinical, cognitive and developmental psychologists all agree that to begin with, babies probably do not distinguish themselves from the person who cares for them. For the tiny but rapidly growing baby, life is mostly being fed, being rocked to sleep and being made comfortable through connection to the caretaker.

Since the mother is usually the primary caretaker, object-relations theorists refer to her as the baby's "primary love object." Boy and girl babies are equally dependent on her and therefore equally "attached" to her emotionally. They do not, for the first two years or so, distinguish her as a "female," any more than they understand what it means to be a male or female themselves. They simply sense that she is the center of their small universe and separation from her for more than a short time generates anxiety.

Dependence and Gender Identity

The fact that mothers, and not fathers, are usually the "primary love objects" of both boys and girls has deep implications for developing gender identity, especially when combined with the high level of fa-

ther absence that characterizes our society. For the first several years
of life, it is usually mother who answers and disciplines the child's
needs. She is all-powerful in the child's eyes and therefore both loved
and feared. Neither the boy nor girl baby has any idea that, in the
world at large, their mother's status and power are really quite low,
because they are barely aware that there is a larger world out there.
And, as I mentioned above, they are not even clear about their own
and other people's sex until between two and three years of age. Thus
mother is not only their first love-object, but also their first role-model.
Because she is so much the center of their world, and so apparently
in control of everything, she is the person with whom both boy and
girl infants are apt to identify—the person they want to be like.

Cognitive psychologists have traced the process by which children
become aware of being male or female. By about age two, most can
answer correctly when asked if they are a boy or a girl—but these are
just personal labels to them, like their own names. They are still far
from understanding the universality and permanence of biological
sex; they cannot grasp that everyone is born either male or female
and that this does not change. A two-year-old will often believe that
a boy has changed to a girl simply because his hair has grown long,
or that she herself could "be a daddy" if she put on her father's
clothes and cut her hair like his. Nor is this early confusion less
among children who understand the genital differences between boys
and girls. Their undeveloped logic still leads them to believe that
superficial change equals complete change. Not until around age two-
and-one-half is the child able to reason, in so many words, "I am a
girl, and I always will be. Once a girl, always a girl; once a boy, always
a boy."[9]

But it is one thing to know rationally that one is a boy or girl, and
quite another to feel emotionally secure, adequate and happy about
that fact. And here is where the role of mothers as almost exclusive
child rearers begins to matter. Mothers, as I have pointed out, are the
primary love-objects of all infants prior to the stage where they understand the meaning of sex differences. When a child does begin to
understand that mother is "like me" (if the child is a girl) or "not like

me" (if the child is a boy), the nature of this primary relationship takes on different meaning for boys and girls.

The Reproduction of Machismo

Little boys, like little girls, are naturally attracted by the nurturance and apparent power of the mother. Being attracted to her, they just as naturally want to be like her. But around age three, along with the boy's increasing certainty that he is and always will be a boy, comes an insistent but confusing message from everyone around him: no, you can't grow up to be like Mommy. You have to grow up to be like Daddy—you know, that big male person you see for a little while most mornings and evenings, and sometimes for a bit longer on the weekends? In other words, the boy discovers that since they are of opposite sexes, he cannot derive his primary identity from his ever-present, nurturing mother, but must instead take as his role model the same-sex father whom he rarely sees!

This produces a kind of "double bind" for boys. They cannot simply stay unambiguously attached to their mothers, yet the role model they are supposed to imitate is largely unavailable. As a result, most boys are forced to learn about masculinity "in the abstract." In the words of one cultural anthropologist, they must identify with a "position," rather than an available "person":

> In most societies, [the father's] work and social life take place further from the home than do those of his wife. He is, then, often relatively inaccessible to his son, and performs his male role activities away from where the son spends most of his life. As a result, a boy's male gender identification often becomes a "positional" identification with aspects of his father's clearly or not-so-clearly defined male role, rather than a more generalized "personal" identification—a diffuse identification with his father's personality, values, and behavioral traits—that could grow out of a real relationship to his father.[10]

Now some developmental psychologists see a cognitive advantage for boys in all this. The unavailability of a personal male role model, they say, forces the little boy to think in terms of masculine "universals."

He must figure out how to behave like a man in a rational, detached manner, uncomplicated by the emotional intensity of a close relationship with any particular male. They also suggest that this early, forced exercise in abstraction may be the root of men's later tendency to be more detached and analytical than women (an obvious advantage in our highly scientized society!).[11] This may be so; but even if it is, there is a price to be paid by everyone involved. For when a little boy lacks a readily available adult male role model, his sense of being "securely and successfully male" is less solid. See-sawing between a desire to be "like mother" (who is constantly there for him) and the vague recognition that he must suppress this in order to be "like father" (who is home very little during the child's waking hours), he may nurse deep and unconscious doubts both about the desirability of being male and his ability to meet the demands of the male role.

Suppressed Fear of Women
But as he grows older and has more contact with the world at large, the boy begins to realize that "being male" is supposed to be a privilege. The message he gets is that men, if they are "real men," are socially more important than women; therefore, if he acts "less than a man" he is acting like the inferior group. This simply forces his earlier ambivalence deeper underground: already somewhat insecure in his masculinity, he must now try all the harder to prove to himself and the world that it is beyond question. How to do this? The safest way is to have as little to do with women and their activities as possible—to repress and deny any "womanly" qualities or impulses in himself. In extreme cases he may do this by openly scorning or even maltreating women. Less extremely, a man may simply avoid women except when he has domestic and sexual needs to be filled, spending the rest of his time in visibly and exclusively male groups. Or paradoxically, he may idealize women, metaphorically "placing them on a pedestal." This too keeps them at a safe distance, but is often accompanied by impossible demands of "womanly perfection" from them as well.[12]

In some cultures, men may see-saw between attitudes of scorn and idealization, a common feature of the "machismo" cult in many Latin American societies. In such cultures aggressive public displays of masculinity may alternate with devotion to the Virgin Mary and heavy-handedness toward the women in one's own family. Whichever of these strategies are used, they allow insecure men to mask what amounts to an unconscious "dread of women." The boy gradually learns that women are not as socially powerful as he once thought. But his earliest, "critical period" associations are still of a mother who seemed all-powerful. When combined with his early deprivation of a male role model, the result may be a deeply repressed yet powerful conviction that women can somehow strip him of an essential part of his selfhood—namely, his masculine identity.[13]

People of both sexes are casualties of such fear and the defense mechanisms that hide it. Although it may partly reflect my prejudice as a psychologist, I suspect that this male "dread of women" is a deeper cause of both the nature/culture and the public/private rationalizations for women's lower status. But men and boys suffer from its effects along with women. For now we can see how this masculine insecurity perpetuates itself from generation to generation. The underfathered boy develops a fragile, ambivalent male identity; to compensate for this insecurity in adolescence and adulthood, he distances himself from women and "women's work." And what is most obviously women's work? Caring for young children. So he avoids nurturant contact with his own sons and unwittingly contributes to their development of insecure masculinity, dread of women, and the compensatory, woman-rejecting behavior that can result.

That this vicious cycle is often an unsatisfying one for the men who seem to benefit from it can be seen in the work of Samuel Osherson, a Harvard-trained psychologist who has directed a long-term study of men who grew up in the 1950s and graduated from Harvard in the 1960s. Most of these men are now the embodiment of the American idea of masculine success: they include doctors, lawyers, executives, bankers, stockbrokers, writers and scientists. By all outward appearances, the American dream has come true for them. If anyone should feel satisfied with their lives, presumably these men should.

What Osherson actually found in his respondents was a double sense of loss, for which their social and economic success were scant compensation. On the one hand, most of these men grew up knowing their fathers as dutiful but distant economic providers who were at best socially and emotionally ineffectual at home and at worst were more childish in their demands and behavior than the children themselves. On the other hand, lacking fathers who were adequate role models of male nurturance (however well they modeled economic upward mobility), Osherson's respondents found themselves repeating the same cycle with their own wives and children. Osherson summarizes his work as follows:

> From these talks I began to see how profound and painful were the consequences of the predictable dislocation between fathers and sons, a separation we take for granted in our society. Many of the male-female skirmishes of our times are rooted in the hidden, ongoing struggles sons have with their fathers, and the varying ways grown sons try to complete this relationship in their careers and marriages. Yet despite their psychological importance, fathers remain wrapped in a mystery for many men, as we idealize, degrade, or ignore them. And in doing so, we wind up imitating them, even as we try to be different.[14]

Lessons from Hunter-Gatherers

It is noteworthy that Osherson uses the triple terms *idealize, degrade* and *ignore* to capture the range of emotions men feel toward the absent fathers of their childhood. For we have seen this same trio of attitudes operating in men toward women as a result of the same pattern of father absence. And if mothers, by virtue of their biology, are always more involved with young children than fathers, there might seem to be no escape from this vicious spiral. But this is not the case. Earlier I pointed out that cultures differ in the extent to which they emphasize the private/public split and give greater value to the latter. I also mentioned that this split is usually least profound among nomadic, monogamous hunter-gatherers, who also have much less status difference between men and women than sedentary, polygamous subsistence farmers. Now what is it about the lifestyle of hunter-gatherers that minimizes the practice of female devaluation? And what is it about their farming neighbors that exaggerates it? To explain this I will draw on my own research experience with the Central African Pygmy and their agricultural Bantu neighbors. But readers who have seen the South African film *The Gods Must Be Crazy*, with its lighthearted portrayal of the Kalahari Bushmen, may already have some appreciation of what follows.[15]

To begin with, nomads necessarily live in small bands: a culture that survives by tracking game and edible plants cannot move around efficiently in a large group. But the very smallness and mobility of the group lessens the likelihood of rigid role specialization. There are just not enough people to have separate classes of basket weavers, arrow makers, palm-oil vendors and so on. In a sense, everyone must be a "Jack (or Jill) of all trades," just as we must when we go on a camping expedition. This does not mean gender roles are absent. Among the Pygmy, women generally build huts, gather plants, process palm oil and cook food. Men kill game, harvest palm nuts and make hunting nets, spears, bows and arrows. But the smallness and mobility of the group require close cooperation among all members. Thus a successful hunting expedition may involve women and younger children scaring the game toward the nets for the men and boys to kill. A woman will call on her husband to care for an infant while she is cooking. Grandparents of both sexes care for toddlers in the camp while their parents go out to hunt and gather. In other words, the public/private split, and the association of men with the former and women with the latter, has very little relevance in such a culture.

By contrast, groups that live by subsistence farming tend to be larger. Since they are not moving from place to place, the only restriction on group size is the availability of arable land. Such groups typically live in large, permanent villages from which they commute to work in nearby fields or plantations. Moreover, the group is large enough and fixed enough to allow for role specialization: there is likely to be a village blacksmith, a basket maker, a palm-oil processor and so forth. And along with this generally greater role specialization

comes greater age group and gender role-specialization. The spheres
of men and women, children and adults, become more strictly defined
and there is much less cooperative activity across them. Wittingly or
unwittingly, conditions are being set for the reproduction of the vicious downward spiral described earlier.

Hazards of Polygamy

A second contrast between subsistence nomadic and farming cultures
is the general practice of monogamy in the first group and polygamy
in the second. The reasons for this difference are not totally understood (it may have something to do with the inconvenience of moving
large households in nomadic groups), but the psychological results
are fairly clear. When a man has more than one wife, he has an
ongoing "backup" system for domestic emergencies. If one wife is
sick, or limited because she is pregnant or nursing, a co-wife takes
over her cooking, child-care and farming duties. In such a situation,
a man may never, even on an emergency basis, have to care for young
children or be seen doing other "women's work." In addition, each
of his wives usually has a separate hut for herself and her children;
anthropologists refer to this as "mother-child sleeping arrangements."
The husband then takes turns sleeping with each wife, though he may
avoid sex with a particular wife for months or even years after she has
given birth. (This by itself is not entirely a bad practice, since it allows
the baby adequate nursing time before a sibling is conceived.) He may
even have the option of sleeping in an all-male compound, totally
away from wives and children.

One result of all this, however, is that fathers in such families are
"spread too thin" among their wives and children. Their lack of contact with young sons, already supported by the greater role-specialization of the culture, is compounded by a polygamous marriage structure. Does this increase men's "dread of women," and the devaluation
that accompanies it? There is indirect evidence that it does. In some
cultures the separation of men from their wives and children is so
complete that boys are simply given the same label as women and girls
until they are initiated into adult male roles during adolescence.

Moreover, there is a fairly strong correlation between the presence of mother-child sleeping arrangements in a culture and the severity of initiation rites for adolescent boys. These rites, often including painful circumcision, are typically conducted by adult male well away from the village, with women strictly forbidden access to what goes on. It is as if the men, knowing only too well the ambiguity of their sons' masculine identity, take strong measures to make them renounce the primary bond with their mothers and be "reborn" as males at the hands of males.[16]

The Fruits of Togetherness
By contrast, the largely monogamous, more role-flexible hunter-gatherers rarely have such complex and secretive initiation rites. Even when forced to take part in them (as the Pygmy are by the Bantu farmers for whom they work when not hunting), they tend to regard such activities with amused contempt. So although the mother-infant bond is necessarily a strong one, it does not inevitably lead to isolation between the sexes and the progressive devaluation of women by men. Also of interest is the fact that hunter-gatherers' gender role flexibility and cooperation is accompanied by greater intellectual similarity between men and women. For example, tests of spatial ability that tend to yield sex differences in our own culture often show none among hunter-gatherers—a finding that is doubly remarkable considering their total lack of practice with Western-style tests! Some of this spatial aptitude may reflect skills acquired in the process of moving from place to place so frequently. But the point, of course, is that males and females are largely equal in their mobility, even though the details of their activities may vary.[17]

Can we learn anything from this about our own situation? Despite the cultural gap that separates us from hunter-gatherers, some cultural anthropologists and object-relations theorists believe so and have written, "Change must proceed in two directions."

To begin with, it would seem imperative to integrate men into the domestic sphere, giving them an opportunity to share in the socialization of children, as well as the more mundane domestic tasks.

What is more . . . women's status will be elevated only when they
participate equally with men in the public world of work.[18]
It is important to understand that such changes do not erase all gender role differences. What is different about the Pygmy and other
hunter-gatherers is not the absence of gender roles (they are quite
clearly present) but rather the degree of proximity, cooperation, economic equality and role flexibility that men and women share. In
addition, as we shall see in the next chapter, even when men and
women do perform a common task—such as child care—they approach it rather differently, and many of these "stylistic differences"
seem to be worth preserving.

What *is* absent in the hunter-gatherer lifestyle is the great gap between domestic and public life, with its limiting of women to the first
and men to the second and the devaluation of the domestic in comparison to the public. And the reversal of such devaluation is of course
one of the things Christians claim to believe in as members of "one
Body." But it is difficult to work out our belief in actual behavior when
the social and economic structure of our society has forced such a rift
between the domestic and public, and between men's and women's
worlds. And it is difficult to match our beliefs and actions to our
feelings when so much of our fear of change is rooted in early family
life and the object relations that typify it in our culture. So far I have
concentrated on the effects of such experiences on boys; but in the
following chapter we will see that the remoteness of fathers and the
constant availability of mothers is a mixed blessing for girls also.

Back to the Nursery
In the meantime we have come a long way from my informal survey
of church nurseries at the beginning of this chapter. But the connection should now be somewhat clearer. To the extent that Christians
consistently integrate males into the work of caring for children, they
are helping to interrupt the continuation of men's tendency to fear
and devalue women. But such changes can happen beyond the
nursery as well. Recently I returned to the city where I had met the
doctor's wife who was concerned about her adult sons' "male chau-

vinism." After my lecture, I recognized her again in the audience, and we spent a few minutes catching up with each other. I heard about her recent return to graduate school and, recalling our earlier conversation, asked how things were going on the home front.

"Well, they've changed quite a bit," she replied. "You know, we also have a third son who's a lot younger than his brothers. And now that I'm back in school, his father has started spending much more time with him. It's been so good for both of them; my husband is much less frantic and stressed about his career and has begun to see what he missed by being away from the older ones so much. And our youngest son has a very different attitude towards women than his brothers!"

"And what do the older brothers make of all this?" I couldn't help asking.

She paused a moment (recalling, no doubt, that critical-period socialization is not easily overcome), but then replied: "I think it's affected them too. They still have a long way to go as far as their own attitudes to women are concerned. But they've definitely noticed their father's change in priorities. And I think it will affect theirs too."

8

The Case
for
Co-Parenting

Recently, at a two-day seminar on gender roles, a man in his
thirties listened to me speak on the relative absence of fathers in our
society, then joined the discussion period in a mood of great agitation.
"Does anyone realize," he began, "just how hard it is for fathers to
be personally involved in their children's upbringing, even when they
want to be?" It turned out that this man was a doctor, a department
head at one of the largest medical schools in the country. As a Christian, he was committed to the priority of his family over personal
career advancement. Consequently, he had told his present employers even before they hired him that he would be a conscientious
worker but did not intend to be an "organization man" who simply
made his family adjust to whatever demands the university made.

I congratulated him for sticking to his principles and getting the best of both worlds anyway. The university wanted him badly enough to hire him in spite of his strange religious priorities. He was a tenured professor and department chairman at a fairly young age. And he had acted on his determination to be a hands-on nurturer of his children and an emotional support to his wife. An academic with a somewhat flexible schedule, this man had been able to manage his research and administrative roles while still being an actively available father. I commented that he was a fine role model for younger Christian men and a good example of someone who had acted on Jesus' admonition to "seek first the kingdom and its righteousness," trusting that God would add everything else needed (Mt 6:33).

But my praise of this man's actual success at role juggling did not satisfy him. He knew all that. He even knew, at an intellectual and confessional level, that he should be happy and grateful for the way he had been able to balance career and family commitments. What he was trying to express when he spoke about the difficulty of being an active father was a much more subtle and deep-seated concern about his life.

The problem was that despite his convictions and his success in acting on them he often felt less than adequate as a male academic. To an outside observer, he appears to be the epitome of career success. But when he compared himself to his classmates in medical school and his peers in the university world, he couldn't escape the uneasy feeling that he was doing "less well." His male colleagues had concentrated more single-mindedly on their careers, and hence had done more research and publishing and had received research grants and academic tenure more quickly. No doubt many had done so at the expense of their families. But male socialization and cultural values being what they are, a man who puts family before (or even on a par with) career is not praised by fellow males for being "more manly"—in fact, usually quite the opposite. And in the competitive world of male careerism, being "second best" or even "more than adequate" at your job is easily construed as failure. There seems to be an implicit pecking order of masculinity, and only to the extent that a man has outdone his peers on the job is he allowed to feel truly successful as a male.

"There are all kinds of support systems for women trying to break out of stereotyped roles and thinking habits," this Christian doctor lamented. "But what is there for men who are struggling to do the same?" He clearly felt bad about his residual attachment to culturally defined masculinity, with its skewed priorities. But he was having difficulty lining up his feelings with his beliefs and behavior. And his feelings kept telling him that he had not gotten the best of both worlds, but that he was failing as a man even while he was succeeding as a husband and father.

A Shared Problem
Women sometimes seem to look for, and get, more emotional support than men as they struggle to reconcile new roles with old entrenched feelings. This is partly because women are permitted to acknowledge and express a greater range of feelings than men. It is also because many women feel more—rather than less—female when they share both problems and their solutions with others. We will explore some reasons for these differences a little later. But for now it needs to be said that women are no strangers to the kind of conflict expressed by this male doctor. Many who are less than full-time homemakers, for example, also feel like failures—this time as wives and mothers—even while they experience success and satisfaction in new roles as students, workers or professionals.[1]

The emotional dynamics get even more complex when both kinds of conflict coexist in one marriage. Lillian Rubin, a psychotherapist who specializes in helping couples cope with gender-role change, writes that even her own professional experience did not prepare her for the feelings that assaulted her spouse and herself when she took over full financial responsibility for the family in order to let her husband realize his lifelong wish to be a writer. It was a change they completely agreed on. As their children grew up and left home, she had finished graduate school and begun a successful teaching and clinical career. Both were convinced it was a golden opportunity to immerse themselves in new vocations each had been unable to realize before. But soon after they made the switch (knowing full well that the husband would earn very little as a novice writer), Rubin reports that her husband "fell into a six-month-long depression, and I into an equally long struggle with my anger":

> Until that moment I never knew what it meant to be responsible for the roof over my own head—let alone the heads of my loved ones. That's what happens when you're born a girl rather than a boy. I had worked in my life, of course, but always as an auxiliary wage earner. . . . Now, for the first time, I was in the position that men know so well: if I didn't go to work today, there would be no money tomorrow. And I hated it.
>
> Suddenly, we had to confront the realization that we were still dominated by the stereotypic images of male and female roles— images we would have sworn we had, by then, routed from our consciousness. He struggled with his sense of failure, with the fear that somehow his very manhood had been damaged. I—the liberated professional woman—was outraged and enraged that he wasn't taking care of me any longer. . . . I knew these feelings came from some very deep part of myself that had learned from earliest infancy to believe that there would always be someone around, preferably a man, to ease my life.[2]

Eventually both her anger and his depression abated, but in Rubin's words, "not without plenty of psychological work for both of us." And, she reports, even among her younger clients "most men still cannot cope with not being able to support the family, and most women still have difficulty in accepting the need to support themselves."[3]

New Roles, New Rules?

These examples of men and women coping with role change anticipate some of the themes we will explore in later chapters. My reason for introducing them in a chapter on parenting is twofold. First of all, I do not think I have to make a theological case for the importance of hands-on fathering. Christians cover a wide spectrum of theological, social and political conviction, even though they are united by a common belief in the Bible as God's Word. Nevertheless, over the past ten years or so, I have been struck by their unanimity on this one issue: if Christian families are to endure, fathers must "turn their hearts toward home" and become involved parents rather than largely absentee landlords who mainly supply the material wherewithal for their wives to raise the children.

Christians may (and do) differ regarding the timing or even the rightness of wives entering the paid workforce.[4] But they are generally agreed about the need for husbands to be a more visible and nurturing presence at home. James Dobson, a popular writer on family issues, has strong criticism for men who leave the burden of parenting to their wives, often isolating them from adult fellowship in the process.[5] And looking back over his long career as an evangelist, even Billy Graham confessed that in his thirties and forties he "tried to do too much." He warned Christian men not to use either their jobs or "kingdom-building" work as an excuse to avoid their children: "The child in the home needs to know she or he is loved and important, and that he or she can count on the undivided attention of the father or mother sometime during the day."[6]

So I do not think it is religious conviction that makes Christian men avoid the challenges and satisfactions of parenting. It is in part the difficulty of overcoming feelings buried deep in their masculine socialization. And, as I pointed out, women also have such struggles. On one level they are rightly unhappy about largely absentee husbands leaving them with the burden of parenting, regardless of how much money those husbands bring home. But on another level, their emotional sense of adequacy as women is closely tied to cultural norms about "perfect" mothering, homemaking and husbandly financial support. And on still another level, there is a sense of power associated with being the most important adult to one's young children, which women are often ambivalent about sharing even when their husbands are ready to do so.

Parenting Research: A Whole New Ballgame

Now believe it or not, parenting research really is a whole new ballgame in psychology. Until very recently there was almost no psychology of parenting, but only of *mothering*—which was assumed to be synonymous with parenting. In fact, until the 1960s almost the only research on fathering had to do with the effects of father absence— due to death, divorce or military service—particularly on sons' gender-identity development. Few researchers ever bothered to wonder about the impact of father-absence on daughters, and virtually no one explored the nature and effects of father presence on either girls or boys.

Of course, trying to understand fathering by studying only father-absent families is rather like trying to understand mothering by studying only institutionalized children who have no mothers! And we have seen how emotionally resistant even the best intentioned people can be to changing entrenched gender roles, with their assumptions about exclusive mothering and largely absentee fathering. In chapter seven we saw how early, critical period experiences help to explain this. Boys who are underfathered at an early age risk becoming adults with a fragile male gender identity. As a result they become overly invested in culturally masculine kinds of behavior and emotionally resistant to whatever seems womanly, including close involvement with their own children. But what are the effects of too-exclusive mothering on daughters? And what are the effects of father presence on both boys and girls, particularly in the first few years of life? These are the questions that will concern us for the rest of this chapter.

Object Relations and Feminine Personality
Let us begin with the impact of the "typical" family on girls' personality and gender identity. We saw in chapter seven that the almost constant presence of mother and the almost constant absence of father are mixed blessings for boys. Now it should be intuitively obvious that the same organization of family life (mother as constant caretaker, father as largely absentee breadwinner) is bound to have somewhat different effects on girls. In early infancy both girl and boy babies are equally attached to the mother as primary caretaker. They have no idea that she is "female" as opposed to "male" or of the

"same" or a "different" sex as themselves. But by age three the little girl has figured out that she is and always will be female, and that the same is true of her mother. At first this is very positive and reassuring knowledge, for in order to learn what it means to be culturally feminine the little girl simply needs to do what comes naturally—that is, stick close to mother. She does not, like her brother, need to wonder if she is getting her gender-specific actions and feelings "right," because she has a constant, same-sex role model who gives her continuous feedback as a developing female. Under these kinds of parenting arrangements, culturally defined femininity is "caught" more than "taught": it is picked up in countless interactions with the person who is simultaneously a same-sex role model and the most valued and powerful person in the little girl's limited experience.

This is not to deny the existence of pathological families, whose mothers are so rejecting or critical that their daughters become very insecure about their probable success as females. But in most families daughters do have an advantage in the ease with which they form their gender identity. This helps to explain why women generally tend to be more comfortable than men in close relationships. Unlike boys, girls are not forced to distance themselves from their primary love object (the mother) at the very time their gender identity is being consolidated. Consequently, as object-relations theorists put it, girls' "ego boundaries" tend to be more "permeable." What this means is that a woman's sense of being a person, separate and distinct from others, may be less strongly developed than is the case with most men. Having been allowed more total identification with their mothers when young, women seem to find it both easier and more enjoyable to form intimate ties with people—to share their own failures as well as successes and to identify with the emotional states of others.

Costs and Benefits

Until recently, the fact that girls grow up less individualized and more connected to other people than boys was seen as proof that they were unfit for the rigors of public life. Both psychoanalytic and cognitive psychologists argued that women lacked the moral and intellec-

tual distance to use universal principles, rather than personal loyal-
ties, as the basis for making just and rational decisions in law, business
or government. C. S. Lewis agreed with this view and advanced it as
one reason for the "natural" headship of husbands over wives, as they
have greater fitness to be representatives of the family to the world
at large.[7] (See also chapter thirteen.)

But more recently such impersonal rationalism has been recognized as the mixed blessing it is. For even in public life decisions are
always made in the context of relationships—between workers and
management, salespersons and customers, lawyers and clients, doctors and patients, political officers and constituents—the list is potentially endless. Breadwinning in the public arena is anything but "impersonal" and purely "task-oriented." Particularly in large institutions,
where people working in many different roles must coordinate their
efforts, there is an increasingly recognized need for empathy, tact and
skill in conflict resolution. Thus women's concern for relationships,
nurtured during the early years of unambiguous attachment to their
mothers, is potentially more of an asset than a liability in public life.

Immature Altruism
There are costs as well as benefits to women's more person-centered
style. The strength of that style is a concern to preserve relationships
and to resolve conflict through dialogue and compromise rather than
the rigid application of abstract principles. But in striving to preserve
networks of relationships, women may neglect to develop a sense of
adult responsibility for their own actions. Harvard psychologist Carol
Gilligan, in a book whose main purpose is an analysis and appreciation of women's "different voice," outlines the problems that result
when women fail to temper their relational impulses with a sense of
individual self-respect and responsibility.

One of Gilligan's studies involved a group of young women trying
to decide what to do about an unplanned pregnancy. The point of the
study was not to urge them toward one course of action or another,
but to discover the ways in which women approach this uniquely
female moral dilemma—one in which two lives are simultaneously

affected because the one is carrying the other. The least mature response, in Gilligan's view, came from young women who made the
decision only on the basis of their own immediate wishes, ignoring
the impact of that decision on all other persons involved (the child,
the child's father, their own parents and so on). But there were also
women who were immature in just the opposite way: they tried to deny
any personal responsibility for the onset or management of the pregnancy by appealing solely to the wishes of someone else. Most had
engaged in unprotected sex in order to "please" or "not lose" someone else (the boyfriend), and they were now prepared to do whatever
"someone else" (boyfriend, parents or the like) wanted—abort or not
abort—in order to preserve the relational status quo.

On the surface of it, such women have progressed from the total
"selfishness" of the first response to a proper concern for the others
involved. But it is obvious that such concern for others masks a profound denial of responsibility. In this case, "I did it for someone else"
becomes a cover for "I don't have to take responsibility for my own
behavior"—a point underlined by the fact that some of the young
women giving this response were contending not with their first, but
second unwanted pregnancy. In Gilligan's words, such women are
"caught between the passivity of dependence and the activity of
care."[8] Consciously or unconsciously, they have convinced themselves
that the essence of femininity is pleasing others, and that if they just
keep doing this, "others" will always take care of them.

When Gilligan contacted these young women a year later, she
found that many of them had experienced a rude awakening in the
interim. Relationships had been disrupted regardless of what they had
done (aborted or kept the child) to try and cement them. And it was
this trauma that pushed many of the young women beyond the kind
of immature dependency for which women have been simultaneously
rewarded and blamed throughout history. Many had acquired a long
overdue sense of vocation and purpose and were working to realize
it. In effect, they came to say "Even though relationships are important, I cannot use them to shift responsibility for my actions, or as an
excuse for not developing and using my own talents." So women's

concern for relationships, nurtured during the early years of uninter-
rupted attachment to mothers, is a mixed blessing. On the one hand,
it is a needed corrective to the generally more impersonal and abstract
male style. On the other hand, it easily becomes an excuse for failing
to develop some aspects of adult moral maturity.

Please do not misunderstand my reasons for sharing this study. It
is *not* to suggest approval of abortion on demand. But Gilligan's study
does indicate that a woman's moral dilemma is not resolved merely
by deciding to carry a child to term. If "immature altruism" led to her
pregnancy in the first place, and if the young woman is not encouraged to get beyond this, then in effect she does not grow up. And
while I wish I could say that churches are in the vanguard of those
helping women "grow up" into a healthy balance of altruism and
independence, I know that this is often not the case. Too many
churches discourage independent thought and leadership in women
as being unfeminine or unsubmissive. Too many respond with pity for
single women who lack husbands to "look after" them—as if a woman
supporting herself in an extra-domestic calling were somehow a
breach of the creation order. And the fact that some women use
church order as an excuse not to exercise independent thought and
action does not make this practice any more laudable. It rather suggests that neither sex has acknowledged the fallenness of such behavior, the way it has been inflated by gender role socialization and the
way in which it is perpetuated by unjust social structures that leave
women so few options for action.[9]

Findings on Fathering
Distorted gender-role behavior, such as that shown by Gilligan's wom-
en respondents, is ultimately rooted in the fall of humankind. But as
we have seen in the crosscultural examples of chapter seven, parenting arrangements can either inflate or help reverse men's propensity
to misuse dominion and women's tendency to misuse sociability. We
learned that in polygamous cultures, where fathers have almost no
contact with young children, separation of the sexes and contempt for
women spiral to alarming levels. In nomadic, monogamous cultures—

where gender roles are less rigid and men are continually involved in parenting—women become more independent, men become more relational, and the sexes are more equally valued.

Because of the social and economic history of our own culture, the typical father in industrial Western society is almost as absent from the early development of his children as the polygamous male in a subsistence agricultural setting. I have pointed out some of the costs to both boys and girls when parenting arrangements center around almost exclusive mothering and marginal fathering. But what is the impact of greater father presence in the lives of young children? We will answer this question with a look at the new and very intriguing work being done in "the psychology of fathering."[10]

The research on fathering has included a great deal of observation of father-infant interaction—in hospitals just after the arrival of a first-born, in laboratory settings aimed at measuring older infants' attachment to their fathers, and during visits to family homes. These methods have the advantage of yielding very "fine-grained" data, from audiotapes, videotapes and systematic written records, which can be analyzed down to the smallest detail. Their disadvantage is that they are susceptible to a "guinea-pig" effect. Because fathers know they are being observed, their behavior may not be typical. However, since other methods (to be described shortly) help to offset this limitation, I will go ahead and summarize the results of these "controlled observation" studies.

During hospital visit studies, where parents are observed interacting with their first-borns, researchers have compared both the quantity and quality of "bonding behavior" shown by fathers and mothers toward their babies. Bonding behavior includes activities such as holding, rocking, looking, smiling, vocalizing, touching and kissing. These studies have found that fathers react essentially the same way as mothers to their newborns, regardless of social class and regardless of whether the father was present at the actual birth. Nor do new fathers and mothers differ in their physiological response to newborns. When their heart rate and blood pressure are monitored, parents of both sexes respond in the same way, and to the same extent, when the baby shows distress. But significantly, they do differ in their more public, verbal responses. On the average, mothers express more interest in babies when they are in a group than when asked privately—but the exact opposite is true for fathers! Contrary to existing stereotypes, fathers are as competent and responsive as mothers toward their newborns, and—unless questioned publicly—express at least as much interest in them.[11]

A second kind of observational study is known as the "attachment paradigm." In this kind of study, parents bring their infant or toddler to a laboratory playroom for an hour or so. The parent is asked to remain with the child at first, to sit and read rather than play actively with the child, but to respond if the child initiates interaction. This allows the researchers to get a "baseline" measure of the child's attachment—by recording how close the child stays to the parent, how often the child brings toys over, vocalizes to the parent, or demands help or comfort. Then the parent is called out of the room for a few minutes, and the child is left to play alone. The degree to which the child stops playing, shows distress or attempts to find the parent (goes over to the door, looks around and so on) is a second measure of attachment. In the third stage of observation, an adult unknown to the child enters the room and tries to play with the child. The degree of distress the child shows toward the stranger (and the degree of "clinging behavior" shown when the parent replaces the stranger) are final measures of attachment.

Until recently, of the hundreds of studies done using this attachment paradigm virtually none involved fathers. This was finally rectified in the 1970s, when several studies systematically compared the attachment behavior of children to both mothers and fathers. The results: up to twelve months of age, there was no difference in the amount and type of attachment behavior shown toward the father as compared to the mother. Children interacted with both parents equally and distinguished both in the same way from the stranger. Earlier theories of child development had assumed that for reasons of sheer survival, infants were instinctively primed for early bonding with mothers alone.[12] Yet it was only in the one- to two-year olds that any

pattern of preference for the mother emerged. This was not surprising, considering that in all the families studied mothers were the
primary caretakers. But even so, a quarter of the toddlers showed
more attachment to the father than the mother, and another quarter
showed equal attachment to both parents. Contrary to popular wisdom, fathers are such important figures in the eyes of their infants
that even their high degree of absence from the home did not reduce
their attractiveness for some of the infants studied.[13]

Finally, researchers have observed father-infant interactions in the
home setting. Probably the most thorough of these studies has been
done by psychologist Michael Lamb, who randomly selected ten first-
borns of each sex from hospital records and studied them during
repeated home visits until they were two years of age. As I pointed out
in chapter seven, infant behavior seesaws between attachment to
caretakers and increasing interest in the wider world. Lamb captured
this tension by distinguishing between the children's "attachment"
and "affiliative" behaviors (although I think the term "cognitive-affiliative" better expresses the latter). Attachment behaviors were those
aimed at gaining comfort and physical contact when the child was
frightened, hurt or otherwise distressed. By contrast, cognitive-affiliative behaviors were used by the children to satisfy their social and
intellectual curiosity and included looking, smiling, laughing, vocalizing and playing. Lamb found that on measures of attachment alone,
children generally did not distinguish between mothers and fathers.
Only if they were tired, or upset by the presence of a stranger, did they
direct more attachment behavior to the mother (again, not surprising
since all but one of the mothers were primary caretakers).

However, when the children were not tired or under other stress—
in other words, when they were maximally able to profit from social
and intellectual stimulation—fathers were generally the preferred
parents at all stages up to age two (when the study ended) and across
all social classes. Lamb concluded that in families where mothers are
primary caretakers, infants value their fathers as "optimally novel
stimuli." That is, fathers are not so unfamiliar as to provoke stranger
anxiety in the children, but they come and go often enough to gen-

erate interest as "exciting novelties" in a way that doesn't happen for total strangers until after age two. Note that such a conclusion doesn't require that mothers always be the primary caretakers and fathers the "optimally novel stimuli." Indeed, as families enlarge, older brothers and sisters (and even pets) also bring out infants' cognitive-affiliative behavior. What it does mean is that the primary caretaker, whoever that is, will probably be the prime target of attachment behavior, but that behaviors aimed at increasing the child's physical and intellectual independence are more apt to be directed at other family members.[14]

But even when both parents engage in cognitive-affiliative behavior with infants, it turns out that they go about it in somewhat different ways. Harvard psychologist Michael Yogman discovered this when he did second-by-second analyses of videotapes recorded over a six-month period in infants' homes. Mothers consistently made more sounds and played more verbal games with their children, particularly games involving imitation and taking turns. Fathers were more likely to engage in physical play with their infants: tapping or patting younger infants, doing controlled "rough-housing" with older ones. Moreover, parents express similar preferences along these lines—that is, mothers express more enjoyment of verbal than of physical games and fathers the opposite. And in fact, children need both kinds of play for social and intellectual development. The mother-infant dialogues encourage language development and turn-taking, while the father's more physically oriented games help develop spatial and motor skills.[15]

Of course, the fact that parents tend to practice and prefer different kinds of play with their children doesn't mean that these differences are reducible to biology. It is noteworthy that they parallel the two cognitive areas in which men and women are apt to differ—when they differ at all. The women are showing slightly superior verbal skills and the men slightly superior spatial skills. But as we have already learned, nurture adds so much to nature in the production of such differences that by adulthood it is quite impossible to separate their contributions. The important point is that by having two highly involved parents, as well as a variety of other secondary caretakers,

the cognitive and social development of the child is likely to be enhanced.

Fathers' Competence versus Fathers' Performance

But the crucial qualifier in my last sentence is the phrase "highly
involved." If we were to go only on the research reported above, we
would end up concluding that fathers are doing quite well. Are they
not competent as parents, and developmentally important to their
children, despite any rhetoric to the contrary? Yes, indeed; but there
is a crucial distinction to be made between competence and performance. The studies reported above tell us only what fathers in our
society can do, not what they usually do when not under scrutiny by
note-taking, camera-toting social scientists. To assess fathers' actual
degree of involvement with their children we need to consult studies
which are less susceptible to the "guinea pig" effect. The least obtru-
sive measures of fathering come from what are called "time budget"
studies. These studies, which can involve thousands of respondents
in several countries, basically require adults to record what they are
doing in each fifteen- or twenty-minute time block throughout a typical weekday. Because no one activity is singled out as being the target
of the study, respondents are less likely to distort the time recorded
for any given behavior, including activities involving children. Of
course, such records only give us estimates of the quantity, not the
quality, of time fathers spend with children. But this is important to
know, because the benefits of fathering for children—including those
involving cognitive, social and gender-identity development—can
hardly be reaped if fathers are largely absent.

Time-budget studies conducted up through the 1980s consistently
show that fathers spend about one-fifth the amount of time as mothers on total domestic work, including child care. Moreover, in North
America this difference remains unaffected by the mother's employment status outside the home. A great many popular arguments
against mothers returning to the paid workforce center around the so-
called deprivation of parental contact children will suffer as a result.
Yet time-budget studies show that mothers, on the average, do not

spend less time with their children when they have outside employment. They simply cut down on other activities they consider less important, including house cleaning, hobbies, socializing with friends and even sleeping. By contrast, the average North American father, while quite competent to parent, actually performs parenting tasks only for ten to thirty minutes per day. And most of this, it turns out, is taken up by chauffeuring children to activities or "keeping an eye on them" while watching television. Perhaps the greatest irony of all is that many divorced fathers report spending more time with their children after they have retained only visiting rights than they did when they lived in the same household with them.[16]

Paternal Presence: What Advantage?

Because high father absence is still the norm even in intact North American families, it is not easy to get a full picture of what high father presence means for children of both sexes. I have mentioned the cognitive and social advantages that result when young children have two parents, each with slightly different styles, with whom to interact. But many of these advantages might not require a "standard nuclear family" in order to appear. A different line of theorizing suggests that it is the *number*, not the *sex* of adults in a family that influences children's intellectual development. There is a tendency for first-borns, as well as children with no siblings, to have higher IQ scores than later-born children in larger families. Some theorists suggest that this is because in large families the total amount of adult intellectual attention is more "thinly spread" among the children than in smaller families. Such findings might actually be a source of relief, especially to single parents, for they suggest that as long as children have plenty of high-quality contact with any reliable and committed set of adults (including grandparents, other relatives, teachers, youth leaders and so on) their intellectual and social development need not suffer.[17]

But intellectual and social development take place in the context of emerging gender identity, and it is in this area that children of both sexes most obviously need involved, available caretakers of both sexes. In the case of boys, traditional wisdom has held that their developing sense of masculinity requires only a father who is a "good provider" and a "strong male" whose power in the family and in the world at large is plain to see. But, in fact, boys who have the most secure sense of masculinity are those whose fathers have been highly involved in child care and who have been nurturant and gender role flexible, rather than punitive and gender role stereotyped toward their sons. So strong and consistent is this finding that parenting researchers have been known to state that it is almost impossible for a father to be *too* nurturant toward his sons. This is an important point to note because it underscores the fact that mere quantity of fathering is not sufficient. One can be a highly involved, but still very gender-stereotyped and authoritarian father who thus perpetuates, rathers than re-educates, both his son's "insecure masculinity" and his later contempt for women.[18]

As for girls, there is now some data available on the effects of both father absence and father presence. Girls who have lost fathers through death tend to grow up overly fearful and inhibited in the presence of men, whereas those who have lost fathers through divorce tend to react the opposite way: they seek proximity and attention from males and tend to become sexually active at an earlier age than daughters of intact families.[19] But whereas the father's nurturing presence has an unambiguously positive effect on son's masculinity, the wrong kind of nurturing can be detrimental to daughters. There is a great deal of research showing that even though they spend much less time with their children, fathers are more insistent than mothers that their children show "proper" gender-role behavior. Thus they are apt to encourage feminine dress, manners and dependence in their daughters. When this pressure is added to a young girl's already well-developed desire to please others and not appear assertive, it can retard her motivation to achieve intellectually.

Women who are top-level business executives and mathematicians have regularly emphasized the influence of their fathers on their choice and pursuit of careers. Most grew up in households where fathers encouraged independence and achievement rather than ster eotypical femininity. It's not that the fathers were emotionally distant or non-nurturing toward their daughters; but what they nurtured and encouraged was what they had achieved themselves—namely, a successful career in the so-called man's world.[20] Nor is it the case that the mothers of high-achieving women have no influence as role models; other studies show that they certainly do. But as one reviewer of the literature has put it,

> the real influence of the Father may be his power to remove the restrictions of socially-prescribed gender roles. . . . The fathers of high-achieving daughters did not convey to their daughters the message that certain activities were the exclusive domain of one sex or another. They gave their daughters the message that sex was not the most significant organizing variable when it came to determining whether or not girls should take part in certain activities.[21]

Of Boys and Babies
It is somewhat distressing that the father should be so able to help remove gender-role restrictions, yet remain the parent who is generally more concerned to promote gender-role stereotypes in both sons and daughters. For not only does this hinder intellectual achievement in girls; it also stifles the development of nurturance in boys. Common wisdom has it that little girls are just "naturally" (biologically) more interested in babies than boys. But a recent series of studies discounts this assumption.

Children between the ages of two and six were individually brought to a room where a six-month-old baby was sitting playing, with its mother reading nearby. The baby was neutrally dressed and randomly labeled a boy or a girl, as in other "Baby X" studies (see chapter three). The baby's mother was asked not to interfere, except to say hello to the visiting child. In the resulting analysis, the sex of the nursery-schooler made no difference whatever to the amount of talking, touching or playing that the children engaged in with the baby, nor did the fact that some children had younger siblings whereas others did not. The *presumed* sex of the child did make a difference, but not always in predictable ways: girls at all ages interacted more with babies they thought were of their own sex, but the same was true for boys only at ages two and three; from ages four to six, boys actually preferred what they thought to be girl babies!

But when the same study was repeated with eight-year-olds, the "common wisdom" stereotypes appeared: girls played with, talked to and touched the baby much, much more than boys. Yet when children of the same age were asked privately whether or not they thought they could care for a baby, and if so how they would do it, boys and girls expressed equal confidence and equal knowledge. So, as with their fathers, it is not competence in child care that boys lack; it is lack of motivation. This conclusion is supported by the fact that when children in a subsequent study were specifically encouraged by an adult to interact with the baby—including helping to dress and feed it—boys and girls of all ages were equally responsive and equally interested in the baby regardless of its ascribed sex.[22]

Of course, babies are not the only possible targets of children's nurturing behavior. When the same series of studies measured the amount of time children of varying ages spent playing with and caring for pets, sex differences completely disappeared. This is encouraging news, because caring for pets is in many ways good practice for infant care—certainly more realistic than playing with inanimate dolls!

But there are still many distortions to be corrected. In chapter one I mentioned a large, centrally organized Christian community where fathers are discouraged from changing their children's diapers on the assumption that their older sons, observing them do "women's work," will grow up with an insufficiently secure male identity. I have often been tempted to send the male leaders of this community (there being no female leaders to speak of) a copy of the study that found the best predictor of toddlers' attachment to fathers was (can you guess?) the number of diapers the father had changed during the previous week.[23] The case for co-parenting is very strong!

9

Marriage, Family and the Kingdom of God

This third section, "Parents and Partners," has concentrated first on parenting because the flow of the argument from part 2 on nature and nurture made this ordering a logical one. It is by parents, after all, that children are nurtured in their critical, formative years— the years when, perhaps above all others, nurture modifies nature. But having concentrated on parenting in the past two chapters, we need now to look at marriage and family in their more general, institutional sense. Because Christians have such a high view of the family, and such great concern for its preservation, we need especially to take a critical look at the accepted shape of the middle class, urban family to which most people in our society have aspired during this century. I hope readers will find that in this as in other areas of gender relations, there is more room for responsible Christian freedom than they may have believed.

Ambivalence about Marriage Roles in Recent History

Marriage and the family have long been controversial topics. But in a society that has seen two decades of feminist activity these topics are generating more discussion than ever. I remember a conversation I once had with a fellow graduate student, in which we were comparing the kinds of families we'd been raised in. My friend recalled making family visits to her grandparents' home back in the 1950s. During the long car trip her parents would take turns driving. But they always made sure it was her father who was (literally) in the driver's seat as they pulled up to the grandparents' house. She even had memories of occasions when her parents changed places in the car only a few blocks from their destination. This practice was quite foreign to my own experience, not because my parents refused to practice such minor deceptions but because my mother never learned to drive at all. Both parents simply took for granted that the burden and privilege of chauffeuring (and I think my father found it as much the former as the latter) were part and parcel of the husbandly role.

Although such anecdotes may now seem quaint, they hint at a profound ambivalence most of us share with regard to marriage and the family. On the one hand, we are fearful of change. As young children, we absorbed a particular set of ideas (those of our parents) about "correct" roles for wives, husbands and children—and these deeply emotional, critical-period associations are not easily shed in adulthood. On the other hand, most of us resent it when we see these roles turning into cages. We rightly sense that our individual gifts and personalities defy pat stereotypes about "the ideal wife" or "the ideal husband," and we wonder why these stereotypes should exercise so much power over us.

In addition, I think it important to emphasize that this ambivalence characterizes men as much as it does women, even though women may be expressing their dissatisfaction more publicly at this time. There is a popular theory, among Christians as well as others, that

North American men and women were perfectly content in their respective marital roles until feminism came along in the 1960s and subverted women into wanting something different. (The prevalence of the theory is suggested by the current nostalgia for 1950s-style family comedies on television.) According to this theory, it was only when Betty Friedan wrote *The Feminine Mystique* in 1963 that women, betraying their best interests and true desires, began to rebel against the role of full-time homemaker, leaving their husbands bewildered and hurt in wake of their ingratitude. But a closer scrutiny of post-World War 2 social history strongly suggests that men were not all that happy with the gender-role status quo either.

Barbara Ehrenreich, a student of popular culture, has noted that the first issue of *Playboy* magazine appeared in 1953, a full ten years before Friedan's book helped to launch the current feminist movement. Most of us associate *Playboy,* and its later clones such as *Penthouse* and *Hustler,* primarily with a strident defense of sexual libertarianism. But there was another theme which appeared regularly in its pages during the 1950s: a castigation of parasitic wives who, while making no money of their own, constantly demanded more and more financial success of their husbands in order to support an upwardly mobile lifestyle. *Playboy*'s very first feature article was an attack on the concept of alimony in particular, and against money-hungry women in general: it was titled "Miss Gold-Digger of 1953." The magazine's first print run of 70,000 virtually sold out, and by 1956 it had over a million subscribers. "From the beginning," writes Ehrenreich, "*Playboy* loved women—large-breasted, long-legged young women anyway—and hated wives "'

It is probably true that *Playboy*'s attack on the suburban American dream did not affect the actual behavior of most middle-class men in the 1950s. (How much it affected their fantasies is another matter.) In addition, the magazine's attack on parasitic wives was at least partly a case of blaming the victim. Women had been pushed out of the high-responsibility jobs they held during World War 2 in order to guarantee employment to returning war veterans. They were told that it was "patriotic" to return to full-time homemaking and offered in-

centives such as low-interest mortgages and free college education for
their husbands via the G. I. Bill. Legal, economic and social pressures
all combined to turn them into the "parasites" *Playboy* was criticizing
less than a decade after the war's end.[2] Still, regardless of these qualifiers, the runaway success of Playboy points to a deep-seated ambivalence in many post-war male breadwinners—an ambivalence about
more than just the restrictions of sexual monogamy. The fact that an
outlet for their resentments appeared on the newsstands a full decade
before *The Feminine Mystique* indicates that the marital role dissatisfac-
tions of the 1960s were not limited to a few middle-class wives
supposedly subverted by feminist doctrine.

Is the "Traditional" Family the Biblical Family?

By the late 1970s, the stability of marriage and the family had declined
considerably. Concerned about this trend, historian Christopher
Lasch wrote a book on the family titled *Haven in a Heartless World.*
Subtitled *The Family Besieged,* the book came as a surprise to Americans
on the political right and left alike. Because Lasch was known to be
a leftist historian, people on the left viewed him as a traitor in his
defense of the nuclear family: he seemed to be arguing for the very
institution which, ever since the sixties, they had been attacking as a
mainstay of both capitalism and women's oppression. And reviewers
from the political right suspected that he had a hidden agenda which
wasn't really pro-family after all.[3]

Where do Christians, with their high view of Scripture, place themselves in this debate? There is little doubt that most are firmly—
indeed anxiously—pro-family. In recent years Christians have produced a veritable explosion of books, films, seminars and organizations devoted to the kind of family they feel is the biblical norm. This
family consists of a breadwinning father who works outside the home
and a non-waged mother who cares for both home and children until
the latter are well into their school years. When the children are older,
she will perhaps take on paid work, provided it doesn't interfere with
her primary role as homemaker. Proponents of this view also agree
with Professor Lasch that the family is meant to be "a haven in a

heartless world," a shelter of love which counteracts the harsh impact
of public life:

> In times such as these . . . the Christian home should be a holy
> refuge. A place of peace. An enclave of loving authority and Godly
> grievances and truth.[4]

> The home is an island of serenity and support and understand-
> ing in a hectic, plastic, often avaricious world. A Christian oasis far
> from the maddening throng and godless currents and pressures.[5]

> Only through the family can we hope to achieve security, a sense
> of well-being and belonging.[6]

> It's in our homes that we are needed, it's to our families that we
> are important. For the home is the last bastion against deperson-
> alization and dehumanization.[7]

> The family is the basic institution which undergirds all else. . . .
> If the family fails, then all the other institutions of society will fail.[8]

> The hope of America today is strong Christian families. Deter-
> mine to make your family a fortress of spiritual and moral strength
> against the shifting tides of moral change.[9]

Biblical Family or Bourgeois Family?

Is this a biblical view of the family? Is the "traditional" family both
a haven in a heartless world and the primary focus of our human
attachments? The above quotations seem to assume so. Moreover,
they seem to imply that such families—at least if they are *Christian*
families—are largely exempt both from the effects of the Fall and
from accountability to any other body. Consequently, what happens
within this "holy refuge" and "island of serenity" is somehow sacred,
and any criticism—or even relativization—of its importance implies
an attack on Christianity itself. But despite the frequency of such
rhetoric in the popular Christian media, there are at least three reasons why we should seriously question the "biblical" status of the
family so described.

The first of these reasons is historical. As we have already seen in
previous chapters, the kind of family many Christians regard as normative is actually historically quite recent—in large part a product of

the urbanization and industrialization trends of the past two centuries. This is not to say that the nuclear family per se is that recent: social historians tell us that it has been the basic family unit in the Christian west since the fourteenth century.[10] But the present, idealized role-structure of the nuclear family—father as commuting breadwinner, mother as full-time homemaker and childrearer, children seen as tender plants in need of special shelter and carefully-paced education—is largely a product of the nineteenth-century urban middle class.

In earlier times the home was for most people both a living space and the hub of work activities in which all family members necessarily shared. People married for practical, not romantic, reasons. In most families it was economically impossible to let children assume adult roles gradually, even if their parents had been inclined to do so. And even among the more leisured aristocracy child mortality rates were so high that it made little sense to get emotionally attached to one's children, as they might die at any time. Thus, in sociologist James Hunter's words, "There has been enough variability in family structure and relations in the last several centuries in the (predominantly Christian) West that it is not entirely clear what the traditional family is."[11]

A second reason for questioning the biblicality of the "traditional" family has to do with the frequent implication that this is the most benign and life-enhancing kind of family possible, both for its own members and for society at large. And yet in recent years we have discovered that although eighty per cent of sexual abuse and family violence occurs in alcoholic families, *the next highest incidence of both incest and physical abuse takes place in intact, highly religious homes.*[12] The offending fathers in such families (for it is overwhelmingly men, rather than women, who practice child abuse) often espouse "old-fashioned values" to the point of rigidity and stuffiness. They emphasize the subordination of women, sometimes to the point of believing that they "own" their wives and daughters. In addition, they believe so strongly in individual self-sufficiency that the family often lacks close contact with other adults who can dilute the father's possessiveness.

If their religious beliefs are judgmental and exclusivistic (stressing the danger of associating with people who "aren't like us"), then the family's isolation is compounded.

Incestuous fathers in such families are often preoccupied with sex, yet afraid to talk about it. They may project their own desires onto their daughters, excusing their own behavior as a case of overwhelming seduction by a daughter who is "just no good." Their wives, fearful of conflict within the family and public censure outside it, often turn a blind eye to these incestuous practices. Indeed, the "traditional" nature of the family, which reinforces the wife's economic dependency on the husband, makes it doubly difficult for her to confront her husband about his behavior. And the fact that such families make up only a small fraction of religious conservatives is quite true but not the point. The point is that having a so-called traditional family—Christian or otherwise—is no guarantee of a "holy refuge" or an "island of serenity." Instead of using such metaphors it would be more accurate if we likened *all* families to the little girl of nursery-rhyme fame: when they're good, they're very, very good; but when they're bad, they're horrid.[13]

Marriage and Family in the Biblical Drama

This brings us to the third and most important reason for questioning the biblical status of the "traditional" family—namely, the Bible's own, very two-edged attitude toward the family as an institution. Here again we need to consider all the acts of the biblical drama, just as we did in chapter two when considering the more general issue of maleness and femaleness.

As we saw in that chapter, women and men were jointly created in God's image. This means that, like the members of the Godhead, they were meant to complement each other and together to exercise accountable dominion over the rest of God's creation. But both of these creational mandates were accompanied by the command that they should "be fruitful and multiply" (Gen 1:28). This command, observes theologian Geoffrey Bromiley, is given "not merely as an end in itself, but in order that the stewardship of God's bountiful creation might be possible." Carrying out the cultural mandate—that is, opening up the possibilities latent in creation—was going to need not just two, but many, many men and women: hence the obvious need for families as well as marriages. Thus, continues Bromiley, "marriage itself goes back to God's beginning with us and ours with God . . . both marriage first and family second have their origin, basis, and goal in the divine purpose, word, and action."[14]

Marriage, then, is part of God's basic creation order. That God intended it to be a lifelong, "one flesh" monogamous union is both affirmed in the creation accounts and reaffirmed by Jesus (Mk 10; Mt 19; Lk 16). Certainly one does not have to marry in order to image God or carry out the cultural mandate in cooperation with others. But neither is marriage simply God's "second best" solution for those who cannot contain their lust well enough to serve him as celibate singles, as some medieval theologians taught. Marriage is part and parcel of what God has approved for human life on earth, reflecting the unity-in-diversity of Father, Son and Holy Spirit, as well as being the vehicle through which future imagers of God are procreated.

Now if we could merely stop with a creation theology of marriage, we might be able to justify (or at least excuse) the idealized descriptions of family life which, as we have seen, some Christians espouse. But, as we know only too well, the Fall has introduced distortions into all aspects of creation, including the relationship between women and men. And the Old Testament is quite unsparing in its documentation of the results. It presents us with accounts of rape, adultery, incest and polygamy gone wild. (King Solomon had seven hundred wives and three hundred concubines!) It adds accounts of further sins aimed at covering up sexual sins, such as King David's plot to murder the husband of the woman he impregnated. And it presents such events not primarily as the acts of pagans trying to undermine Israelite society, but as the acts of God's own people. Nor are these abuses of creational sexuality limited to men. We have accounts of women scheming to get their favorite sons into positions of primacy in the family (Rebekah) and to get heirs in the first place by means God has forbidden—through incest, as in the case of Lot's daughters or by mating a husband with a servant, as in the cases of Sarah, Rachel and Leah.

None of this, of course, is meant to portray God's intentions for marriage and family life. Rather, in Gretchen Gaebelein Hull's words, it is "the true record of a false idea"—an accurate portrayal of fallen men and women, "warts and all."[15] Just as importantly, it is intended to show the Israelites that, despite their special status as the nation through which the Messiah comes, they cannot save themselves by trying to manipulate their bloodlines—let alone by departing from God's norms for faithful marriage. When the Messiah comes, he comes in God's time and by God's means—and although his coming and his message reaffirm the creational shape of family life, they also *relativize* it for the rest of human history, in the interests of bringing God's kingdom to completion.

First Family, Second Family

The sovereignty of God and the relativization of marriage and family are shown both in Jesus' coming, and in his life and teachings. Geoffrey Bromiley summarizes the first of these very aptly:

> The virgin birth, foreshadowed in Genesis 3:15 with its specific reference to the seed of the woman, forms the last and most extraordinary link in a series of unusual births that extends from Isaac to John the Baptist. During this period children often come to aging parents, contrary to normal expectations. In some instances God chooses apparently unsuitable mothers, such as the foreigner Ruth and the adultress Bathsheba. But now in the incarnation he sets aside not only marriage (except in a purely formal sense) but also the ordinary process of human reproduction to initiate the work which will undo the fall. "The power of the Most High" brings about this birth of the child that "is set for the fall and rising of many in Israel." (Lk 1:35; 2:34)[16]

Moreover, Jesus' own life and teachings underscore the fact that marriage and family now take back seat to the universal proclamation of God's salvation and the formation of a new "first family"—a worldwide kingdom-building company, in which membership depends not at all on bloodlines, but on faith in the Messiah. Note that though he radically affirms women's worth, Jesus himself stays unmarried in order to better fulfill his mission. Although he confirms God's intention for monogamous marriage and performs his first miracle in the context of a marriage feast, he announces that the final, eternal state of humanity will *not* include the marriage bond (Mk 12:25). Moreover, he demands that his disciples place marriage and family loyalty second to their allegiance to him, "If anyone comes to me and does not hate his own father and mother and wife and children and brothers and sisters, yes, and even his own life, he cannot be my disciple" (Lk 14:26).

None of this is a license for Christians to treat the marriage bond casually. Although the disciples "leave all to follow him," nowhere is there evidence that this meant literally hating or abandoning their wives. In fact, just after Peter's call, Jesus goes to the latter's home and heals his mother-in-law. Later, after Jesus' resurrection and ascension, we learn that Peter and various other apostles took their wives on missionary journeys. What Jesus' teaching does mean, for both women and men, is that commitment to Christ and his kingdom comes before any other commitment. "The radical mistake of the human race," writes Bromiley, "is that of pushing God into second or third or last place . . . of giving a higher value to other goals than to the purpose of God."[17] In doing so, ironically, humans lose the means by which those other goals, including marriage and family, can become most satisfying. For it is only by making God's kingdom their primary commitment that humans avoid worshiping "the created, rather than the creator," a sure recipe for disappointment in the end.

The problem, then, with Christian romanticization of the "traditional" family is not primarily that it tries to freeze a particular set of gender roles in time (although this is certainly a problem) nor even that it underestimates the sin and violence that can take place in the family (although this too is a problem). *The root problem is one of creeping idolatry—of putting first what should come, at best, second.* Look again at my earlier quotations from popular Christian literature on the family. Do we "achieve security, a sense of well-being and belonging *only* through the family"? The first question of the Heidelberg Catechism asks: "What is your only comfort in life and death?" Answer: "That I am not my own [nor, by implication, my family's] but belong, body and soul, in life and death, to my faithful savior Jesus Christ."[18] Is the family our "last bastion against depersonalization and dehumanization"? If so, then the family of God—the church universal—is in bad shape, and is not fulfilling its radical, kingdom-building function. Is the family "the basic institution that undergirds all else"? No, not in any of the acts of the biblical drama. God's covenant with humanity, first in creation, then in salvation, is the basis on which Christians build everything else.

Roles versus Priorities

None of this is meant to imply that the institutional church is potentially any freer than the family from corruption and self-worship. The New Testament does not identify the kingdom of God with the church per se, but with the restored rule of God over all things. Thus abusive, authoritarian families such as those referred to earlier often find their way into churches whose leadership style mimics and reinforces the least healthy aspects of their own family life. Nor am I trying to suggest that families per se are unimportant—either psychologically or in the economy of God's kingdom. I am so convinced of the family's importance for children's development that I have made as strong a case as I can for increased fatherly involvement in childrearing (see chapter eight). But I would be most distressed if anyone mistook my case for co-parenting as a license for isolated, family self-centeredness— "Molly and me, and baby makes three," in the words of an old sentimental pop song. The point, in Rodney Clapp's words, is simply this: "For the Christian, church is First Family. The biological family, though still valuable and esteemed, is Second Family. Husbands, wives, sons, and daughters are brothers and sisters in the church first and most importantly—secondly they are spouses, parents, or siblings to one another."[19]

And Clapp goes on to point out that "exactly as family is how the New Testament church behaves." It extends hospitality to a wide range of Christians and others. Its central sacrament draws on the analogy of a family meal. At their best, both "first" and "second" families are a magnet for unbelievers who are drawn to the love that is shared within and beyond their boundaries. Indeed, in marriage even genital sexuality is to be placed in the larger context of kingdom service: ,

> Sexuality in service of the kingdom . . . is substantially freed of its destructive possibilities. It is freed from service to compulsive promiscuity, dissolution, or trivial hedonism, and instead binds one person to another in love and continuing commitment. On one level, married sexuality is simply enjoyment of God's gracious creation, male and female. But on another level, it is the base for a stable home from which to minister to the wider Christian community.[20]

We should also note that by restoring the family to its secondary, biblical place we can come a long way toward recovering a biblical respect for singleness. For despite the fact that Christians pay lip service to the equal value of married and single people, their near-idolatry of the family over the past century has made single Christians feel like second-class citizens at best and moral failures at worst. But when both states are evaluated in kingdom terms, their functions are clearly complementary: a stable Christian family may have a missionary advantage in providing hospitality. But the single person, unencumbered with family duties, often has the missionary advantage of mobility. And both are vital to the spread of the church.

So the root issue is not primarily one of "proper" gender roles for husbands and wives, if by "proper gender roles" we mean some historically fixed way of structuring family economic, domestic, and childrearing tasks. The root question is one of priorities. How can a given Christian family, with its particular constellation of talents, limitations and needs, so structure itself that it contributes to the advancement of God's kingdom on earth? As one woman put it in response to Clapp's article: "Perhaps the best environment for children is not one in which the mother stays home, but one in which the whole family, as part of the larger family of God, reaches out to meet the needs of others."[21] Just *how* an individual family accomplishes this at various stages of family life is a matter of responsible Christian freedom. There is no one, "best" answer that fits every case.

When I reflect on my own situation, and the fact that both my husband and I are Christian academics, I suspect that God has called us to combine aspects of both the "hospitality" and "mobility" strategies. Because our children are still young, it is easier for us to extend hospitality at home than to travel widely. Nevertheless, we both do travel—to lecture, to preach, to fulfill editorial and board functions for Christian and scholarly organizations. And this means that each of us has to "single parent" for the other at times. Moreover, the fact that we are not a "traditional" family has, to our surprise, added to our hospitality ministry. For there are many hurting, marginal people in and outside the church who do not always feel comfortable in "traditional" homes, no matter how healthy. I cannot say that we consciously planned it this way. But in retrospect we can see how our combined gifts and choices have led to a particular family structure which, we trust, complements others in the advancement of God's kingdom.

Sewing as a Subversive Activity

That it is kingdom priorities, not family roles, that are the issue was brought home to me very graphically as I began writing this chapter. The wife of a colleague phoned to ask me if I would like to meet a visiting South African woman whose husband, a Dutch Reformed theologian, was on a lecture tour of America. This woman, she explained, had been working for over a dozen years to improve the status of black South African domestic workers, and wanted, if possible, to raise some support for this work in America. I was happy to accept, because I knew from other sources just how rare it is for white, Afrikaner Christian women to question the status quo in South Africa. "What it comes down to," wrote one woman academic from that country, "is that women are so accustomed to the idea of men taking leadership that they never learn to think for themselves. In a society so conscious of Scripture, they have been taught that this is biblical. On the whole, I don't think Afrikaner women understand the impli-

cations of apartheid or think much about it. We have produced a race
of women in blinders."[22]

The woman I met over coffee was certainly no flaming political
radical. She was in many ways the epitome of the middle-class pastor's
wife: carefully dressed, mild-mannered and (in her own words) "not
a theologian, just a housewife—no, I mean a Christian first, then a
housewife." But that telling self-description set the stage for what was
to come. Over a decade ago, she and a group of fellow Afrikaner
church women were led to find a way to improve the independence
and self-esteem of the many black women domestics who worked in
the white homes of their city. But, as unwaged homemakers themselves, what could they do for black women in order to achieve these
goals? Soon the answer came. They could set up a dressmaking-and-
tailoring school in the church, to which the women could come in
their hours off.

It should be noted that even in an industrialized country like South
Africa quality manufactured clothing is still quite expensive. Consequently, when people acquire sewing skills they are at least able to
save on the cost of their own and their family's clothing. In addition,
they may have a marketable skill in making clothing for others. So the
local church understood the potentially subversive implications of this
proposal, and many of its members disapproved. Not only would it
mean racial mingling on church property (unheard of at the time),
but it might also "give ideas" to the black women domestics about
"rising above their station." Nevertheless, cautious permission was
given for the project to begin, but with little financial support other
than the use of the church hall. Undaunted, the white homemakers
dug into their own sewing supplies, canvassed fabric dealers for remnants of cloth and persuaded sewing machine manufacturers to do-
nate equipment. They began classes catering to various levels of sewing skill, always closing each class with a short Bible study and
devotional period.

In all of this the black women were encouraged to develop leadership skills as well as sewing expertise. Indeed, they had to, for the
students came from several language groups, each of which needed

spokespersons to help the others understand directions and to organize the school as it grew. Now, twelve years later, between one and two thousand women have acquired basic or higher-level sewing skills in this informal school, which is still housed in the church and still run on a shoestring by women who are "Christians first, and housewives second." So successful has the venture been that the school may soon sign a contract for manufacturing school uniforms.

Running such a project is satisfying but hardly romantic work, according to my informant. Because of the cumbersome and often unjust bureaucracy of apartheid, the school's teachers frequently find themselves called to play the role of advocate for their students beyond the classroom. Often they feel that their efforts are merely a drop in the bucket, given what needs to be accomplished in this troubled land. But in their own steady way, they are advancing the cause of racial reconciliation, even as they share Christian teaching and economically valuable skills. Clearly their identity as homemakers is lodged within their larger role as ambassadors for Christ.

Domesticity and Mental Health

The previous paragraphs have, I hope, reassured readers that I am not trying to advance my own particular blend of career and family as the "truly" biblical model. If we have been made free in Christ, if he came to give us not less, but more, abundant life, then a variety of family role patterns can be used to build God's kingdom within the framework of faithful marriage. But because of the Christian tendency to romanticize, if not idolize, the "traditional" family, we also need to look at the relationship between this type of family and the mental health of its members. Since we have looked at some effects on girls and boys in previous chapters, we will now focus more on findings concerning their parents. When we do, we find what sociologist Jessie Bernard called a "double paradox," one concerning husbands and the other concerning wives.

Common wisdom holds that men view marriage as a trap for themselves and a prize for their wives (recall the "gold digger" motif of *Playboy*'s first issue). But statistically speaking, traditional marriage is good for men—physically, socially and psychologically. That is the first paradox. By contrast, almost all women want to marry and most want to become mothers. But on the average, childless marriages (including those in which the children are grown and gone) are happier than those with children. Additionally, women in traditional marriages show more symptoms of physical and mental distress than unmarried women—despite the social stigma that has traditionally been attached to being single. That is the second paradox.[23]

Marriage: His and Hers

Around the turn of the century, pioneer sociologist Emile Durkheim observed that "the regulations imposed on the woman by marriage are always more stringent . . . she loses more and gains less [than her husband] from the institution."[24] Since then a large body of research on the traditional (that is: urban, middle-class, single-earner) family has confirmed and elaborated on Durkheim's statement.[25] To begin with, when single and married men are compared in terms of mental and physical health, the married men as a group consistently score higher. Now this finding is based only on survey data, so the direction of causality is unclear. One could argue, for instance, that only the healthiest men manage to attract wives in the first place (rather than that acquiring wives is good for their health). But if this is the case, how are we to explain the opposite finding with respect to women in traditional marriages—namely, that they consistently score lower on mental and physical health indices than single women? It is difficult to believe that marriage, as an institution, selectively favors the healthiest men, while at the same time catering to the least healthy women!

And in fact, studies of women at various stages of their married life strongly suggest that it is marriage per se which is responsible for their lesser state of health. Newly married women do not differ, on the average, from their single women peers in terms of health indicators; but the longer they are married, the greater the gap becomes. All of this strongly suggests that traditional marriage is generally a more positive experience for men than for women. Nevertheless, when traditionally married couples are asked to give a global statement about their happiness, almost no differences are found between the self-reports of husbands and wives. Why should this be so? One could surmise, as Freud did, that women are inherently masochistic, that they enjoy suffering. But there is an equally plausible alternative explanation. In Bernard's words:

> Could it be that [traditionally married] women report themselves as happy because they are oversocialized, or too closely integrated into the norms of our society? . . . Until recently women were indoctrinated with the idea that their happiness lay in devoting their lives to their husbands and children. Could it be that because married women thus conform and adjust to the demands of marriage, at whatever cost to themselves, they therefore judge themselves to be happy? Are they confusing adjustment with happiness?[26]

The Need for Reform

Bernard rightly adds that "adjustment" is not always a sign of psychopathology. If only a few possible lifestyles exist, the "happiness-as-adjustment" mindset is a healthy one to adopt, regardless of one's sex. Healthy people do come to terms with the unchangeable. Our pioneering ancestors of both sexes did so as they labored to make isolated frontiers livable for future generations, changing the landscape to be sure, but putting aside dreams of urban cultural and educational opportunities in the process. But as I noted in the very first chapter of this book, our society has for a long time been educating men and women equally, at least through high school and in the middle class beyond high school as well. We have implicitly treated education as a window of opportunity for men in terms of the work possibilities it opens up. At the same time, however, we have assumed that education for women is primarily a means for meeting more suitable marriage partners and only secondarily an avenue for job training—just in case (God forbid) the woman should "fail" to marry.

This double message to women ("get educated, but don't take it very seriously") was bound to backfire eventually. And given the job conditions of traditional full-time homemaking, it is perhaps a wonder it didn't backfire earlier. Much household work is repetitive, unskilled, tiring and done largely in isolation from other adults. There is no clear standard for "good" housekeeping, yet no apparent end to the work of meeting everyone else's physical and emotional needs. ("Man's work goes from sun to sun, but woman's work is never done," reads an old proverb.) Moreover, a large body of literature on gender role stereotypes reveals that most of the "feminine" qualities we expect of marriageable women are also the ones we generally consider socially undesirable at best and clinically immature at worst. Until recently, both lay people and professional clinicians agreed that the "ideal" woman was (among other things) unambitious, dependent, emotional, submissive, naive, indecisive, illogical, passive, unselfconfident and home-bound. But when asked to judge these labels in a non-gendered context, clinicians also agreed that this constellation of traits was just the opposite of what makes a healthy "adult"![27]

Given all this, is it any wonder that traditional homemakers, despite their self-reports of happiness, show increasing signs of psychological distress as the marriage progresses? This is not to say that there are no truly happy and healthy homemakers: the above findings are based only on averages. But other research suggests that, to maintain both happiness and good all-round health as a full-time homemaker, certain other conditions need to be met. Chief among these are regular contact with other adults (such as family, friends, fellow members of organizations), and respect, affirmation, and support from family members in general and the husband in particular.[28] One hopes, of course, that this is routinely the case in Christian families. But as we have seen, it is by no means a foregone conclusion. And even the healthiest of traditional marriages still has the problem of chronic father-absence from the day-to-day routine of childrearing. We saw in previous chapters that this high degree of father-absence (no matter how sincerely motivated in terms of fulfilling the breadwinner role) runs the risk of turning sons into misogynists and daughters into underachievers.

Moreover, in the long run, something else is needed; it is not enough to be affirmed and supported in the homemaker role if the society one is helping to perpetuate is blatantly unjust. The pre-Civil War American South, Nazi Germany, present-day white South Africa—all these societies have supported, even glorified, women's role as keeper of the home and transmitter of values to the next generation. But in all of them it has been understood that women are not to question the societal status quo. To do so was considered biting the hand that fed them and violating accepted notions of male authority. In each of these societies the comfort and privatization of "traditional" family life in the dominant group has helped to retard desperately needed societal reforms.[29] In each of them, thankfully, there have been women who insisted on being "Christians first and housewives second" and men who supported them in that vision. They helped run the underground railroad during the American Civil War and hid Jews in Nazi-occupied Europe. Today they are operating inner-city food pantries, opposing abortion on demand and working for reform of the criminal justice system, among other things. Again, it is priorities, not roles, that are crucial.

Lessons from the Farm
As we close this chapter on marriage and the family, we will consider one other set of findings which may help us to regain some flexibility in our thinking about marital and family roles. It is ironic that many who support the norm of the urban, middle-class, single-breadwinner family are people whose own parents or grandparents were none of the above. A particularly pointed example is that of a California man who spent years publicly protesting the fact that a woman was chosen over him for the job of county road dispatcher. That her test scores and previous experience were comparable to his cut no ice with him. Nor did the fact that she was a widow supporting four children. Road work is hard manual labor, he insisted, and men, not women, should be getting a family wage for doing it. His own mother, however, helped to run a large farm—drove tractors, baled hay and even kept the farm afloat when her husband died during the Depression. "I guess she was a pretty strong woman," her son conceded, without recognizing that his own family history contradicted his argument

about "women's natural place."[30]

Farmers as a group are largely ignored by North American social scientists, and farm women are perhaps the most neglected group of all. It was not until the early 1980s that a national study of farm women's work and family life was conducted, drawing on interviews with 2,500 farm women and a comparison sample of 500 farm men.[31] The results give us a picture of family life much more organically unified than that of the "traditional" family in the urban, industrial setting. To begin with, the farm is a family business in which both husband and wife are equally active. Gender roles do exist. For example, husbands are generally more involved than wives in marketing decisions, and wives are more involved than husbands in farm accounting. But there is still much more gender role flexibility than is the case in "traditional" urban marriages, with wives highly involved in farm labor and fathers more available for child care between chores.

Furthermore, childbearing reduces women's participation in farm work only when children are below school age. Once children are themselves old enough to help with the operation (taking on a degree of responsibility seldom matched by urban children of the same age), their mothers are actually more, not less, involved in all aspects of the farm. In addition, the survey results confirm and update an old proverb: if you want something done, ask a busy woman. The farm women most likely to be involved in voluntary organizations, political work and church activities were those with the largest farms, a job outside the farm and school-aged children. And perhaps the best test of their co-partnership in the operation was the conviction of over half the women sampled (and the concurrence of most of the men) that the wife could carry on the farm if death or disability overtook the husband.

A "traditional" family structure? Hardly, although it is one which most traditional, urban families remember with pride from their own family history. We cannot, of course, reproduce the exact details of such a lifestyle in the city. But its basic dynamics—a more equal sharing of economic and childrearing responsibilities by parents, the delegation of real responsibility to children as they are able to handle it—these are available to most families who care enough to organize their lives and their priorities accordingly. There is nothing unbiblical about traditional family roles, provided the family is healthy in other ways. But neither is the traditional family the only (or always the best) way to organize such roles for marital health, adequate parenting and kingdom service. So let us, in this vocation as in others, be prepared to exercise responsible Christian freedom and allow others to do likewise.

PART 4

Achievement
and Attraction

10 Gender, Work and Christian Vocation

"What happens when feminists turn up on both sides of the courtroom?" This was the headline of an article appearing in *Ms.* in the mid-1980s. The event was a sex discrimination case mounted by the U.S. Equal Employment Opportunity Commission (EEOC) against Sears, Roebuck and Company. A ten-year investigation of the company's records revealed that proportionately more women than men began, and stayed, in sales positions involving small items with no commissions attached (clothing, jewelry, greeting cards). By contrast, a greater percentage of men ended up selling big-ticket items—things like large appliances, power tools or car tires—which netted them hefty commissions on top of their basic hourly wage. And since even first-year commission salespersons have median earnings almost twice those of all non-commission workers, the EEOC announced that Sears was guilty of a systematic "pattern or practice" of sex discrimination.[1]

So far, it sounds like a routine anti-discrimination case, similar to ones brought against corporations like General Motors, General Electric and AT&T. All of these groups settled out of court, agreeing to give millions of dollars in back pay to the groups discriminated against and/or to set up affirmative-action programs making salary and promotion policies more equitable. What was unique about the Sears case was not just that the company decided to fight it out in court. What was newsworthy were the "expert witnesses" Sears and the EEOC brought in to testify, in each case a well-known feminist history professor from a prestigious Eastern university. And although their arguments were historical, the issues behind them are also psychological. They point to questions about men's and women's differing priorities, whether these are rooted more in nature or in culture, and what they might mean (and allow for) in the workplace.

Sears's lawyers argued that the relative lack of women in big-ticket sales did not reflect systematic discrimination or even lack of encouragement by the company. Their surveys had shown that most women didn't want the pressure, competition and extra responsibility of these jobs. Testifying in the company's defense was Rosalind Rosenberg from Columbia University. "Historically," she explained, "men and women have had different interests, goals, and aspirations regarding work. Because housework and child care affect women's labor force participation even today, many women choose jobs that complement their family obligations over jobs that might increase or enhance their earning potential."[2] Men and women just naturally have different priorities, Rosenberg seemed to be saying. And these will be reflected in different patterns of employment that are not, for the most part, due to organizational discrimination.

Testifying for the EEOC was another social historian, Alice Kessler-Harris of Hofstra University. Justifying a segregated workforce by appealing to women's "natural" choices was just a timeworn excuse for continued discrimination, she asserted. In reality, "women's choices can only be understood within the framework of available opportunity." Our notions about "suitable" work for women shift as societal needs change. In this century, for example, women have been alternately encouraged and discouraged to take banking jobs, depending on the rate of unemployment among men. When men didn't want to be bank tellers, women were told they were "good at figures" and welcomed to the banks; when men began to need such jobs (during the Depression, for example), banks stopped hiring women "because they were poor at figures." The argument that women don't want certain jobs, Kessler-Harris concluded, is actually a smokescreen for discrimination, subtly or not-so-subtly veiled by negative propaganda and working conditions. If women then reject such work conditions, they are said to have "chosen" to leave in response to some innate female personality trait, when in fact the trend has been mainly engineered by males working to preserve male interests.[3]

Sorting Out the Issues
This case highlights important issues concerning women, men and work. Rosenberg implied that gendered patterns of work are the result of personality differences between women and men: women "just naturally" pattern their work life around the care of home and children, and men "just naturally" cope with the stress and competition of commission sales better than women. Kessler-Harris countered that it is the forces of society, not personality, that best explain why men and women end up doing different work for different pay. Can we choose between these two explanations? Are there other factors we need to consider as well?

To answer these questions we need to clarify what is meant by the word *work*. So far I have glibly used terms like *workforce* and *workplace* without even saying what work is. I have also spoken of paid work (such as sales jobs), unpaid work (such as parenting) and implied a distinction between physical work (like housekeeping) and mental work (like doing history). What counts as work, anyway, and what attitude should the Christian take toward it? If, as in previous chapters, we are to look at this topic within the framework of a biblical worldview, then we need to begin with a theology of work. We will do this by surveying pre-Christian and Christian views of work and its place in human life. Then, having already seen in chapter eight how families benefit from men's greater involvement in the work of childrearing, we will consider some research on women involved in so-called men's work.[4]

Work in Historical and Theological Perspective

Work has been given different meaning, and consequently different value, throughout history. To the ancient Greeks, work was whatever had to be done to keep the human body going—feeding, cleaning, sheltering and protecting it. Since mere animals also do these things, Aristotle concluded that there was nothing uniquely human about such drudgery and that it should be avoided wherever possible. Human beings were unique and god-like inasmuch as they were rational, said Aristotle. So it was the philosopher's life of the mind that a person should value and covet most. Plato agreed. To him, the body was an unfortunate encumbrance that dragged down the mind, or soul, from its eternal, spiritual, prenatal state where formal knowledge was clear and complete. Struggling back to such a state, and becoming fully fit for it again after death, required renunciation of bodily indulgence and a constant cultivation of the mind through philosophical exercise.[5]

But even philosophers must eat. And the Greeks, like the biblical Hebrews, believed that human beings were by nature social and interdependent. But they also believed in a "natural" division of labor based on people's relative intelligence. Philosophers, the most diligent seekers after moral and intellectual truth, were considered the people best suited to rule society. They would, of course, rather be doing philosophy, but their heightened moral sensibilities would lead them to take on political responsibilities as well. Below the class of philosopher-rulers, in Plato's scheme, were the "Auxiliaries"—those who functioned as police, soldiers and civil servants in response to the ruler's directives. And at the bottom of the scale were the workers who produced the material necessities of life—farmers, craftsmen, traders and so on. In *The Republic*, which develops this social theory, Plato claimed not to be doing any one class of people any favors (after all, even the philosophers had to take on duties they'd rather avoid). It is the good of the whole community Plato was promoting, convinced that this depended on each class knowing its place and willingly staying in it.[6]

In Aristotle's *Politics* there was also a class of "natural slaves"—those whose rational capacities were the least developed. These persons, wrote Aristotle, were fitted by nature to do the "maintenance work" that allowed their more intelligent masters to engage in political or philosophical activity. And where did women fit into this scheme of things? According to Aristotle, women's rational capacities were inferior to men's; consequently, "the male is by nature superior and the female inferior; the one rules and the other is ruled."[7] Women could belong to any level of society by virtue of their role in bearing children for their husbands (though even here, women's wombs were considered merely the soil in which the man's seed grew, not contributing to human life, but merely nourishing it). They could have limited domestic authority over slaves and workers if they were fortunate enough to marry well. But civic life and philosophy were closed to them, because both depended on a level of rational development which women were assumed to lack.

Medieval and Renaissance Views of Work
The Christian gospel was first preached in a Greek cultural and intellectual milieu. As a result, many of the church fathers and their medieval descendants developed the implications of the gospel in terms of the Greek philosophical framework in which they had been trained. Just as the Greeks had seen in the life of the mind the highest of human activities, so medieval theologians like Thomas Aquinas regarded the contemplation of God as religiously superior to the physical work of caring for one's own—or even other people's—bodily needs. The latter, it was said, merely helped to maintain that which would pass away with death, whereas prayer and religious study, as activities of the eternal mind, would endure eternally.

Hence the medieval distinction between the "active" and the "contemplative" life. The active life included all that Plato had assigned to workers and auxiliaries—namely, the work of meeting bodily and societal needs. To be a farmer, a parent, a merchant, a knight or a city official—these were "good" in the medieval economy of salvation: given the material nature of earthly life, somebody had to do these things. But from the early church fathers right through the Middle Ages (and in Catholic thinking until more recently), the message was clear. The active life is merely temporary, while the contemplation of God lasts forever; consequently, the contemplative life is religiously "better." Indeed, only the latter was referred to as a "vocation" or "calling" from God. Work might have a negative value in disciplining the flesh to a state more fit for contemplation, but otherwise it was just a regrettable necessity.

Of course, the medieval church differed from the Greeks in allowing both women and men to choose between active and contemplative lives. And although in theory women were more evil and less rational than men (and thus could never become priests), in practice things were often different. High-born, educated women carried their sense of privilege and authority with them to the convents, often becoming powerful administrators of people and property. And despite the growth of church bureaucracy, medievals retained the sense that, as in Christ himself, God's power was most reliably displayed in weak individuals. Thus women recluses and mystics, living austere lives and claiming direct visions from God, sometimes acquired a prophetic role which made them the confidantes and advisors even of kings and archbishops. And despite the lower religious status of merchants, craftsmen and peasants, the women of these classes had close to a functional equality with men. Their labor was essential to the success of the family enterprise, the law protected their inheritance rights, and forced marriages were rare. Widows in particular had a great deal of autonomy, especially if their husbands left them substantial estates, and there are also records of independent single women and of married women who had large stakes in family businesses.[8]

Nevertheless, both productive and reproductive work were seen as religiously inferior to the life of prayer and contemplation. It was not until the Renaissance of the fifteenth century that this began to change. At that time, the longstanding view of God as a solitary, self-sufficient mind was replaced by an emphasis on God as active creator and sustainer of the universe. In this view human beings became like God not merely by thinking, but by the productive activity that had earlier been so downgraded. Philosopher Lee Hardy summarizes this newer view: "To be created in the image of God meant not only possessing an intellect, but hands as well. God created nature out of nothing. Humankind would now create a world out of nature and thus become a demi-god."[9] The ideal human being was no longer the philosopher or monk who merely contemplates, but rather the artist, who both contemplates an idea and shapes materials to express it.

In chapter two we pointed to dominion and sociability as aspects of the image of God in all people. Certainly the Renaissance thinkers were recovering a respect for the first of these in their emphasis on God and persons as "makers." At the same time, some philosophers put so much stress on human creativity that they released human beings entirely from their dependence on God. Indeed, three centuries later Karl Marx was writing squarely in this tradition. Workers under capitalism might be alienated from their own labor, but after the revolution they would jointly own all the means of production, and freely control a world entirely of their own making. From the Greek and medieval view of work as a disagreeable necessity, Renaissance thought began to regard it as the peak of autonomous, human self-expression. It was the Protestant Reformers who tried to steer a fine line between both of these unbiblical extremes. In the process they recovered and developed the meaning of work in terms of the biblical drama. But at the same time they limited gender roles in a way anticipating the divorce of public and private spheres that was to come with the nineteenth-century Industrial Revolution. The result has been a mixed blessing for both women and men.

The Reformation: A Mixed Legacy
The heart of the Protestant Reformation's message was that neither

the active nor the contemplative life can save us: we are saved by the
grace of God, not through our own work, whether religious or secular.
In fact the Reformers cut right through the medieval distinction between the sacred and the secular, extending the definition of religious
vocation to include any activity by which a person could serve his or
her neighbor in Christian love. Both Luther and Calvin saw human
work as partaking of all the acts of the biblical drama. They did not
deny that work was often made onerous and repugnant by the Fall.
But, they insisted, its fallen aspect was neither its beginning nor its
end in God's eyes. Our ability to work is part of the creation order,
imaging not only God's dominion and creativity, but also the chief way
in which he continues to care for us. "Having fashioned a world filled
with resources and potentials, God chose to continue his creative
activity through the work of human hands. Through our work, humble though it may be, people are brought under God's providential
care. As we pray each morning for our daily bread, people are already
at work in the bakeries."[10]

In this view work also extends God's redemptive activity in Christ.
Although we have biblical assurance about its final outcome, the cosmic battle between good and evil still produces many casualties. But
we combat evil in the power of God not by abandoning earthly activity
for a life of pure religious contemplation. Without neglecting prayer
and worship, we are to cultivate the fruit of the Spirit by accepting
both the pleasant and unpleasant aspects of work as our service to
others. Seen in this light, any work that serves our neighbor—paid or
unpaid, domestic or public, mental or physical—can be a vocation
imbued with divine dignity. Seen in this light, to use a more contemporary Reformational saying, "all of life is religion."[11]

So far, so good. According to the Reformers, work neither debases
us to the level of beasts nor elevates us to the status of gods. As we
exercise accountable dominion and sociability in our work, we develop
two important aspects of God's image in us. Through work, we share
in God's providential care for his creation and follow Christ's example
of redemptive suffering on behalf of the young, the poor and the
downtrodden with whom he identified. Moreover, in the past century

or so there has been a remarkable convergence of Catholic and Protestant thought on the nature and meaning of work.[12] And it is important that Christians have a clear theology of work, for we live at a time when its meaning has become very distorted. For too many working-class people work is the mindless repetition of tasks in the production of goods or services of dubious value. For too many middle- and upper-middle-class people it has become the pursuit of wealth and power, regardless of its effect on family, friendship, the environment or the long-term good of society. And for all of us it has become overly identified with earning wages—so much so that even some Christians and some feminists (Christian and otherwise) still distinguish between "working women" and "housewives"—as if homemaking were not one of the most demanding occupations going!

Gender Roles and the Reformation

Did the status of women improve as a result of the Reformation? Protestants and Catholics have tended to give opposite answers to this question. Protestant historians point to the Reformers' insistence that all vocations are equally part of God's kingdom work, thereby putting marriage and family life on an equal spiritual footing with the so-called religious vocations. Catholics, on the other hand, point out that the Reformation removed women from all the religious offices which were created for them by the medieval church without setting up any officially sanctioned substitutes. This, they say, has left Protestant women in a kind of ecclesiastical limbo where they are floundering even today.[13]

There is truth in both these views. The Reformers' notion that all of life is religion certainly made it possible to see marriage and parenting as ways of serving God that were no less important than being a monk or nun. Their stress on the priesthood of all believers meant, in theory, that even the most humbly situated man or woman could approach and listen to God directly, without mediation by a church official. And because the Reformers saw Scripture as the sole source of doctrinal authority, they had good reason to encourage literacy in all believers, for only by understanding God's Word could each co-equal "priest" understand God's ways and God's will.

But in the case of women these Reformational principles were honored more in the breach than in the observance. It is true that Luther decried the Greek/medieval assumption that woman is more evil and less God-imaging than man. "Still," he wrote, "she [is] only a woman. As the sun is much more glorious than the moon (though also the moon is glorious), so the woman was [created] inferior to the man both in honor and dignity, though she, too, was a very excellent work of God."[14] And although the German Reformer had a very progressive view of female education (in contrast to Calvin, who thought that oral instruction in the catechism was enough for women), Luther denied women the right to preach or administer sacraments except in emergencies, such as the baptism of dying newborns by midwives—itself a carry-over from medieval Catholicism. The so-called priesthood of all believers remained, in terms of church offices, a priesthood of only male believers.

A similar ambiguity pervades the attitudes of other Reformers. In both his *Commentaries* and his *Institutes* John Calvin came to the conclusion—surprising for his time—that Paul's restrictions on women were not in the realm of eternal law, but only a matter of human governance. Scripture, he wrote, neither forbids nor requires women in church office. But this being the case, Calvin was not about to become a pioneer integrator of these offices. Since he regarded social upheaval as anti-biblical, and since expanding women's church roles would certainly be a divisive issue, Calvin left women on the fringes of Genevan church polity.[15] And although the Anabaptists, like their medieval predecessors, respected both male and female mystics, they generally held to very traditional views on women with regard to both marriage and ministry. A biographer of Menno Simons comments that his most radical action on gender relations was the denial of a husband's right to beat his wife, and another sixteenth-century Anabaptist leader actually argued for the re-institution of Old Testament-style polygamy. Women had been "wearing the trousers" too long, he wrote, and the best way to reassert men's God-ordained authority would be through the practice of polygamy [16]

Sliding into Separate Spheres

Although women's place in the church is an issue Christians debate constantly (and one to which we will return in chapter twelve), we now turn to the Reformers' views on women's and men's work spheres outside the institutional church. Luther may have had a high view of marriage and family life, but he did not always have great respect for women even within that sphere, nor did he think them fit for much beyond it. "Women ought to stay at home," he wrote. "The way they were created indicates this, for they have broad hips and a wide fundament to sit upon, keep house, and bear and raise children."[17] Elsewhere he commented: "Take women from their housewifery and they are good for nothing. If women get tired and die of childbearing, there is no harm in that; let them die as long as they bear; they are made for that."[18] And Menno Simons, the Anabaptist Reformer, was adamant about women staying almost as cloistered at home as nuns formerly were in their convents: "Remain within your houses and gates unless you have something of importance to regulate, such as to make purchases, to provide in temporal needs, to hear the Word of the Lord, or to receive the holy sacraments, etc. Attend faithfully to your charge, to your children, house, and family."[19]

To be fair, we need to realize that the restriction of women to their households was partly motivated by a concern to preserve the young Protestant church from accusations of loose living. And such restrictions might not have been so serious if households had remained places where women and men shared both childrearing and a family business. Under such circumstances women's work remained a clearly defined part of the productive economy, and although women might not have ventured out into the world as often as their husbands, the local world came to them, thus decreasing the risk of social isolation. In such a social arrangement gender roles remained flexible in practice, even if not in theory. Children of both sexes had more equal access to adult role models of both sexes, and the self-esteem of both women and men benefited from each having a clear role in the economy.

But of course most households did not stay this way. In the nineteenth century, as the factory system gained momentum, more and more men left their families at home while they went off to earn what was supposed to be a "family wage." The home, formerly a unit of production, now became merely a unit for consuming things produced elsewhere, and women's role in the cash economy was reduced to that of choosing which goods and services the family would spend its money on. Instead of sharing economic productivity with their husbands, women became unwaged consumers and caretakers. Rather than sharing the work of childrearing with husbands and other family members, they ended up doing it largely alone. And the crowning irony (as we saw in chapter nine) is the vehemence with which many Christians claim this to be the one, true, "biblical" pattern for family life, rather than a middle-class, industrial-society ideal which is both historically recent and, for single parents and families unable to survive on a single wage, an unattainable lifestyle anyway.[20]

I have often wondered how this is justified theologically. Most Christians would agree that accountable dominion and sociability are part of the image of God in persons. But I suspect that many Christians, unconsciously adhering to purely cultural norms, proceed to divide these up. They maintain that, really, it is men who are mostly made for dominion (which is then equated with waged labor, no matter how lacking in creativity and responsibility), and it is women who are mostly made for sociability (which is then equated with raising children, no matter how much this fosters economic dependency and isolates them from other adults). In the process they also conclude that it is unnecessary for men to be closely involved with child-rearing, and that it is "unbiblical" for women to aspire seriously to much else!

But we saw in chapter seven that the rigid separation of domestic and public spheres has unhappy consequences for parents and children of both sexes. And we learned in chapter eight about some of the positive consequences that occur when men relearn the work of hands-on parenting. But what about women who are in the waged economy? How are they faring? In answering this question, let us look at a couple of kinds of research on an increasingly visible minority, namely professional and managerial women.

Laboring under Handicaps: Professional and Managerial Women
There are still relatively few women in management and professional careers, and as we learned at the beginning of this chapter, there are two competing explanations of this scarcity. The first is the "person-centered" explanation, which holds that, whether through nature, nurture or both, women have failed to develop the personality traits needed for managerial or professional success. They may fear that achievement will defeminize them, that the demands of a career will make them poorer mothers or that competition with fellow workers is too stressful. One recent volume argued that men learn essential management skills—like planning strategy, cooperation and competition—on the sports teams of their youth, in which most women show only a spectator's interest.[21] What links all these explanations is the implication that women somehow deserve their lower-status, lower-paid jobs. Unless they belong to that small minority of women who conform more to the stereotypical male personality profile, they are reaching beyond their grasp if they aspire to a career-track job. And most women, it is argued, recognize this and happily set their sights lower.

By contrast, a "situation-centered" explanation emphasizes the role played by the organization in holding women back. This theory argues that differential hiring and promotion practices, exclusion from informal information networks, lack of mentors and role models in higher positions, and even subtle or direct sexual harassment are among the externally imposed handicaps that make women's career advancement difficult and only ambivalently attractive.[22] Is there a way we can put these rival theories to the test? In fact there is, with a large body of studies to go with it.

Perceptions of Competence: Women Need Not Apply
You will remember from previous chapters what we called the "Baby X" research strategy, which shows that most people react to a neutral-ly clothed infant of either sex according to the stereotypes they hold

of its presumed sex. To test for the presence of discrimination against women in professional and management jobs psychologists have developed what we might call the "Product X" strategy. Its methodology is as follows: a particular "product," such as a painting, a piece of writing, a graduate-school application or a career résumé is circulated for evaluation (for example, among potential employers, artistic judges or graduate-school admissions officers). In half the cases, the "product" is said to be the work of a man ("John T. MacKay"); in the other half, the product is said to be a woman's ("Joan T. MacKay"). With the sole exception of this sex-labeling, exactly the same product is circulated among the entire sample of judges.

Does the same product get judged differently, depending on whether it is thought to represent a man or a woman? The answer, unfortunately, is a resounding yes. The results of close to forty studies, using various products and judges in various parts of North America, show that in most cases a product, application, or work history thought to be a woman's is judged more negatively than if thought to be a man's.[23] Nor is this prejudice against women limited to male judges; in some of the studies women judges also rate the "female" product lower than the "male" one. There are, however, some moderating factors. For instance, people are more likely to be prejudiced against women's achievements when they have less-detailed information about the nature of those achievements. In such situations, judges seem to fall back on the easy habit of gender role stereotyping. But if there is detailed information to go on—a painting is said to have won a prize or a woman applicant to have worked for a company closely related to the judge's—then the product is apt to be judged less on the basis of its sex-labeling. In addition, people of both sexes who hold to more traditional gender stereotypes are more apt to be prejudiced against woman-labeled products. Also, expert judges (of art works, for example) tend to be more prejudiced than non-experts.

While all of this is useful information to the social scientist, it is hardly comforting to women trying to break into non-traditional jobs. For it is precisely in such situations that they are likely to be judged by experts rather than peers, by older people holding more traditional gender role stereotypes (particularly in the business world) and on the basis of incomplete information (with no firsthand observations of actual performance). Indeed, some studies have shown that an employer would prefer to hire a clearly less-qualified man over a better-qualified woman for the same position!

Moreover, there is another large group of studies demonstrating that even when women and men show clearly equal success at a task, observers of both sexes tend to conjure up different explanations for their success. Men's success is usually deemed to be the result of ability and effort—stable, internal factors that suggest consistently good performance in the future. Women's success is usually explained as a matter of "luck" or "the ease of the task"—factors that are unpredictable and certainly not a stable possession of the woman herself! And when people are asked to guess why a woman or a man failed on a given task, the opposite pattern usually emerges. Men's failures are attributed to transitory factors, such as "having a bad day" or being given a task that is unrepresentative of their job description, while women's failures are attributed to intrinsic lack of ability or motivation—traits which they will presumably carry with them to other tasks. Whether they succeed or fail at a task, women are judged by harsher standards than men.

Of course, some people may reply, most women don't have any confidence in themselves, do they? So why should they expect potential employers to feel any differently? But studies which compare men's and women's own explanations of their success or failure actually show minimal sex differences. It is the attributions of other people that reveal such contrasts.[24] As in many areas we have examined, sex differences in professional self-confidence exist less in real life than in the eye of the beholder. This is not to say that person-centered factors are never at work in an individual woman's (or man's!) lack of job mobility. But recall our example of female engineers at the end of chapter four. There we pointed out that, by strictly mathematical calculations, even if spatial ability were totally sex-linked, we would still expect about a third of all engineers to be women, when in fact only about three per cent of women are. Likewise, the results of the "Product X" and attribution studies suggest that situation-centered explanations account much more for the scarcity of women in professional and management jobs than person-centered ones.

The attribution studies I have just described are limited by being mostly laboratory studies, in which feedback about success and failure is deliberately manipulated and participants work on rather artificial tasks. And the "Product X" studies are limited by demonstrating sex prejudice in job and school admissions, but not in job evaluation once a person is actually employed. However, the results of both types of studies agree with an increasingly large body of literature on the actual performance evaluation of male and female business executives by their peers, superiors and themselves.[25]

In a previous chapter we learned that men and women approach some aspects of their parenting tasks differently, and it has often been argued that the same is true of men and women in high-level management positions.[26] This is an argument that can be used either to keep women out of such jobs, on the grounds that they "don't have what it takes" or to let them in, on the grounds that they will complement men's styles and bring balance to the corporation. But although the latter argument is now quite fashionable, it is not supported by any systematic studies of executive style, which actually show that executive men and women differ very little in terms of personality, IQ or behavior in problem-solving groups. Nor do ratings by their subordinates, peers and bosses show any sex differences in executive styles. Instead it turns out that successful executives of both sexes share qualities that are a mix of the stereotypically male and female: for example, empathy, sociability, tactfulness and a concern with one's image (supposedly female traits); dominance, rationality, self-discipline and the ability to cope with high levels of stress (supposedly male traits!).

But when it comes to job progress (as opposed to job style at any given level of the career ladder) executive women must cope with more imposed handicaps. When powerful company "insiders"—those who can make or break the careers of subordinates—are asked what factors are essential to executive advancement, they list almost twice as many requirements for women as for men. As well as having all the skills traditionally required of male executives, women also have to seem "appropriately feminine" and non-threatening to males. Given the competitive nature of corporate business, this requires a tricky balancing act. Indeed, according to one set of researchers, the "hoops" women executives must jump through often involve contradictory requirements: take risks, but be consistently outstanding; be tough, but don't be "macho"; be ambitious, but don't expect equal treatment; take responsibility, but follow others' advice.

Moreover, all of this hoop-jumping takes place in a fishbowl atmosphere amid much hoopla: executive women "are thoroughly scrutinized by senior management, male peers, women at lower levels, their relatives, head-hunters [who are often anti-feminists eager to see women fail in the workplace], the media, and so on."[27] All of this adds to the stress of career progress. And, as we know from the time-budget studies of chapter eight, the married woman executive is not likely to have much respite on the home front, since the average husband still takes over very little domestic and childcare responsibility when his wife enters the waged economy. Given all these externally imposed handicaps, perhaps we should be surprised that there are not fewer women rising to the top. There is a humorous feminist poster that reads: "A woman has to be twice as good as a man to get just as far. Fortunately, this is not difficult." It appears that the first part of this statement is only too true. But the second—if taken as referring to external rather than internal hurdles—is anything but true. "Getting just as far" is still an uphill battle and very difficult, for most women.

Toward a Theology of Work and Gender

There are, of course, Christians for whom the above research summary will make no difference. Unless a woman is single, they believe, her place is not in the paid workforce. It makes no difference how competent she is. At the heart of such resistance, consciously or unconsciously, is usually a theology that assumes the immutability of a certain pattern of social roles. Such persons believe, along with Luther and Calvin (and with the Greek philosophers), that there is an inflexible "creation order" divinely prescribed for society as a whole, and that departure from it—except in times of dire emergency—constitutes rebellion against God. According to this belief pattern, work within one's ascribed station, however high or humble, is indeed a divine and dignified calling. But the desire to change or expand one's work sphere, especially if it results in social unrest or even mere social change, is seen as selfish at best and anti-biblical at worst. Both men and women must simply "bloom where they're planted."

Thus for Luther the church, the home and political life were co-equal "creation orders" in which Christians were called to participate; but not everyone was to have equal access to all these orders. Luther simply took for granted that princes should never tolerate revolt from the low-born peasants (no matter how burdensome their laws and taxes). And he took for granted that women should hold neither political nor ecclesiastical office, but rather realize their divine calling almost totally within the home. Similarly Calvin, although he seems not be have been opposed to women's ordination on theological grounds, was certainly opposed to it on social grounds: social disruption was anti-creational. Therefore, the hostility and divisiveness that would most surely accompany women's entry into church offices must be avoided.

Now I am all for having a strong creation theology; indeed, it is my own Reformed creation theology that makes me want to unpack what it means to be "created in God's image" and what it means to be a gendered human being. But it is precisely on the basis of creation theology that I argue for change. For if both men and women were created for both sociability and accountable dominion, then any theology that defends an exaggerated separation of male and female spheres, with the "domestic mandate" effectively limited to women and the wider "cultural mandate" to men, is not an adequate creation theology at all. It is rather an accommodation to those social forces which have carelessly ripped apart the organic unity of homes and communities and turned us into a society of commuting wage workers (mostly men) and domestically isolated homemakers (mostly women).

A Post-Industrial Alternative?

One effect of our segregation of male and female spheres has been the over-investment of women in homes and children and the over-investment of men in the workplace. One response to this, implied in the previous pages, is to move women into the waged workplace in a manner that allows them the same opportunities as men. But must the public, wage-earning sphere always remain geographically separate from the private, domestic sphere? That, it seems to me, is a Faustian bargain we have made with the Industrial Revolution whose full price we are just beginning to realize. We have traded a progressively higher standard of material living for fragmented and emotionally problematic relations between the sexes and generations. And as we have built an industrial economy around the model of the commuter-father, we have also multiplied our environmental problems: too many cars, too much duplication of heated or cooled space and too much concentration of energy use during the nine-to-five workday.

In response to this, there is now a considerable drift back to home-based wage employment by both men and women. According to the U.S. Bureau of Labor Statistics, some eighteen million adults now perform some waged labor at home, and within a few years fifteen to twenty per cent of the total labor force will be home-based, much of it the result of developing computer and fax machine technology.[28] To facilitate this trend, state and local governments have begun repealing prohibitions against home-based labor and considered giving tax breaks for equipment, for work space that doubles as living space and for dependents who live at home, especially preschool and elderly ones. All of this merits reflection as a Christian alternative to the separation of work and family life, especially for men. In the past it has been taken for granted that young Christian women will choose paid work which complements family life the best. We have not asked the same of men, but simply assumed that father-absence from the domestic scene is the only way to support a family economically.

Of course, for academics like my husband and myself, writing and doing class preparation at home has been an obvious way to share domestic responsibility—one which is admittedly not possible for everyone. And having consciously tried to equalize wage-earning and homemaking responsibilities between us, we may never have as much money or prestige as we might have if we had decided only one of us should "go for the gold" career-wise. But we have the satisfaction of knowing that our sons have grown up being nurtured by a father as well as a mother, that the burden of material provision is not concentrated on one family member, and that both of us are responding to God's call to be Christian scholars as well as Christian parents. In the area of work there is again much room for Christian freedom. If we can agree in principle that women's and men's spheres need considerable desegregation, then there is more than one way to make progress in this regard.

Sexual Values in a Secular Age

"Have you written it yet? Have you written the chapter about singles and gays—those 'invisible minorities' in the church?" Hardly a month has gone by in the past year when I haven't had that question, by phone or letter, from a friend who has good reason to want to test my conclusions on such matters. She is single, gay and Christian, a woman who, since her conversion in the 1950s, has been a celibate lesbian with a quite public ministry to fellow gays. She is also a fellow writer, and so has followed my progress on this book from the time when it was little more than an outline for the publisher. I had planned to devote this chapter specifically to the topics of singleness and homosexuality, topics to which the church has devoted too little attention—or perhaps too much attention of the wrong sort. But the more I read and thought about these matters, the more convinced I became that something else, something more basic, was needed.

"Most Christians lack the freedom to talk openly about their sexuality," a counseling colleague once remarked to me. "And even those who have the freedom don't have the vocabulary." By "sexuality" he meant much more than the biological functions which I have discussed in others parts of this book. About mere sexual biology most of us are now fairly well informed. Most of us know where our cervix is (or our prostate gland or our ovaries) and are able to talk about such things in a medical or hygiene-related context without too much awkwardness. What my colleague meant by sexuality (and what I will mean by it in this chapter) is that complex of feelings, thoughts and behaviors that constitutes sexual attraction and arousal in each of us, from its first stirrings to its final resolution.

From Repression to Obsession

What our present society lacks is a moral and psychological context in which to place sexual feelings, thoughts and behaviors. In the space of a few decades we have gone from an official stance of sexual repression to one of pluralism and licentiousness, hardly taking time to draw breath between the two. And this is supposed to be a change for the better. Like our constitutional right to freedom of speech, the freedom of consenting adults to do whatever they want sexually is more and more taken for granted. Sexual tastes, like tastes in food, are seen as a private matter set apart from the domain of public morality. In the words of a recent Western head of state (himself rumored to be bisexual), "The state has no business in the bedrooms of the nation." And on this account, the Christian ethic of heterosexual monogamy and celibate singleness is at best an anachronism and at worst a case of one group trying to impose its subjective, arbitrary morality on everyone else.[1]

I agree that government regulation of adult sexual morality is largely inappropriate, if only because it doesn't succeed (or alternately, because its success requires the repression of too many other freedoms). Christians must indeed address sexuality—like sex and gender—within the outlines of the biblical drama. But their primary aim in doing so will be to apply the results to their own behavior. None of this guarantees a receptive audience among non-Christians. But it may help Christians to better understand and deal with the tensions among what is creational, fallen and redeemed in their sexuality. Moreover, since the biblical drama is the ultimate drama in which all human beings act out their lives (whether they acknowledge it or not), a more nuanced treatment of sexuality within a biblical world view may strike an answering chord even in non-Christians. It may especially do so in readers for whom the promise of the sexual revolution has begun to turn sour for reasons they cannot—but very much want to—understand.

I will begin the chapter with a biblical analysis of sexuality. Then I will enlarge it with some psychological considerations, drawing on concepts introduced in previous chapters. Such treatment—on a topic which merits volumes in itself—is bound to be introductory and incomplete, but one can hardly finish a book on sex and gender without at least trying to grapple with the issues of sexual feeling, activity and orientation. What is lacking in my own treatment will be enriched by the references provided.[2]

Sexuality and the Biblical Drama

Mrs. Stanley Baldwin, the wife of a post-Victorian prime minister, instructed her daughters to close their eyes and think of England as the best way to endure sexual intercourse. According to the middle-class morality of that era, a desire for sexual intercourse was something decent, godly women didn't have. It was part of the fallenness of male nature and, regrettably, the only way to have babies. By these standards, the most fortunate women were those whose husbands did not prevail upon them too frequently. Indeed, in some middle-class and aristocratic households a double standard of sexual behavior was discreetly tolerated. Men could go to lower-class women for routine sexual release, and thus make fewer demands on their wives—perhaps only for the purpose of having legitimate heirs. At the same time it was assumed that true ladies would remain faithful to their husbands, both by natural breeding and moral conviction.

It is not surprising that in such an atmosphere the positive biblical themes about sexuality were ignored or reinterpreted. Indeed, the assumption that sexual passion is a result of the Fall rather than of creation goes at least back to Augustine, who dismissed the very idea that there might have been "unregulated excitement" in the Garden of Eden.[3] The Song of Solomon, by anyone's reckoning a very sexy book, was for centuries regarded by most theologians only as an allegory of Christ's spiritual love for his church, not as a God-approved celebration of passion between committed lovers. Of course, the Song may very well be both: metaphors of wooing and marriage are often used of God's relationship to his people. But even so, things remain what they symbolize after the symbolic value is attached. In Rodney Clapp's words: "Physical love may symbolize spiritual love, just as a wooden crutch can symbolize dependence on God. But it must first actually support the crippled man's weight when he leans on it."[4] So too, the language of sexual love in the Bible often symbolizes God's stubborn love for Israel. But it would not be used in such a positive way if sexual love were not originally part of God's good creation.

Sexuality and Creation

Theologian Lewis Smedes suggests three reasons why we should view sexuality first and foremost as a creational good. The first has to do with God's intention to make us body-persons. In the creation accounts, Smedes points out, "God is not pictured making a soul and wrapping a body around it. The soul does not drive the body around like an angel driving an automobile. The biblical story is not about the creation of a soul that is encumbered by a body; *it is about a body that comes alive to God.*"[5] We humans are intimately part of material and organic creation, all of which God pronounced "good" as he made it. Most of us have no trouble accepting the joy of eating as part of God's creational plan. We concede that our relationship to food may become distorted, addictive or laced with fear. But few of us would agree that the medieval mystics who virtually starved themselves were thereby getting closer to the pre-Fall state intended by God for them. Their radical discipline perhaps accomplished something for God's kingdom. But in the new heaven and the new earth, as in Eden, we will be body-persons with body-appetites. And we will no more be alienated from our genitals than we are from our stomachs.

The second reason for seeing sexuality as a creational good lies in the sociability that is part and parcel of the image of God in us. As the Godhead is intrinsically social, so are the creatures made in God's image. We cannot become or remain complete human beings on our own; we need other people at all stages of life. Even the medieval recluses were united to others in their prayers (and, of course, were raised in communities to begin with). But there is more: in the paradoxical words of Genesis 1:27, "God created humankind in his own image; in the image of God created he him; male and female created he them."[6]

One humanity, one unified image of God, but two sexually distinct embodiments. It is not just that human beings need other people in general; they need a sense of female/male complementariness to be complete and to image God fully. The theologian Karl Barth thought that this sexual complementariness was the total image of God in human beings.[7] This is probably an oversimplification. Our maleness/femaleness is bound up with accountable dominion and a more general sociability, and all three are "image of God" themes in Scripture. But Barth's insight, coming in the wake of Victorian sexual repressiveness, was certainly a needed corrective—in Smedes's words, "not only to prod us to take the simple statement [of Gen. 1:27] seriously, but to get us to re-examine our own feelings about the place of sexuality in our lives."[8]

Sexuality as part of God's image, Smedes continues, "is the human drive toward intimate communion." More than a mere physical itch that needs scratching, it urges us "to experience the other, to trust the other, and to be trusted by [that other person], to enter the other's life by entering the vital embrace of his or her body."[9] Of course, this urge toward mutual trust and self-disclosure is also present in friendships and family relationships at their best. But with the urge for

sexual intercourse there comes the added dimension of passion, ec-
stasy and the throwing-off of restraint. Thus sexual intimacy involves,
at one time, the maximum degree of risk (if it goes badly) and the
maximum promise of communion (if it goes well).

This brings us to a final reason for seeing sexuality as a positive
creational good—namely, its place within marriage. Sexual intercourse is obviously not the whole meaning of marriage. Nor do people
have to marry to experience good sexual complementariness. In fact,
the day-to-day demands of marriage so risk eroding sexual excitement
that it sometimes becomes easier for spouses to feel that excitement
toward people they have never slept with. (Remember the old song
"Chicago, My Kind of Town"? In this most extraordinary of cities,
writes the lyricist, "I once saw a man who danced with his wife!") Still,
marriage is not marriage without the desire for sexual intercourse.
And, as C. S. Lewis once observed, sexual attraction is the essential
spark that gets the engine of marriage going in the first place, even
though it is a quieter, steadier agapic love that fuels it for the long
run.[10] Catholic and Protestant theologians alike now acknowledge that
sexual activity is *not* merely God's "reward" to married people for the
pain and inconvenience of having children. Smedes, working from a
strong creation theology, puts it as follows:

> To make reproduction the essence and ultimate goal of sexuality
> is a put-down of God's creation. But the tie between sexual union
> and conception of life suggests how deeply the sex act is rooted in
> humanity. [Sex and procreation] are the best conceivable combi-
> nation; but it is not as though sex is only a tool for procreation and
> not a gift in its own right.[11]

Now Christians who live with a legacy of negative teaching about
sexuality may still be suspicious of these arguments. If sexuality is such
a great, creational gift of God, why would Jesus announce that in
heaven we will not marry, but rather be like the angels? (Mk 12:25)
Does this not mean that there will be no sexual activity in the new
heaven and the new earth—that sexuality (like death and taxes, perhaps) is one of the passing features of this age? Frankly, it is difficult
to understand the significance of Jesus' remark about "heavenly non-

marriage," since there are no similar sayings with which to compare it. But this has not stopped people from trying to apply quite opposite interpretations of this verse. For instance, among the communal, nineteenth-century American millennial movements (those which believed that the new heaven and earth had either already arrived or were about to), the Shakers believed Jesus meant that no man would ever have sex with any woman. So they remained celibate, feeling sure that their numbers would expand purely by recruitment from the outside. (Needless to say, the movement didn't flourish, its numbers never exceeding about 6,000).

By contrast, the Oneida community insisted that Jesus meant just the opposite: that *monogamous* marriage was a passing thing and that the true millennial goal was that every man automatically be the husband of every woman and every woman the husband of every man. This they practiced, under the name of "complex marriage," although not with the total license the principle seems to imply. Mutual consent was required for any sexual activity, and only those pairs permitted by the community could actually conceive children. The others were expected to practice contraception in the form of male withdrawal before ejaculation. I once toured the quite handsome remnants of the Oneida buildings in upstate New York. My guide was a Quaker lady whose great-grandparents had led an internal mutiny against the community some thirty years after its beginning. Their complaint: they wanted to be monogamous! In fact, the Oneida community recruited even fewer people than the Shakers, and both its socialist structure and complex marriage system broke down less than forty years after its founding. So much for the durability of free love, nineteenth-century millennial style.[12]

Sexuality in the Restored Creation

Obviously we lack the biblical data to know definitely what Jesus meant when he said there would be no marriage in the age to come. But an adequate creation theology would hold that whatever was good in creation to begin with will not be destroyed but actually enhanced at that time. Freed from both sin and physical death, we who can each

barely manage one committed union on earth may be capable of
boundless intimacy when all things are made new. Whether such
intimacy will be sexual in the sense that we understand it now is
another question. But whatever it is like, it cannot be less than the best
we have known on earth.

My own theory (and it is, of course, speculation) is that it may be
like those moments Christians experience during Spirit-anointed worship or prayer together. At such times, not just relationships but everything seems intensified and enhanced, from colors and music to conversations and meals. And at such times, in my own experience, the
male/female dynamic seems stronger, yet safer and more relaxed
than is usually the case in our post-Fall world.[13] Of course, we know
from the history of spiritual revivals that such experiences, handled
wrongly, can also lead to sexual license. But my point is simply this:
since God did not make us asexual creatures to begin with, we are not
likely to be that way when all things are finally made new.

Factoring in the Fall

Of course, our treatment of sexuality cannot appeal only to the first
and last acts of the biblical drama. Despite the goodness of creation,
despite the realities of redemption and Pentecost and their promise
of all things made new, we still struggle with the legacy of the Fall in
our sexuality as in every other area of our lives. And it is in our
understanding of these struggles that we can be helped by psychological as well as biblical considerations.

In chapter nine I referred to the Bible's blunt catalog of sexual
abuses to which even God's own people were prone. These abuses—
from accounts of rape and incest in Israel to those of adultery and
lustful homosexuality in Corinth—were contrary to God's creation
order and hence stood under his judgment. But so too did sins such
as gossip, gluttony, drunkenness, greed, theft and idolatry (see, for
example, 1 Cor 6). It is we humans who try to grade sins according
to our own emotional rank-orderings, predictably making light of the
sins to which we ourselves are prone and coming down heavily on
those we could never imagine ourselves committing. But God will

have none of this. Sin is not to be likened to ink in clear water, with God excluding from judgment all those who have added only a few drops of the "better brands." God's notion of sin is more accurately compared to missing a bus or train: whether I've missed it by one minute or six hours, I've missed it. It is wishful thinking to assume that because I missed it by less time or for apparently better reasons than my neighbor, I will thereby be assured of getting to my destination. It is only by God's grace in Christ that any of us get "home free." That is why all our righteousness, in Isaiah's words, is no better than "filthy rags" (Is 64:6).[14]

It is also why, when we encounter persons with any form of unusual sexual compulsion, we had better draw a deep breath and say "There, but for the grace of God, go I." This is not to say that the sexual behaviors of such persons should all be rendered legally and morally neutral. Nor do I mean in any way to underrate the tremendous damage done to victims of the sexual aberrations of others, especially since most of these victims are women and children. But it does mean that we need to make a distinction between the direction of a person's sexual desires and the compulsive acting out of those desires. It means that we need to understand just how complex and easily disrupted is the process of acquiring a normal gender identity and repertoire of sexual desires. Finally, it means we need to repent both individually and corporately of the practice of excluding, not just from Christian fellowship but apparently from membership in the human race, persons who cope with major sexual struggles. For in doing so, we violate the second of the great commandments, which calls us to love our neighbors as ourselves.[15]

Such repentance and compassion do not come easily. Many Christians consider it romantic and noble to minister to some kinds of "lost sinners" but decidedly not to others. The friend whom I mentioned at the start of this chapter began her journey toward God not just as a lesbian, but as an alcoholic. Whenever she came to her office job with a hangover, a Christian fellow-worker, anxious to show acceptance and compassion as part of her witness, would help her balance her books. But when that same fellow worker found out via a third party that she was dealing not just with an alcoholic but a homosexual, all help was summarily withdrawn. Such isolation, with its covert judgment that the person is nothing more than his or her sexual orientation, simply drives the individual deeper and deeper "into the closet." Eventually, in desperation and loneliness, that same person may end up joining a subculture that not only accepts, but glorifies, the sexual inclinations for which he or she was written off by the church—the same church that is called to show God's love to all persons, but particularly to those whom the world at large treats as "non-persons."

Sexuality as an Idol

How is it that we act this way—treating some sins as worthy of compassion and others (especially sexual ones) as implicitly beyond both God's mercy and our own? I think it is partly due to the way we have learned to deal with sexuality in our own Western culture. Most of us have learned to regard sexuality in only one of two ways: we have treated it either as a positive or negative idol.

I have a theologian friend who periodically suggests that we should understand original sin more in terms of idolatry than pride. He says this partly because the original human pair tried to replace God with themselves as their source of meaning and the measure of good and evil. But he also points out that human beings do not always idolize themselves when they reject God's supremacy. Many instead focus on some other part of creation, certain in their own minds that this is what will save them and give meaning to their lives. This false god, which in its right place may be a valuable reflection of God's creation order, may be their own work, a particular social, artistic or political movement, another person, a human appetite, a system of theology, a national or racial myth—the list is potentially endless. Moreover, professing Christians are not exempt from being functionally idolatrous with regard to any of these things. I may verbally profess that God is at the center of my life but still be obsessed with some idol in my fantasies and/or behavior.

Sexuality per se, cut off from its larger context of human and divine meaning, is one idol which our culture is being persuaded to worship. "It is simple to make an idol," writes Lewis Smedes in his book *Sex for Christians*. "Just slice one piece of created reality off from the whole and expect miracles from it." We make a positive idol of sexuality, he continues,

> by first isolating one dimension [of it]—the genital. Then we expect everything from it that we need to be happy. One harmful illusion is that if we find the one sexual partner made in heaven for us, our genital experience will bring heaven on earth. Of course this places a burden on genital sex that nothing, not even the most ecstatic orgasm in history, can bear. How can you be sure that your partner is giving you everything you really need or might want? Or how can you be sure that you are providing your partner with his or her great expectations? The biblical statement about the folly of trusting idols is an apt warning about illusions concerning sex.[16]

The problem with idols, Smedes implies, is that sooner or later they are going to let us down. Because only God himself can satisfy our longing for ultimate meaning, anything else, no matter how creationally positive and redeemable, is only a relative good beside him. When we elevate one part of creation—a relative good, such as sexuality—to an absolute status, then it is invariably the devil who has the last laugh. Like a skilled drug pusher, he keeps altering our thresholds upwards, so that we need progressively more (and often more bizarre) stimulation to give us even passing relief. This truth constitutes a strong warning to all who have placed a particular sexual obsession at the center of their lives, whether that obsession is heterosexual or homosexual, adult or child-oriented, kept in the closet or flaunted in public. And it is not just a warning about the high risk of exploiting other people while acting out one's own compulsions, although that too is very important. It is a warning that such compulsions, however they may have come about, may seriously block our path to the living God—not because they are worse than other sins in God's sight, but because, like all idols, they promise a peace they cannot, in the end, reliably deliver.

But the problems of sexual idolatry do not stop with open worship-

ers at the shrine of eros. As we know from recent scandals in the
American televangelism business, some of the strongest condemnation of positive sexual idolatry has come from preachers later caught
in the very acts they so insistently condemned. One cause which
psychologists cite is the defense mechanism of reaction formation.
The mind tends to transform unacceptable impulses into their opposite, as when a preacher secretly obsessed with pornography mounts
a crusade against it. They also suspect the defense mechanism of
projection, in which the mind attempts to deny unacceptable impulses
in oneself by attributing them to other people, often quite inaccurate-
ly.

Now it is quite true that some sexual impulses are distortions of
God's creation norms, so we should not be surprised if our minds try
to keep them out of awareness by means of defense mechanisms. But
the trouble with much specifically "Christian" crusading against sexual sin is that it is more likely to be driven by an anti-creational fear
of sexuality per se than by a sincere desire to restore sexuality to its
creational place in people's lives. For an idol can work either way: the
miracles we expect of it may be either positive or negative. If I expect
positive blessings from my idol, I will keep it in the forefront of my
mind; I will play with it, glorify it or manipulate it in any way that
seems to bring even temporary gratification. By contrast, if my idol is
one which I believe has great power to harm me, then I will place a
taboo on it, perhaps refuse even to talk about it. I will repress or
displace any suggestion of its activity in me and may even become self-
righteous about exposing others who have not, in my estimation,
totally "boxed up" this negative idol in their lives too. In Smedes's
words, "we make an idol of sex [when] we either expect everything
from it that we need to be happy, or when we fear that it will hurt
us."[17]

Moreover, the compulsion to crusade against my negative idol in
other people's lives can itself become addictive. When driven by such
an idol, I can no longer trust God to convict people of sexual sin; I
am compelled to dig it out, root and branch, on God's behalf with only
my own tunnel vision to guide me. In such anti-sexual crusades sim-

plistic ends often justify dubious means, and people made in God's image quickly become mere battle statistics.

Sexuality and Accountability

I have tried to weave together several significant themes in the previous sections—for example, the concept of positive and negative idolatry and the suggestion that idolatry of either sort is the spiritual root of addiction. But I also made a very important qualifier: no matter how it has originated, sexual idolatry is still a condition for which we are responsible. It may have roots in faulty childrearing, early exploitation by others, or even biological predisposition. But the fact that it can hurt other people, dominate all other aspects of life and crowd out God means that all of us must come to terms with the sexual or anti-sexual obsessions of our lives. This is true regardless of their direction and regardless of how frequently they leave the realm of fantasy and erupt into behavior.[18]

We should note that in some respects positive sexual idolatry is like alcoholism. Recent research strongly suggests that there may be a genetic predisposition toward alcoholism in some people. But alcoholics who finally recognize the seriousness of their condition do not look for excuses in their biology; they seek help in controlling the effects of that biology which have interacted with learned habits of drinking. From a biblical perspective, the reason that Twelve Step groups such as Alcoholics Anonymous have been as successful as they have is at least twofold. First of all, they require an admission of human limits—that life has become unmanageable because of the addiction and that the help of a "Higher Power" is needed to restore sanity. Second, they require an admission of moral accountability—that whatever the origin of the addiction, the addict is still responsible for the way he or she has handled it, and the harm it has occasioned others.[19]

It is significant that the Twelve Step model originated by Alcoholics Anonymous has now been adapted to deal with other addictions—certain eating disorders, compulsive sexual behavior of many kinds, and "relationship addictions," to name a few. I do not think this is

simply a bandwagon phenomenon. I believe it signals an unconscious recognition that there is no aspect of creation, however good
in its place, that cannot become distorted and tyrannical in our lives.
It is also a recognition that we cannot view addictions the way we view
eye color—as something irreversible that "just happens" to us. However much nature and nurture have contributed to their emergence,
we have a responsibility to get addictions under control. Moreover,
because we are so irreducibly social, most of us cannot do this alone.
Not only do we need God's "higher power" in our lives, we need the
"tough love" of people who understand our problem from the inside
and who can provide emotional support and practical help in overcoming it. This often requires one-on-one psychological help. But
even so, the support and hope which come from a group of recovered
and recovering addicts can be a valuable adjunct.[20]

Sexuality in Developmental Perspective
My aim so far has been twofold: to lay out a positive, creational view
of sexuality and to point out that in the wake of the Fall many
distortions of sexuality can occur in the form of positive or negative
idolatry. All such distortions are under God's judgment, and none can
be condoned by simply appealing to the inexorable mechanics of
nature or nurture in our lives. However, if I had to judge which kind
of sexual idolatry is doing more harm among Christians in Western
society at this particular point in history, I would point to the excesses
of negative rather than positive idolatry. Because so many Christians
have a legacy of anti-creational teaching about sexuality (and are thus
fearful of their own sexuality getting out of control), they often pass
judgment far too hastily on persons struggling with sexual problems.
In addition, psychologists and human biologists have just begun to sort
out the developmental complexities of sexuality. So even the best-
intentioned laypersons do not know how easily, and at how many
points, the development of normal sexuality can go awry. If we are
to be compassionate helpers of the sexually distorted or addicted, we
need to learn more about this.

In chapter three, we were introduced to some of the complexities of prenatal sexual development. We learned that apart from sex-chromosomal differences, male and female fetuses are physically indistinguishable in the first trimester of pregnancy. If the genetic programming of sex-hormone ratios unfolds normally during the rest of pregnancy, there will be a step-wise correspondence of chromosomal sex with gonadal sex (such as the ovaries or testes), with the internal reproductive organs (such as the uterus or seminal ducts) and with the external genitals. In chapters four and five we encountered some of the ways in which this delicate orchestration can go awry. The results can be genetic girls who are born with masculine-looking external genitals but a female reproductive system, or female external genitals but no uterus or ovaries. Moreover, even when children are completely normal at birth, we must wait until adolescence to confirm that the correct hormone ratios will re-emerge to produce secondary sex characteristics and fertile ova and sperm.

My students are always amazed to learn how complex these developmental processes are and in how many ways they can be upset. They comment that it seems a wonder that any of us arrive at adulthood with all of our sexual anatomy and physiology coordinated with our genetic sex and sexual orientation. But there is more. As we learned in chapter five, sex-hormone ratios influence the developing fetal brain even after a child's sexual anatomy is completely and normally formed. One result may be certain sex-based behavioral tendencies that are then enhanced—or, alternately, re-directed—during childrearing. The language analogy is again a helpful one. All normally formed human beings are biologically "prewired" to learn the complexities of language. But whether they learn to talk, what language they learn and how well they learn it depends on the language community to which they are exposed during a critical period after birth. Likewise, sex researchers now suspect that the brains of all normally formed children are hormonally primed to tilt their gender identity in the direction that matches their biological sex. But, as with language learning, the completion of this process (including the development of sexual preferences) depends on critical-period experiences in the years after birth.

Current research suggests that two processes, working separately or together, may interfere with this matching tendency. First, the disruption of normal hormone circulation to the fetal brain in late pregnancy may mean the brain fails to match the pattern that earlier established a normal male or female sexual anatomy. In fact, when such a mismatch is deliberately engineered in animals, the result is an anatomically normal male or female whose adult sexual behavior is like that of the opposite sex. Of course, human behavior is far from being this rigidly dictated by biology. Thus a second process—namely faulty critical-period socialization—contributes as much or more to inappropriate gender identity and sexual orientation. So it is not a case of nature *or* nurture. It is nurture (adequate or faulty) building on nature (normal or faulty) during certain critical periods when the mind is as primed for fixing certain sexual patterns as it is for acquiring a first language. And, as with language, while further learning is not impossible and individual differences in facility exist, it is never again as easy.[21]

Homosexuality: A Case Study

A few weeks ago my work on this chapter was interrupted by a conference at which I shared material on the relationship of father absence to the development of insecure gender identity and misogyny in boys (see chapter seven). Afterwards a young man approached me with a question of personal relevance to him: Did I know the work of Elizabeth Moberley on the genesis of homosexuality, and if so, what did I think of it? According to Moberley, homosexual activity is an unconscious attempt to regain the same-sex parent, with whom there was inadequate emotional bonding in childhood.[22] The young man was a member of Homosexuals Anonymous, a Christian adaptation of the Twelve Step movement which uses Moberley's theory to help persons wishing to leave a homosexual lifestyle. His question was a logical one in light of my talk. For if the standard amount of underfathering in our culture makes it hard for boys to form a secure male gender identity, would it not follow that extreme underfathering (or fathering of a very off-putting, authoritarian sort) might make it even harder, even tilting gender identity away from normal masculinity with its usual adult sexual preference for women?

My response to the young man was to say, in effect, "If the shoe fits, wear it!" Given the research summarized in the previous section, homosexuality may result from a variety of causes working separately or together. That is why (in combination with the political heat surrounding this topic) the literature on homosexuality is so equivocal. If the Moberley model and its associated therapy seemed to fit his case, by all means (I said) run with it—the more so since Homosexuals Anonymous and groups like it are undergirded by a Christian world view and couched in empathetic Christian fellowship of a sort almost impossible for homosexuals to find in the institutional church. Aside from pointing out that no single theory could cover all cases, I expressed a second reservation. Whatever its causal origins, homosexual orientation (like one's first language) is often acquired, without the child's will or knowledge, at a fairly young age. And as with second-language learning, the longer one waits to attempt redirection, the more difficult the process and the more equivocal the results.

I say this not to discourage any individual or movement from working toward change in both homosexual behavior and orientation; clinical statistics show a rate of anywhere from thirty to sixty per cent success in reorienting highly motivated adults to fully heterosexual functioning.[23] Nor do I doubt the power of the Holy Spirit to bestow quantum leaps in sexual healing in the same way that has sometimes happened with substance addictions. My caution is born simply of psychological realism. It also stems from a concern that Christian homosexuals not experiencing a complete reorientation of both behavior and feelings, no matter how long they have prayed or how hard they have tried, not conclude that they have somehow "failed" before God as human beings. Quite the contrary: in the words of C. S. Lewis, those "poisoned by a wretched upbringing [and] saddled, by no choice of [their] own with some sexual perversion are among the poor whom He has blessed":

Do not despair. He knows all about it. He knows what a wretched machine you are trying to drive. Keep on. Do what you can. One

day (perhaps in another world, but perhaps far sooner than that)
he will fling it on the scrap heap and give you a new one. And then
you may astonish us all—not least yourself: for you have learned
your driving in a hard school.[24]
The "hard school" of which Lewis speaks is not just the homosexual's
struggle with the unwilled effects of nature and early nurture. It is
equally against the seductive call of the gay subculture on the one
hand and the rejecting moralism of mainstream society on the other.
I have a colleague who, having written on issues of substance addiction, understands at least by analogy how difficult it is for the Christian homosexual to be continually on guard against his or her inclinations. His indignation is kindled when, as a Christian ethicist, he
talks to representatives of the New Christian Right who proclaim that
only persons who are wickedly and willfully perverse will experience
homosexual inclinations. Under the banner of "a return to the old-
fashioned morality of the Ten Commandments," such would-be
Christian spokespersons ignore the fact that the Decalogue, which
does indeed condemn sexual immorality, equally condemns false witness against one's neighbor. "Truthfulness is very dear to the heart
of God," writes my colleague. "We do not serve that God well when
we misrepresent the people whom we are criticizing."[25]

A very high percentage of homosexuals know of no choice they
made to be the way they are; their orientation was, rather, something
they finally acknowledged after years of turmoil and bewilderment.
We do them no favor—indeed, we make their Christian walk more
difficult—when we presume a willfulness which was not originally
within many of them. As with alcohol and tobacco dependence, homosexuality needs to be viewed as a predisposition to which, given the
crucial mix of nature and nurture, many of us would be prone. There
is little evidence that active homosexuality by itself leads to an inability
to function in ordinary work and social relationships. Thus it cannot
be labeled a psychopathology in the same sense as, say, schizophrenia
or a phobic disorder. But neither can Christians regard it simply as
a "lifestyle variation," as morally neutral as preferring drama to sym-
phonic music. In the words of one reviewer of the literature,

Homosexuality must be regarded as a problematic erotic orientation that contemporary social science can help us understand. One
can take such a stand without regarding it as a psychopathology *per
se.* Such a stance permits one to support the ordination of celibate
persons of homosexual orientation who are otherwise suited and
called to the ministry, in that homosexual orientation cannot be
equated with diagnosing the individual as "neurotic" or "psychot-
ic."[26]

Christians have slowly learned to replace condemnation with practical
aid and emotional support for people with alcohol and tobacco de-
pendencies—often as a result of having to face such problems in their
own families. But the church as a whole is still far from doing the
same for homosexuals and other sexual strugglers. We have much to
repent of, and much to learn.

Gender, Sex and Singleness
All of the above presupposes that genital activity is not an absolute
requirement for human happiness, either in homosexuals or hetero-
sexuals. I believe this not in spite of, but because of the strong creation theology with which I began this and other chapters. Throughout
this book I have tried to lay the foundations of a biblical view of
persons that would adequately include sex and gender without reduc-
ing us to either of these aspects of humanness. Sex and gender, I have
argued, are lodged within our more basic call to have accountable
dominion over the earth, to live in mutually helpful relationships, and
above all to worship God. Our male/female complementariness does,
and should, nuance all of these activities. But that is a far cry from
saying that sexual activity, marriage and childbearing are essential to
full personhood.

Society, of course, has been telling us for some time that active
sexuality is both a right and a necessity. But the church has not done
much better by implying, in its organization, if not its theology, that
marriage and family are the norm and that singles (like "shut-ins"
perhaps?) are a marginal group whose "problems" will be taken into
consideration only if there is time and energy left over to devote to

them. I have argued (in chapter nine) that for Christians even family life is to be seen as a specialized expression of life in the family of God. This being the case, the phrase *single Christian* is a contradiction in terms. By definition, there are no single Christians (nor, for that matter, are there any "shut-ins"). We belong to each other long before and long after the specialized demands of marriage and parenting (and of sexual desire) have had their say in our lives. And we continue first and foremost to be variously gifted members of "one body"—the church—even during the years when we are "one flesh" in marriage.

Singleness and Mental Health

Of course, some people do remain unwillingly single because of personal or social problems they seem unable to overcome. But then, many people jump blindly into marriage for exactly the same reasons, often with disastrous results in the long run. The state of being married is no guarantee that we have reached maturity and wholeness, though we automatically tend to see it this way in our culture. Furthermore, as we saw in chapter nine, traditional marriage is generally stressful for women, despite their disclaimers of happiness. Women about to be married do not differ from their single female peers in overall indicators of mental health, but the gap widens the longer the former group remain married.

In fact studies have shown that in terms of *absence* of pathology, never-married women as a group come first, followed by married men, married women and never-married men. The reason for the extremes of mental health represented by never-married men and women are explained by sociologist Jessie Bernard in terms of a societal "marriage gradient." Since women are traditionally expected to marry men who are "older, richer, smarter, and taller," never-married women are apt to include many gifted "cream of the crop" women who have priced themselves out of the marriage market as traditionally defined. Conversely, the pool of men who never marry is apt to include those whom society judges to be "the bottom of the barrel" in terms of "masculine" adequacy; thus, so dull, poor or problem-ridden that they can't qualify as "a good catch" for any woman.[27]

Bernard's theory is not meant to fit all cases, either for never-married men or never-married women. It is simply a reasonable explanation of the discrepancy in average mental health for these groups. Nor does it fit the profile of divorced people, whose situations are so various that we do not yet have an adequate body of theory to account for them. My point is simply this: we have neither biblical nor psychological warrant to marginalize single persons, most of whom are rendering as much kingdom service as married persons, often in more varied ways simply because of the greater flexibility of their lifestyle. And only when we have renounced the idolatries associated with both sexuality and marriage will we be able to do proper justice to all of God's children, regardless of sexual orientation or marital state.

12 All Things Made New

One of my incidental roles as a writer is that of consulting editor to a rather widely circulated Christian magazine. In that role I sometimes receive suggestions from colleagues and others who read the magazine and want to help improve it. But what is ordinarily a trickle of comments became something more like a deluge a few months ago. The triggering event was the appearance of the Danvers Statement. This two-page spread in the very center of the magazine announced the formation of a group called *The Council on Biblical Manhood and Womanhood,* "established for the purpose of studying and setting forth Biblical teachings on the relationship between men and women, especially in the home and the church."[1]

The immediate reason for the deluge of inquiries was the magazine's failure (later corrected) to identify the two-page spread as an advertisement, rather than a statement to which the editors themselves were committed. And the statement had obviously generated strong feelings in the minds of biblical feminists. These Christians of both sexes affirm not just the spiritual equality of men and women, but equality of access to offices in the church and mutual submission—rather than husbandly headship—within marriage. By contrast the Danvers Statement of this newly formed Council explicitly deplored "the increasing promotion given to feminist egalitarianism." It went on to affirm that "Adam's headship in marriage was established by God before the Fall, and was not a result of sin . . . [that] in the church, redemption in Christ gives men and women an equal share in the blessings of salvation; nevertheless, some governing or teaching roles within the church are restricted to men."[2]

Male Headship: A Confessional Issue?

The Danvers Statement said much more than this. But two of its recurring themes were the biblicality of male headship in the church and in marriage and a concern that "the noble Biblical vision of sexual complementarity [might] yet win the mind and heart of Christ's church." The detailed meaning of sexual complementarity was not spelled out, but included (for women) a strong emphasis on motherhood and vocational homemaking. And the Council's president, when interviewed, added the group's belief that "childcare is the primary responsibility of the wife."[3] There was not a single reference in the statement to men's responsibilities as fathers, although there were many references to male "headship," "leadership" and "authority" in both home and church settings.

Even if nothing else had disturbed me about this document, its assumption that parenting is primarily mothering would have been enough set off alarm bells in my mind. But the people who telephoned or wrote to me in wake of the Statement's publication had not, in fact, picked up on this particular feature of it. They were more concerned with the statement's assumptions about the biblical basis of male headship in the home and church. Now a closer reading of the document shows that these were actually labeled "affirmations," not "doctrines," "beliefs" or "confessions." Thus the members of the Council stopped short of turning belief in male headship into a test of Christian orthodoxy. In fact, they were careful to recognize "the genuine evangelical standing of many who do not agree with all of our convictions."[4]

"There is a tendency to think that biblical feminism is the only biblical view," the council's president explained during a press conference just after the Statement's publication.[5] But the very phrasing of his remark betrays a recognition that one's position on the male-headship-versus-gender-equality debate cannot be turned into a litmus test of Christian identity. Like the perennial debates on pacifism versus "just war" participation, strict versus flexible Sabbath observance, and Christians' cultural involvement versus cultural separatism, the debate about gender roles continues to be fraught with ambiguity simply because the Bible itself speaks ambiguously on these issues. It even speaks ambiguously about slavery, an institution whose demise contemporary Christians never question on biblical grounds. Yet in the pre-Civil War American South, Christian defenders of slavery often had surprisingly cogent exegetical arguments for its continuation—arguments which were by no means always a mere smoke-screen for economic self-interest.[6]

Because beliefs about gender role relationships cannot be turned into tests of Christian orthodoxy, I have resisted tackling the "headship" issue directly in earlier chapters. I have resisted doing so even though I have a personal stake in the debate, being a member of a church (the Christian Reformed Church in North America) which does not ordain women to any office above that of deacon. Furthermore, the discussion on gender roles among Christians has been largely *limited* to the question of headship, with a consequent neglect of the burgeoning literature on sex and gender development, parenting, cognitive sex differences and other issues treated in earlier chapters of this book. And while Christians must certainly evaluate this literature according to a biblical theology of humanness (including a theology of human authority), they cannot cast it aside as irrelevant without totally denying the value of general revelation. That is why, as a psychologist, I have done my best to present this research in a critically Christian manner that nonetheless gives credit to science where it is due.

Kingdom-Building as a Cooperative Venture

Despite the above qualifiers, it is obvious from previous chapters that I have taken an implicit stand on the male-headship-versus-gender-equality debate, in favor of the latter interpretation. I have not assumed that the Bible is either silent or hopelessly ambiguous on this matter, but rather that it is an unfolding drama in which God's salvation is made available to more and more groups previously considered marginal. Salvation and equality of access to its privileges and responsibilities, is not just for Jews, but for non-Jews; not just for free persons, but for slaves; not just for men, but for women—and so on, in keeping with the principle Paul enunciated in his original letter to the Galatians (3:28).

Moreover, the inclusiveness of God's salvation is not meant to result in an anxious competition for progressively scarcer resources, as if kingdom-building were like a static business with only so many slots available for executives, managers and lower-level workers. True kingdom-building, according to Jesus, works like yeast. Rather than shrinking the lump of dough, it expands it. Or like a mustard seed: far from staying small and self-contained, when planted in the right soil it becomes an ever-growing tree. It is not what social scientists call a "zero-sum game" in which no one can win without someone else losing. At its best it is a cooperative, or "non-zero-sum," endeavor in which the growth of God's kingdom enhances the growth of each imager of God within it, at the same time as the latter make their individual contributions and sacrifices for the kingdom.[7]

Thus, in the words of New Testament scholar Don Williams, "if redemption is real the warfare between the sexes is over. Male dominance, egotism, patriarchal power and preferential priority [are] at an end. At the same time, female seduction, manipulation, and domineering [are] also over, for 'you are all one in Christ Jesus.' "[8] Or as the apostle Paul wrote to the Corinthians: "If any one is in Christ there is a new creation. The old had passed away, behold, the new has come. All this is from God, who through Christ reconciled us to himself and gave us the ministry of reconciliation" (2 Cor 5:17-18).

Biblical Hermeneutics: Where the Real Differences Lie

But if I have already acknowledged the Bible's ambiguity on the headship issue, how can I justify my own confidence that its main thrust is toward the leveling, not the maintenance, of birth-based status differences? Here we enter the territory of hermeneutics—the discipline that has to do with principles of textual interpretation, especially biblical interpretation. And it is on hermeneutical issues, not the issue of Scripture's infallibility per se, that subordinationists (those who believe in male headship) and liberationists (those who believe in gender equality) really differ. For hermeneutical questions, as summarized by theologian Willard Swartley, include the following:

1. How are the two Testaments related to each other?
2. How is the authority of Jesus related to all of Scripture?
3. What is the relationship between divine revelation and the culture in which the revelation is given and received?
4. Does Scripture mandate, regulate, or challenge certain practices, such as those associated with slavery, war, and the subordination of women?
5. Does the Bible say only one thing on a given subject, or does it sometimes show differing, even contradictory, points of view?
6. What does it mean to take the Bible literally? Is that a vice or a virtue? Does "literal" signify the intended meaning of the author or a meaning that seems natural to us?
7. To what extent does an interpreter's predetermined position, even ideology (such as partriarchy or feminism), affect the interpretive task?[9]

It is these "questions behind the question" of male headship versus gender equality that really divide subordinationists from liberationists. It is not enough for either side to say "I believe in the Bible" or "The Bible says. . . ." The Bible is a collection of sixty-six separate books compiled over a period of thousands of years and finalized in its present, canonical form many centuries ago. And it is an incarnate revelation in the sense that it takes seriously the audience, time and place to which each of its books is addressed. Certainly its writers are trying to portray the radical "otherness" of God, and of the people whom he calls. This is what one missiologist has called the "pilgrim principle" in Scripture: the constant reminder that God's people, no matter what culture or era they live in, are (in the old-fashioned words of the King James translation) a "peculiar people" who will always be at odds with the world around them. They will always be judging it by the standards of the new heaven and earth toward which they are traveling.[10]

But this "pilgrim principle" of Scripture is in constant, creative tension with what Swartley calls its "missionary principle"—namely, the Bible's constant tailoring of its message to real people in real, culturally diverse situations. Such diversity is a strength of biblical revelation, not a weakness. It is consistent with the nature of God as One who is encountered in the nitty-gritty of human history, both individual and corporate. Scriptural diversity is

> the natural result of the one true God's graciously relating to humans, drawing humans into a relationship inviting free response and full engagement. . . . Biblical truth is concrete, shaped usually by specific contexts, needs, and opportunities. Interpretation should affirm and celebrate this feature of divine revelation, communicated through many different writers in different linguistic, cultural, and political contexts. The variety itself becomes the missionary's textbook [for] the biblical text spoke God's Word in a variety of cultural, economic, political, and social settings.[11]

What the "missionary principle" affirms is that, for the sake of advancing God's kingdom in a given time and place, temporary compromises can and often must be made with the societal status quo. For example Jesus told the Pharisees (Mt 19:3-10) that Moses had allowed men to divorce their wives "because of the hardness of [their] hearts." That was a compromise that lasted for many centuries. But now, Jesus continued, it was time to restore God's original creation norm for

marriage: husband and wife are one flesh, and any man who divorced
his wife for anything except adultery was himself guilty of adultery if
he remarried. It is not enough to quote the Mosaic law, Jesus was
saying. You must know where the redemptive/historical line is moving and be ready to move along it at the right time, even if it means
an unfamiliar way of structuring human relationships.

Thus the missionary principle, by which Scripture is accommodated
to the cultural setting of its varying audiences, is constantly being
augmented by the pilgrim principle, which calls those same persons
to be more than they once were as they move toward the vision of
God's coming kingdom. Indeed, Jesus' elimination of the sexual double standard was so surprising to his disciples that they concluded it
would be safer not to marry at all! They had thought they had the
marriage game nicely tied up in a set of unchanging, self-serving
legalisms. Yet with the coming of the Redeemer the original norms
for marriage were not only restored, but even relativized. In heaven,
Jesus announced, even the "one flesh" of marriage would be tran-
scended (Mk 12:25; see also chapter eleven).

The Parallel with Slavery
Because of the Bible's strategic diversity (the missionary principle) as
well as its movement forward to God's final kingdom of perfect peace
and justice (the pilgrim principle), we may not simply treat it as a "flat
book," whose every pronouncement on a given topic is equally authoritative at all times. We may not, in other words, use the Bible to
play what one of my colleagues calls "proof-text poker." Indeed, even
subordinationists who do try to reduce Scripture to a set of timeless,
equally authoritative, "propositions" do not, in the end, treat all parts
of it equally. For if they did, they would have to be no less concerned
about the demise of slavery than they are about the demise of male
headship.

The apostle Paul states in 1 Timothy 6:1-6 that his teaching on the
maintenance of slavery is based on "the words of our Lord Jesus
Christ." In fact, he says that "anyone [who] teaches otherwise and
does not agree with the sound words of our Lord Jesus Christ . . . is

puffed up with conceit, knows nothing [and] has a morbid craving for controversy." Elsewhere (1 Pet 2:18-21) the apostle Peter makes an even stronger pronouncement: slaves are to obey not only "kind and gentle" masters, but even "overbearing" ones. Both of these texts were used in the pre-Civil War American South by Christians supporting slavery. Even though the institution of slavery did not go back to creation, they argued, the fact that Paul based its maintenance on a revelation from Jesus himself meant that anyone wishing to abolish slavery (or even improve the slaves' working conditions) was defying timeless biblical norms for society. Albert Bledsoe, a professor at the University of Virginia, wrote the following in 1860: "The history of interpretation furnishes no examples of more and violent perversions of the sacred text than are to be found in the writings of the aboli- tionists. They seem to consider themselves above the Scriptures: and when they put themselves above the law of God, it is not [surprising] that they should disregard the laws of men."[12]

Moreover, the pro-slavery writers strengthened their arguments by comparing the subordination of slaves to the subordination of wom- en. They invoked a kind of "domino theory," warning that if slavery were abolished, soon women would "quit the retirement of domestic life . . . [and] come forth in the liberty of men, to be our agents, our public lecturers, our committee-men, and our rulers, in studied insult to the authority of God."[13] Indeed, it was argued, "in this country we believe that the general good requires us to deprive the whole female sex of the right of self-government. They have no voice in the forma- tion of the laws which dispose of their persons and property."[14] If restricting the rights of women was deemed a biblical and social ne- cessity, they argued, it would be inconsistent as well as unbiblical to press for the freedom of slaves.

Of course, Christian men and women in the abolitionist movement had noticed this parallel too, and many eventually concluded that to be consistent and biblical they should press for the emancipation of both slaves and women. Indeed, the so-called first wave of American feminism arose out of the nineteenth-century abolitionist movement, to be followed by a second wave in the 1920s (when women's suffrage was finally achieved) and a third wave in the 1960s, whose momentum continues right up till now. Christian abolitionists rested their herme-neutical case not just on what decontextualized, individual passages of Scripture said but on their perceptions of where scriptural revela-tion in its entirety was heading. In the words of theologian Cornelius Plantinga:

> Despite what Paul says to slaves about obedience, despite what Peter says about obedience even to bad masters, the bigger histor-ical-redemptive line of Scripture tells us that humans made in God's image cannot be owned by anyone but their maker, that we ought to love our neighbors as ourselves, that we ought to do to others what we would have them do to us, and especially, that Jesus Christ came to set at liberty those who are oppressed.[15]

Thus the early church, even while tolerating slavery for the sake of the missionary principle, pointed to a vision of Christian justice and community which would eventually leave slavery behind. So too, Christian feminists argue, does the Bible point beyond the patriarchy tolerated, yet progressively modulated, throughout salvation history to a vision of mutuality between brothers and sisters in Christ in mar-riage, church and society.

Actions Speak Louder than Words

Earlier in this chapter, I was careful to say that one's position on the headship issue—whether subordinationist or liberationist—should not be used as a doctrinal test of Christian identity. I said this not only because I believe it, but also because I sincerely desire dialogue be-tween Christian feminists and those committed to a more "traditional" reading of gender relations. For either side to dismiss or caricature the concerns of the other is not only a breach of essential Christian unity but also a poor witness to the world at large. Nevertheless, I now want to contend that even those who adhere in theory to the tradi-tional model have great difficulty practicing it consistently. And their very inconsistency suggests that despite the lip service they pay to the male-headship principle, they are on their way to an affirmation of gender-status equality which is more in keeping with the redemptive/

historical line of biblical revelation.

Earlier in the chapter I noted the nineteenth-century parallel between slavery and women's subordination. At that time most Christians took it as natural and biblical that neither women nor slaves should have a voice in shaping the laws that regulated their own persons or possessions. For a woman to hold civic office was quite unthinkable: the most she could hope for was treatment at the hands of men which would be in her "best interests," as men defined these. For a woman to be in any kind of authority over a man—whether in church, home or society at large—was (as noted earlier) seen as a "studied insult to the authority of God." It was simply assumed to be biblical, for men have "universal headship"—or headship in all spheres of life—over women.

There are entire Christian denominations who still officially espouse the universal male-headship principle.[16] But I know of none who are able to practice it consistently. Indeed, with the advent of Margaret Thatcher to British politics it has become a very difficult position to maintain. For aside from her anatomy Mrs. Thatcher strikes many politically conservative evangelicals as the epitome of what a conservative (and professedly Christian) head of state should be. Nor have I heard of any "universal headship" adherents mounting campaigns to unseat Roman Catholic Corazon Aquino from her presidency of the Philippines on the grounds that no Christian woman should be in such a position of political authority. And, as we noted in a previous chapter, there are also present or recent female heads of state in Pakistan, Iceland, India and Israel. Yet to my knowledge not even fundamentalist dispensationalists (who give a pivotal place to both males and to the state of Israel in salvation history) complained about Golda Meir's headship there.

Moreover, a consistent universal headship principle would disallow women to be in authority over men in any work situation. As recently as a few decades ago, Christians took this to mean that only husbands should earn a family wage, that women should be in the paid workforce only if they lacked husbands to support them, and then only as the lower-paid auxiliaries of male bosses. Rarely is this assumed to be

biblically immutable today. Contemporary Christians may still argue
about the timing of a woman's entry into the paid work force, particularly if she has young children. But once there, it is generally agreed
that she should be paid whatever a man of her training and experience would get and have the authority that goes with the job regardless of the sex of her subordinates. In short, I know of no group of
Christians espousing the principle of universal headship who are
actually ready to place all women under the authority of all men in
every sphere of life, even within their own ranks.

What about Male Headship in the Church?
But if the concept of universal male headship is no longer honored
in practice, surely principle and practice are more consistent when it
comes to male headship in the church and its related institutions. For
example, there are Christians who hold that women must not teach
biblical doctrine, since like Eve (so the argument goes) they are more
easily led astray than men. I have a colleague who teaches at a seminary which still adheres to this belief. Consequently, she is allowed
to teach church history and courses which survey religious cults. But
she would not be allowed to teach doctrinal courses—for example, a
course involving the exegesis of Paul's letter to the Romans, his most
obviously doctrinal writing.

But a moment's reflection reveals that this practice is not as consistent as it sounds. For it is impossible to teach church history without
making normative pronouncements about past church doctrines. After all, what was the Protestant Reformation about if not about the
priority of Scripture over church and tradition and the priority of faith
over works—both highly doctrinal issues? And it is impossible to de-
fine what constitutes a cult without reference to what constitutes the
normative range of doctrines in a true church. So it turns out that my
colleague is teaching doctrine anyway. Or to take a more common
example, if women are not to teach doctrine to adults, it is not clear
why it is any safer to let them teach it to children, whose tender years
and gullibility surely put them at even greater risk of being led astray.
Yet the very churches who place doctrinal teaching restrictions on

women rely heavily on these same women to staff their Sunday-school classes.

Moreover, if women are not to be in teaching authority over men in the local church setting it is not clear why—even (indeed, especially) in the most headship-conscious churches—they are encouraged to go to foreign mission fields, where they often have a great deal of teaching authority over male nationals. How is this inconsistency justified? It will not do to invoke a technical separation of the roles of evangelist and teacher; it could just as reasonably be argued that potential converts, like young children, are the very last people who should be exposed to the risk of doctrine-twisting by women, since they do not yet have the biblical literacy to combat it.

Nor will it do to argue that women missionaries are ultimately answerable to male authorities. Most of us know of women missionaries who spend months at a time in remote locations without the immediate oversight of male superiors. What they could accomplish by way of heresy-spreading in such a time span should strike terror in the hearts of principled subordinationists, but apparently it does not. One is tempted to conclude that a complex mixture of sexism, racism and territorialism is what is really at the root of this inconsistency. It is not the idea of women in authority per se that is feared, but women having authority over men of *their own* race on *their own* home turf. Again it seems that kingdom activity is being treated as a zero-sum game where one group's success in a given sphere of influence is automatically seen as entailing another group's eclipse.

Even so, practice seems to be running ahead of theory. But not always. For yet another inconsistency is that subordinationists' present concern to keep women out of the pulpit and the pastorate is actually contrary to the historical practice of most of their own churches. Church historian Janette Hassey, in her book *No Time for Silence,* has shown that American evangelicals both advocated and practiced women's ministries before and after the turn of the century to a degree unheard of today. She points out that

Evangelical women entered the pulpit because significant elements of Evangelical theology supported such a practice. At interdenominational Bible institutes and conferences, many turn-of-the-century Evangelicals rubbed shoulders with groups like the Salvation Army, Evangelicals among the Quakers, and the United Brethren, whose theology promoted an egalitarian concept of women in ministry. In addition, the interaction of holiness churches and even some Pentecostal groups with other branches of Evangelicalism significantly influenced views towards women. For example, Moody Bible Institute opposed Aimee Semple McPherson's Pentecostal doctrine of healing—but not her right to preach or pastor.[17] Hassey's study undermines two arguments regularly invoked by those opposing equal access of men and women to all church offices. First, the argument that biblical loyalists have always agreed on the unacceptability of women in pastoral and preaching roles, and second, the argument that current Christian feminism is simply a misguided mimicry of the secular feminism flowing from the 1960s. It is now clear that biblical loyalists gave women more, not less, scope for ministry in late nineteenth- and early twentieth-century America, and that much current Christian feminism is an attempt to recover that honorable heritage. Over the past sixty years fundamentalist, evangelical and even Pentecostal women have been progressively barred from positions of authority in which they were previously welcomed. This is so often the case that another American church historian once told me that if she had not first researched the roles of evangelical women in the nineteenth century, she would have found it too depressing to study them in the twentieth. Many churches have moved the equivalent of three steps forward and two steps back in their attitudes toward women's ministries during this century. But even so, as we have seen from our earlier examples, their women still do more in practice than they are allowed in theory.

Headship versus Equality in Marriage

We have already seen that Christians are disagreed as to the extent of male headship. Is it universal in scope? Limited to the institutions of church and marriage? Only to marriage—or none of the above? They also cannot agree about its origins. Is male headship part of the

creation order and therefore immutable? Or is it an "emergency
order," given in the wake of the Fall and therefore (perhaps like the
human political order) a temporary necessity for maintaining the
peace that will pass away along with marriage in the age to come?[18]
Or is it (like thorns, thistles and pain in childbirth) nothing more than
a tragic result of the Fall and therefore to be overcome with as much
determination as we have overcome the pain associated with getting
food from the ground and children from the womb? Notice that this
gives us four different views on the extent of male headship, multiplied by three different views about its origins. That gives us a total
of *twelve* possible theologies of gender roles, most of which have been
advanced as "the" biblical view at some time or other.

We can go further still: Christians past and present have disagreed
about the actual qualities that should characterize male headship,
even when they have agreed that it is normative. And unless we reject
the "flat book" approach to Scripture, who is to say that present views
of male headship as loving "servant-leadership" are more biblical
than the older view that women must be punitively controlled because
it was through them that sin entered the world? This is an important
point, because Christians who do endorse male headship tend to
agree that even if it remains operative nowhere else in the world, it
is operative in marriage. But as we saw in chapter nine, next to alcohol
and drug abuse the most reliable predictor of wife battering is zealous,
conservative religiosity. It would seem that for some Christian men
punitive headship is the normative doctrine.

Hence the doctrine of husbandly headship, whether defined as part
of the creation order or merely a necessity in wake of the Fall, seems
to many Christian feminists to be a case of putting the fox in charge
of the chicken coop. For even those interpreters who make husbandly
headship a temporary way of maintaining order in a fallen world
leave unexplained why the greater authority should be given to the
more violence-prone member of the human pair.[18] Is it because things
would be just that much worse if the wife didn't have a husband to
protect her from the incursions of other men? But if this were the
rationale, we would expect Christian men to make sure that absolutely

every Christian woman had a husband to protect her—which does not seem to be a program of perceived urgency among supporters of husbandly headship. Moreover we would also expect, at the very least, a lower rate of wife abuse among Christian men, who presumably know more clearly than non-Christians just how fallen they are and how much they need God's help to keep their violence in check. Yet we have seen that, far from being a ticket to better treatment, conservative religiosity is currently the second-best predictor of wife abuse.

Wifely Rebellion or Godly Accountability?

But let us assume that such difficulties can somehow be explained away by those committed to husbandly headship, in marriage. There remains a yet more basic problem. I was happy to note that even while affirming husbandly headship the Council on Biblical Manhood and Womanhood explicitly denied the authority of husbands to press their wives into sinful acts. "In all of life," the Danvers Statement reads, "Christ is the supreme authority for men and women, so that no earthly submission—domestic, religious or civil—ever implies a mandate to follow a human authority into sin."[19] But here is the problem: aside from obvious violations of the Ten Commandments, who is to say what constitutes a "sinful" enough act to justify wifely rebellion? Depending on her reading of Scripture and her convictions about her own calling at a given time, any number of things might qualify—so many, in fact, as to make judgments about the actual scope of husbandly headship almost impossible.

Some examples may illuminate this problem more clearly. In my Psychology of Women course I often show a documentary film entitled *The Willmar Eight*. Although not made either by or specifically for Christians, this film is about eight Christian women from a conservative, heavily Christian Midwest town who in the late 1970s embarked on the longest bank strike in American history. They simply got tired of training men for positions they themselves were never allowed to fill. Nor did the bank deny its practice of sex-segregated job allocation; in fact, the bank president publicly invoked a natural theology of sex differences to defend it. So they went on strike—much to the indignation of most of their fellow citizens, for whom disrupting the status quo, forming unions and engaging in unladylike picketing were much the greater sins.

Of the seven married women involved, six had husbands who stood by them in their almost two-year-long strike action, despite deep disapproval by relatives, pastors and fellow citizens. The marriage of the seventh, whose husband did not support her participation, failed to survive the duration of the strike, and her pain over its break-up is evident when she is interviewed in the film. What should she have done, according to the principle that she be a submissive wife yet not be pressed into sinful behavior? Sided with her husband in the name of wifely submission? Or invoked her more primary calling as a Christian and resisted (at great personal and financial cost, as it turned out) a chronically unjust situation? It is now generally agreed that the Willmar bank strike, although small and geographically isolated, was a vital step toward reversing the banking industry's practice of segregating jobs by sex. Nor can this be dismissed as the case of a weak Christian woman being subverted by secular trade-unionist politics, as some might wish to conclude. It was a case of eight Christian women, with the support of six Christian husbands, who were barely unionized when the strike began and most of whom had done nothing more political in their lives than voting.

To this day, most of "Christian" Willmar sees this episode—and these women—as a disgrace to their town's image. (I know this because the Willmar area is fairly heavily populated with members of my own denomination.) Many of their pastors told them they were doing wrong. And I do not deny that, in the case of the woman not supported by her husband, a painful judgment call was involved. But here is the crucial question: should it be seen as a judgment call involving the limits of husbandly authority? Or is it simply an example of a Christian person (sex irrelevant) having painfully to decide, as we all must at times in a fallen world, between the lesser of two evils?

By way of analogy (and a second example), my own parents-in-law spent much of World War 2 helping the Dutch Underground smuggle Jews out of Holland. Now it is estimated that only about fifteen per cent of the Dutch population was involved in the Underground, while about the same percentage actively collaborated with the Nazi occupiers. The rest (Christians among them) simply steered a safe middle course and, like most of the citizens of Willmar, went about their business as best they could until the disruption of their lives ended. Of course, I am very glad that both my in-laws joined the resisting minority. And, knowing my mother-in-law, I suspect she would have done so out of her convictions about wifely obedience, even had she preferred the less risky route of marking time until the war's end. But had her husband not wanted to join the Underground movement while she, out of Christian conviction, felt that she must—with the result that her husband left her—how then should she be remembered by her grandchildren? Primarily as a rebellious wife, or primarily as a Christian person who happened to be a woman and who, in the midst of a difficult situation, took her accountability to God seriously?

Beyond Ideology: The Test of Servanthood
The thrust of my argument—and of other parts of this book—is that male headship can be invoked neither by Christian men to preserve their positions of privilege nor by Christian women to avoid responsibility for their choices. In chapter two I argued that both these propensities—which the rest of the book has shown to be alive and well in the human race—are tragic results of the Fall, rather than timeless norms of creation. In chapter three we learned that appeals to biology are quite insufficient to justify a particular set of gender roles for either men or women, especially if we are to take human freedom and moral accountability seriously. I concluded that while gender roles in themselves are not wrong (indeed, that at their best they have a positive, sacramental quality) they cannot be reduced to a rigid (even limited) list that is valid for all times and places. This conclusion was reinforced in later chapters, where we examined the psychology of gender roles in our own and other cultures. Finally, in this chapter I have tried to show that even those who have a formal theory of male headship seem unable to apply it consistently in prac-

tice. I have also argued that women are no less responsible than men before God for carrying out difficult decisions in difficult situations, regardless of their marital state.

You will recall that one of the hermeneutical questions listed earlier was about the extent to which people's ideologies, or preferred ways of seeing reality, influence their interpretations of Scripture. I am certainly as vulnerable to reading Scripture through the lens of ideology as anyone else. But although I am a feminist, I have tried very hard to avoid feminist triumphalism throughout this book. I have not assumed (as some radical feminists seem to) that male sexism is the original sin, or that women are somehow more exempt from the effects of the Fall than men are. I have argued that the Fall seems to have had somewhat different effects on men and women in general, men becoming more prone to turn dominion into domination and women more prone to turn sociability into social enmeshment of an unhealthy sort. But the basic impulse behind the Fall—the desire to be independent of God—is no respecter of persons. Feminists and patriarchalists are equally in need of redemption.

Theologian Willard Swartley has suggested a good test of the degree to which our ideologies warp our reading of Scripture. That test is our willingness to be changed by what we read, to let the Bible function as "window" through which we see beyond self-interested ideologies, rather than a "mirror" which simply reflects back to us what we want it to show.

> Biblical interpretation, if it is worthy to be so called, will challenge the ideology of the interpreter. It can and will lead to change, because people do not come to the text thinking as God thinks, or even as the people of God thought in serving as agents of divine revelation. Interpreters [must] listen to the text carefully enough not to like it. [When they do so] it powerfully demonstrates that the text's message has been heard and respected.[20]

Thus believers in male headship may insist that "Scripture must harmonize with Scripture." But this can easily degenerate into a mirroi game, in which readers ignore the diversity of Scripture and force all the relevant passages to say the same thing, thereby cutting off any possibility that God may be asking them to change their own thinking and behavior. By contrast, feminists may say that our interpretation of Scripture must reflect the progressively more inclusive scope of salvation history, in which first non-Jews, then slaves, then women (and by extension all other marginal groups) are freed for full Christian citizenship and responsibility. But this too has a danger—namely, that of ignoring the missionary principle, which calls us to adjust the achievement of justice for ourselves to the larger agenda of advancing God's kingdom in a given historical setting. Thus both women and men are sometimes called to set aside their "just desserts," however responsibly each may be reading these from the Bible. Like Christ himself, they must be willing to become servants for the sake of the kingdom.

Gretchen Gaebelein Hull, a very wise, older Christian woman, has written a book about men and women titled *Equal to Serve.* As you can guess from the title she, like myself, sees Scripture as pointing toward equality and mutual submission between the sexes, rather than the preservation of male headship. Yet, in keeping with Swartley's principle that good scriptural interpretation must be able to disturb us, she adds the following warning:

> Today, like James and John, so many people pluck at Christ's sleeve: dogmatists, traditionalists, egalitarians, feminists, liberationists, all sorts of activists. They all say the equivalent of "Seat me nearest You, Lord; show those other people that my system is best." As they pluck at Christ's sleeve, thinking that places at His right and His left will bring them honor and power and worldly recognition, He looks at them—and at all of us—and still asks: "Can you drink my cup? Don't you see that whoever stays nearest Me must . . . go where I go, serve where I serve? Don't you see that, loving the world as I do, I must serve it to the uttermost?"[21]

This, she continues, can lead to hard questions for Christian men. For example, can they bring themselves to serve in a situation where a woman may be department head, committee chair, chief of medical staff or even Bible teacher or church leader? Can a man accept the fact that his wife's gifts may make her more visible than he? Can he "dare to be like Joseph," who was certainly a bit player in comparison to Mary on the stage of salvation history? "If not," she asks, "what prevents you from being willing to appear secondary in the eyes of the world? Peer pressure? Pride of place? A sense of entitlement to a preferred position?" But her admonitions do not end with men. If Christian servants are not to be higher than their master, there will be some hard questions for women as well:

> Can you drink the cup of submission? Yes, I realize full well what many of you are thinking: That's all we've ever done. But I would ask of you: Can you now drink the cup as Christ means you to drink it? Not because you must, but because you choose to? Would you be willing to put aside your legitimate rights, if the time to exercise them is not yet right in your particular circumstances? Would you be willing to put your career on hold, if that is in the best interests of your family or your cultural milieu? Will you work for change in a patient and loving manner, rather than sinking into anger or bitterness? Will you commit yourself to work in a Christ-like way, even if you are in un-Christ-like situations?[22]

When all is said and done, Gretchen Hull is reminding us, the struggle for Christian freedom is not between men and women, nor even between feminists and traditionalists. The struggle is within each one of us, male or female, between the old person and the new person, between the flesh and the Spirit, between the impulse to be first among all and the call to become the servant of many. Debates about sex and gender will be around for a long time to come, both in the community of the church and the community of social science. But long after our current questions have been settled or forgotten, the radical words of Jesus to his followers, both women and men, will ring down through history from the Gospel of John: "Unless a grain of wheat falls to the ground and dies, it cannot bear fruit." And this is a saying which will rightly continue to offend us all.

Notes

Chapter One: Why Read This Book?

[1]Kamin, as quoted in "The I.Q. Myth," narrator, Dan Rather, CBS Documentary Films, 1975.

[2]It is important to realize that such tentativeness is built into the structure and conduct of even the "hardest" of the natural sciences, such as physics, and is not merely a characteristic of the "softer" social sciences. For a good introductory overview of this and related questions, see Del Ratzsch, *Philosophy of Science: The Natural Sciences in Christian Perspective* (Downers Grove, Ill.: InterVarsity Press, 1986).

[3]See for example Betty Friedan, *The Second Stage* (New York: Summit Books, 1981); Germaine Greer, *Sex and Destiny: The Politics of Human Fertility* (New York: Harper and Row, 1984) and Sylvia Ann Hewlitt, *A Lesser Life: The Myth of Women's Liberation in America* (New York: William Morrow, 1986).

[4]Versions of the ERA that do allow for protective legislation for women were proposed in the 1950s by Senator Carl Hayden, and again in 1970 by Senator Sam J. Ervin, but rejected by the U.S. House of Representatives. Phyllis Schlafly has said that if Congress had retained these provisions, she would have no qualms about supporting the ERA. For further details, see Hewlitt, *A Lesser Life,* chap. 9.

[5]See for example Kenneth J. Gergen, "Social Psychology as History," *Journal of Personality and Social Psychology* 26 (1973):309-20.

[6]As reviewed by Alice Eagly, "Sex Differences in Influenceability," *Psychological Bulletin* 85 (1978):86-115.

[7]Piaget's naturalistic world view comes through strong and clear in this aspect of his work. See especially *The Child's Conception of Physical Causality* (London: Kegan Paul, 1930).

[8]On the psychology of women alone, it has been estimated that close to 100,000 books and articles were published between 1967 and 1987. This does not include the growing gender-related literature on men, nor does it include materials produced by sociologists, economists or political scientists. See Margaret W. Matlin, *Psychology of Women* (New York: Holt, Rinehart, and Winston, 1987), chap. 1.

[9]See for example Jay Adams, *Competent to Counsel* (Grand Rapids: Baker, 1970) or Dave Hunt and T. A. McMahon, *The Seduction of Christianity* (Eugene, Ore.: Harvest House, 1985). Somewhat less separatist (but still skeptical of mainstream psychology) are William K. Kilpatrick, *Psychological Seduction* (Nashville: Thomas Nelson, 1983) and Paul C. Vitz, *Psychology as Religion* (Grand Rapids, Mich.: Eerdmans, 1976). A Christian separatist stance toward other social sciences (economics, politics, sociology) is taken especially by those in the Christian Reconstructionist, or Theonomist, movement. See for example Greg L. Bahnsen, *By This Standard: The Authority of God's Law Today* (Tyler, Tx.: Institute for Christian Economics, 1985).

[10]See for example Arthur Holmes, *All Truth Is God's Truth* (Grand Rapids: Eerdmans, 1977) and Albert M. Wolters, *Creation Regained: Biblical Basics for a Reformational Worldview* (Grand Rapids, Mich.: Eerdmans, 1985).

[11]Psychologists who hold that the Bible cannot be used as a source of "control beliefs" for judging scientific theories include Donald MacKay, *Human Science and Human Dignity* (London: Hodder and Stoughton, 1979) and Malcolm Jeeves and David Myers, *Psychology through the Eyes of Faith* (San Francisco: Harper and Row, 1987). For a more general statement of this position from a natural scientist, see Howard J. Van Till, *The Fourth Day* (Grand Rapids: Eerdmans, 1986).

[12]Christian scholars who agree that theorizing should be guided by biblical control beliefs include Nicholas Wolterstorff, *Reason within the Bounds of Religion* (Grand Rapids, Mich.: Eerdmans, 1984); Stanton L. Jones, *Psychology and the Christian Faith* (Grand Rapids, Mich.: Baker, 1986), and C. Stephen Evans, *Preserving the Person: A Look at the Human Sciences* (Downers Grove, Ill.: InterVarsity Press, 1977). See also Mary Stewart Van Leeuwen, *The Person in Psychology: A Contemporary Christian Appraisal* (Grand Rapids: Eerdmans, 1985), and Sidney Greidanus, "The Use of the Bible in Christian Scholarship," *Christian Scholars Review* 11, no. 2 (1982):138-47.

Chapter Two: Male and Female in the Biblical Drama

[1]Interpreters differ regarding the significance of Paul's remaining restrictions on women as mentioned in the Epistles. For readable discussions of the issues involved, see for example Gilbert Bilezikian, *Beyond Sex Roles* (Grand Rapids, Mich.: Baker, 1985); Mary J. Evans, *Woman in the Bible* (Downers Grove, Ill.: InterVarsity Press, 1983); James Hurley, *Women in Church Leadership* (Grand Rapids, Mich.: Zondervan, 1982); Alvera Mickelsen, ed., *Women, Authority and the Bible* (Downers Grove, Ill.: InterVarsity Press, 1986); and Aida B. Spencer, *Beyond the Curse: Women Called to Ministry* (Nashville: Thomas Nelson, 1985). See also chap. 12 of this book.

[2]Kari T. Malcolm, *Women at the Crossroads* (Downers Grove, Ill.: InterVarsity Press, 1982); see also Janette Hassey, *No Time for Silence: Evangelical Women in Public Ministry around the Turn of the Century* (Grand Rapids: Zondervan, 1986), and George Rawlyk, *Ravished by the Spirit* (Montreal: McGill-Queen's University Press, 1984).

[3]Malcolm, *Women at the Crossroads,* p. 132.

[4]For a further discussion of gender role stereotyping see Joanna Bunker Rohrbaugh, *Women: Psychology's Puzzle* (New York: Basic Books, 1979), chap. 7, or Margaret W. Matlin, *The Psychology of Women* (New York: Holt, Rinehart, and Winston, 1987), chap. 8.

[5]For example, Donald MacKay, *Human Science and Human Dignity* (London: Hodder and Stoughton, 1979), pp. 114-15.

[6]For a more detailed discussion, see Mark Noll and David Wells, eds., *Christian Faith and Practice in the Modern World* (Grand Rapids: Eerdmans, 1989), especially chapters 2B and 2C by Evans and Plantinga.

[7]See for example Sallie McFague, *Metaphorical Theology* (Philadelphia: Fortress Press, 1982); Valerie Saiving Goldstein, "The Human Situation: A Feminine View," in Carol P. Christ and Judith Plaskow, eds., *Womanspirit Rising* (New York: Harper and Row, 1980), pp. 25-42. Judith Plaskow, *Sex, Sin and Grace* (Washington: University Press of America, 1980) and Carol Gilligan, *In a Different Voice: Psychological Theory and Women's Development* (Cambridge, Mass.: Harvard University Press, 1982). A good overview can also be found in Randy Maddox, "Towards an Inclusive Theology: the Systematic Implications of the Feminist Critique," *Christian Scholar's Review* 16, no. 1 (September 1986), pp. 7-23.

[8]For a more exhaustive listing see Donald G. Bloesch, *Is the Bible Sexist?* (Westchester, Ill.: Crossway Books, 1982).

[9]Phyllis Trible, *God and the Rhetoric of Sexuality* (Philadelphia: Fortress Press, 1978), p. 100.

[10]For example, Tim LaHaye, *Understanding the Male Temperament* (Old Tappan, N.J.: Fleming-Revell, 1977).

[11]Anne Atkins, *Split Image: Male and Female after God's Likeness* (Grand Rapids:

Eerdmans, 1987), p. 222.

[12]In fact, at the end of the biblical drama, when God's reign is totally re-established, we are told that "the glory and the honor of nations"—the best that they have opened up in creation—will be brought to the city of God (Rev 21:23-27). It may have to be purified first; the swords will certainly have to be beaten into plowshares, for "no unclean thing can enter." But the risk of contamination is no excuse for Christian men and women not to be participating in the cultural mandate. It is part of their creational responsibility. See also chap. 6.

[13]Trible, *God and Rhetoric of Sexuality*, p. 92.

[14]Trible, *God and Rhetoric of Sexuality*, p. 120.

[15]Trible says that a more accurate translation of the second part of the verse is, "For your man is your desire, but he will rule over you," p. 127.

[16]Gilbert Bilezikian, *Beyond Sex Roles: A Guide for the Study of Female Roles in the Bible* (Grand Rapids: Baker, 1985), pp. 55 and 229. For a more traditionalist interpretation (but one which does not take all three appearances of the word *desire* adequately into account), see Susan T. Foh, *Women and the Word of God* (Grand Rapids: Baker, 1979).

[17]Atkins, *Split Image*, pp. 168 and 169.

[18]On the biblical meaning of *shalom*, see *The International Standard Bible Encyclopedia*, ed. Geoffrey W. Bromiley, vol. 3 (Grand Rapids: Eerdmans, 1986), pp. 731-33.

[19]This is only a sampling of books of this type. The author and publisher information for the four mentioned is Natalie Shainess, *Sweet Suffering: Woman as Victim* (New York: Bobbs-Merrill, 1984); Robin Norwood, *Women Who Love Too Much* (Los Angeles: Jeremy Tarcher, 1985); Penelope Russianoff, *Why Do I Think I Am Nothing without a Man?* (New York: Bantam, 1982), and Susan Forward and Joan Torres, *Men Who Hate Women and the Women Who Love Them* (New York: Bantam, 1986). For a very sophisticated feminist psychoanalytic treatment of these issues, see Jessica Benjamin, *The Bonds of Love: Psychoanalysis, Feminism, and the Problem of Domination* (New York: Pantheon, 1988). For a theological treatment, see Valerie Saiving, "The Human Situation: A Feminine View," ed. Carol P. Christ and Judith Plaskow, *Womanspirit Rising* (San Francisco: Harper and Row, 1979).

[20]Leonard Swidler, *Biblical Affirmations of Women* (Philadelphia: Westminster, 1979).

[21]Ed. Gilbert Barnes and Dwight Dumonds, *Letters of Theodore Dwight Weld, Angelina Grimke, and Sarah Grimke, 1822-44*, vol. 1 (Gloucester, Mass: Peter Smith, 1965), p. 432. Quoted by Malcolm, *Women at the Crossroads*, p. 122.

[22]Oscar Cullman, *Salvation in History* (London: SCM Press, 1967).

[23]The "pilot plant" analogy is used several times in Schaeffer's *The God Who Is There* (Downers Grove, Ill.: InterVarsity Press, 1968).

Chapter Three: How to Think about Sex and Gender

[1]For a more detailed discussion see John Money and Patricia Tucker, *Sexual Signatures: On Being a Man or a Woman* (Boston: Little-Brown, 1975).

[2]For a review of such studies, see Anne Fausto-Sterling, *Myths of Gender: Biological Theories about Men and Women* (New York: Basic Books, 1985), especially chap. 5. Fausto-Sterling, a genetic embryologist, has written a detailed but very readable book about current research advances and problems in the biological study of sex. In addition, she has a competent grasp of the psychological literature.

[3]A more complete treatment of both methodology and results of studies can be found in Eleanor E. Maccoby and Carol N. Jacklin, *The Psychology of Sex Differences* (Stanford, Calif.: Stanford University Press, 1974), Julia A. Sherman, *Sex-Related Cognitive Differences: An Essay on Theory and Evidence* (Springfield, Ill.: Charles C. Thomas, 1978) and Fausto-Sterling, *Myths of Gender*.

[4]See Sherman, *Sex-Related Cognitive Differences*, chap. 2, for a more complete review of these studies.

[5]Put technically, statistical meta-analysis, when applied to the results of accumulated studies of verbal ability, indicates that the differences between women and men account for only about one per cent of the variance in verbal ability.

[6]Fausto-Sterling, *Myths of Gender*, p. 29. See also Janet Hyde, "How Large are Cognitive Differences? A Meta-analysis Using Omega and d," *American Psychologist* 36 (1981):892-901.

[7]See Money and Tucker, *Sexual Signatures*, chap. 2; Fausto-Sterling, *Myths of Gender*, chaps. 3-4; R. C. Lewontin, Steven Rose and Leon J. Kamin, *Not in Our Genes: Biology, Ideology, and Human Nature* (New York: Pantheon, 1984), chap. 6; Perry Treadwell, "Biologic Influences on Masculinity," in Harry Brod, ed., *The Making of Masculinities: The New Men's Studies* (Boston: Allen and Unwin, 1987), pp. 259-85.

[8]See for example David Barash, *The Whisperings Within: Evolution and the Origin of Human Nature* (New York: Harper and Row, 1974); George Gilder, *Men and Marriage* (New York: Pelican, 1986); Stephen Goldberg, *The Inevitability of Patriarchy* (New York: Morrow, 1976); and Edward O. Wilson, *Sociobiology: The New Synthesis* (Cambridge, Mass.: Harvard University Press, 1975).

[9]Lewontin, Rose and Kamin, *Not in Our Genes*, p. 155. Testosterone (one of the androgenic group of hormones) is essential for sexual potency in males, and is also correlated with sexual arousability in females. That is why "chemical castration" of repeated sex offenders (for example, child molesters) achieves its purpose in controlling the behavior that got them into trouble in the first place. But the use of chemical castration to control specifically violent, non-sex-related behavior has been largely unsuccessful in human

beings, although the causal relationship between testosterone and aggression in rats is more clear-cut (and often glibly invoked as "proof" of a similar relationship in human beings). Fausto-Sterling, *Myths of Gender*, chap. 5, includes a review and bibliography of the pertinent literature.

[10]David H. Hubel and Toren N. Wiesel, "Receptive Fields, Binocular Interaction, and Functional Architecture in the Cat's Visual Cortex," *Journal of Physiology* 160, no. 1 (January 1962):106-54.

[11]Melvin Konner, *The Tangled Wing: Biological Constraints on the Human Spirit* (New York: Holt, Rinehart and Winston, 1982), p. 61. See also Mark R. Rosenzweig, Edward Bennett and Marion C. Diamond, "Brain Changes in Response to Experience," *Scientific American* 226 (1972):22-29 and Hubel and Wiesel, "Cat's Visual Cortex."

[12]Konner, *The Tangled Wing*, p. 61.

[13]Karen E. Paige, "Women Learn to Sing the Menstrual Blues," *Psychology Today* 7, no. 9 (September 1973), pp. 41-46.

[14]On crosscultural comparisons of menopausal depression, see Pauline B. Bart, "Depression in Middle-Aged Women," in Vivian Gornick and Barbara K. Moran, eds., *Woman in Sexist Society: Studies in Power and Powerlessness* (New York: Basic Books, 1971). The Rohrbaugh quotation is from Joanna B. Rohrbaugh, *Women: Psychology's Puzzle* (New York: Basic Books, 1979), p. 402.

[15]See Fausto-Sterling, *Myths of Gender*, chap. 5, for a review of the pertinent literature, both in humans and primates.

[16]Stanley Schacter and Jerome E. Singer, "Cognitive, Social, and Physiological Determinants of Emotional State," *Psychological Review* 69 (1962):379-99.

[17]Some have argued that human freedom is compatible with biological and social determinism by redefining a free action as one which is uncoerced. Thus, any action which I am not forced by someone else to do is "free" in this "compatibilist" sense. However, when viewed more closely, this definition of freedom is not sufficient to require moral accountability, since it considers even those behaviors which are externally uncoerced as internally determined by my present and accumulated brain-states. For a further discussion and critique, see C. Stephen Evans, *Preserving the Person: A Look at the Human Sciences* (Downers Grove, Ill.: InterVarsity Press, 1977) and Del Ratzsch, *Philosophy of Science: The Natural Sciences in Christian Perspective* (InterVarsity Press, 1986).

[18]Evans, *Preserving the Person*, p. 74.

[19]Even in Old Testament Israel, with its intense concern about the biological continuity of the covenant, there are hints that God's people understood the importance of the marriage bond even without children. Recall for example Elkanah's attempt to comfort his wife, Hannah, in her barrenness: "Hannah, why do you weep . . . and why is your heart sad? Am I not more to you than ten sons?" (1 Sam 1:8).

²⁰Elaine Storkey, *What's Right with Feminism?* (Grand Rapids: Eerdmans, 1986), p. 49.

Chapter Four: Genes and Gender

¹For further reading on the history of this assumption that male is "standard" and female is "other" or "substandard," as it appears in various disciplines, see for example: Simone de Beauvoir, *The Second Sex* (New York: Knopf, 1970); Anne Fausto-Sterling, *Myths of Gender: Biological Theories about Men and Women* (New York: Basic Books, 1985); Genevieve Lloyd, *The Man of Reason: "Male" and "Female" in Western Philosophy* (Minneapolis: University of Minnesota Press, 1984), and Evelyn Fox Keller, *Reflections on Gender and Science* (New Haven, Conn.: Yale University Press, 1985). Paul Jewett's *Man as Male and Female* (Grand Rapids: Eerdmans, 1975) provides a summary of such thinking in church history, as does Faith Martin's *Call Me Blessed: The Emerging Christian Woman* (Grand Rapids: Eerdmans, 1988). More detailed extracts from primary sources, both legal and ecclesiastical, can be found in Lauro Martines and Julia O'Faolain, *Not in God's Image* (New York: Praeger, 1973). Finally, Dorothy Sayers's two witty essays, "Are Women Human?" and "The Human-Not-Quite-Human," reproduced under the title *Are Women Human?* (Downers Grove, Ill.: InterVarsity Press, 1971) are highly recommended as timeless (and satirical) critiques of this attitude.

²It is important to understand that feminist critiques fall into several different categories. The argument for women's moral superiority is most often found in strands of radical feminism, although occasionally in what is known as liberal feminism as well. Rosemary Tong, in her very clear survey titled *Feminist Thought: A Comprehensive Introduction* (Boulder, Col.: Westview Press, 1989), presents a typology of no fewer than seven different forms of feminism: liberal, Marxist, radical, psychoanalytic, socialist, existentialist and post-modern, while also acknowledging that individual feminists often straddle more than one position. For another philosophical introduction to varieties of feminist thought, see Alison M. Jaggar, *Feminist Politics and Human Nature* (Totowa, N.J.: Rowman and Allanheld, 1983).

³Fausto-Sterling, *Myths of Gender*, p. 61.

⁴R. C. Lewontin, Steven Rose and Leon J. Kamin, *Not in Our Genes: Biology, Ideology, and Human Nature* (New York: Pantheon, 1984), p. 150.

⁵For more on sex-chromosomal abnormalities (SCA's), see John Money and Anke Ehrhardt, *Man & Woman, Boy & Girl: The Differentiation and Dimorphism of Gender Identity from Conception to Maturity* (Baltimore: Johns Hopkins University Press, 1972) and Stephen Smith, ed., *Genetics and Learning Disabilities* (College Hill Press, 1986).

⁶For a further discussion of the controversy surrounding the definition of "intelligence" in psychology, see for example Leon Kamin, *The Science and*

Politics of IQ (Potomac, Md.: Erlbaum, 1974) and Mary Stewart Van Leeuwen, *The Person in Psychology: A Contemporary Christian Appraisal* (Grand Rapids: Eerdmans, 1985), chap. 8.

[7]Robert G. Lehrke, "A Theory of X-Linkage of Major Intellectual Traits," *American Journal of Mental Deficiency*, 76 (1972):611-19. It should be noted that this article is accompanied by three critiques from well-known psychologists, all of whom find major flaws in Lehrke's argument that the latter, in his counter-response, does not adequately answer. Robert Stafford's work, which is independent of Lehrke's, is reported in "Sex Differences in Spatial Visualization as Evidence of Sex-Linked Inheritance," *Perceptual and Motor Skills*, 13 (1961):428, and is subject to the same criticisms.

[8]I say "almost" impossible, because there is one exception. Identical twins are genetically the same because they result from an embryo which splits into two individuals after a single sperm and egg have united. If such twins are separated at birth and raised in different environments, the degree to which they stay similar, as compared with identical twins and various other kinds of siblings raised together or apart, gives us a rough measure of the contribution of genetic heredity separate from that of environment.

But even with a heritability index based on separated identical twin studies two qualifiers must be made. First of all, the heritability index so obtained measures only *group* variability of the trait in question. Therefore, it cannot be rigidly applied to any given individual in the gene pool on which the twin studies were based and provides no grounds for forming social policy with regard to members of that group. Secondly, heritability indices are limited to the gene pool from which the pairs of separated identical twins were originally drawn and cannot be reliably generalized to any other gene pool. For both these reasons it is misleading (and pernicious, when done by scientists who should know better) to use heritability indices (for example, of I.Q. scores) determined from Anglo samples to draw conclusions about the meaning of the lower I.Q. scores of blacks (or other non-Caucasian groups) who were never included in the twin studies to begin with, and hence whose I.Q. score heritability index is still an open question.

In addition, such a methodology is of no help in settling the question of sex-linked abilities in men and women because identical twins can only be of one sex!

[9]J.C. Somogyi and H. Haenel, eds., *Nutrition in Early Childhood and Its Effects in Later Life* (Basel: S. Karger, 1982), as quoted in Fausto-Sterling, *Myths of Gender*, pp. 74-75.

[10]Recall from chapter three that males are more physically vulnerable than females before, during and after birth. Thus, their greater susceptibility to prenatal and birth-related brain damage is sufficient to explain their higher rate of learning disabilities, without invoking more specific, female-favoring

genes. The Scottish study mentioned in the text is reported in Anne Anastasi, "Four Hypotheses with a Dearth of Data: Response to Lehrke's Theory of X-Linkage of Major Intellectual Traits," and in Walter E. Nance and Eric Engel, "One X and Four Hypotheses: Response to Lehrke's Theory of X-Linkage of Major Intellectual Traits," *American Journal of Mental Deficiency* 76 (1972):620-625.

[11]Fausto-Sterling, *Myths of Gender*, p. 33.

Chapter Five: Hormones and Hemispheres

[1]Edgar Berman, M.D., "Letter to the Editor," *New York Times*, July 26, 1970.

[2]Ellen Goodman, "Estrogen on Patrol," *Boston Evening Globe*, March 30, 1976.

[3]Steven Goldberg, *The Inevitability of Patriarchy* (New York: Morrow, 1974), p.36.

[4]Edward O. Wilson, *Sociobiology: The New Synthesis* (Cambridge, Mass.: Harvard University Press, 1975).

[5]See in particular George Gilder, *Men and Marriage* (Gretna, La.: Pelican, 1986), although Gilder revises sociobiology to give women the freedom (and the responsibility!) to "save" men from their hormonally driven, promiscuous ways. For a too-easy acceptance of this form of sociobiology as "natural revelation," see Jan Dennis's review of Gilder, "Taming the Sexual Barbarians," in *Christianity Today* 31, no.4 (March 5, 1987):35-37 and for a critique of both, see Mary Stewart Van Leeuwen, "Selective Sociobiology, and Other Follies," *Reformed Journal* 38, no.2 (February 1988):24-28.

[6]Critiques of sociobiology include Fausto-Sterling, *Myths of Gender*; Stephen Jay Gould, *The Mismeasure of Man* (New York: Norton, 1981), and R.C. Lewontin, Steven Rose and Leon J. Kamin, *Not in Our Genes* (New York: Pantheon, 1984).

[7]It should be noted that many sex hormones, as well as their natural mutants and synthetic approximations, are so close in molecular structure that very small differences can have very large effects.

[8]John W. Money and Anke A. Earhardt, *Man & Woman, Boy & Girl* (Baltimore: Johns Hopkins, 1972), chap. 6.

[9]June M. Reinisch, "Prenatal Exposure to Synthetic Progestins Increases Potential for Aggression in Humans," *Science* 211 (1976):1171-73. A more popular summary of this work can be found in Elizabeth Hall, "A Profile of June Reinisch: New Directions for the Kinsey Institute," *Psychology Today* 20, no.6 (June 1986):33-39.

[10]Donald M. Broverman, Edward L. Klaiber, Yutaka Kobayashi and William Vogel, "Roles of Activation and Inhibition; in Sex Differences in Cognitive Abilities," *Psychological Review* 75 (1968):23-50.

[11]Sharon Golub, "Premenstrual Changes in Mood, Personality, and Cognitive Function," in Alice Dan, Elizabeth Graham and C. P. Beecher, eds., *The*

Menstrual Cycle 1 (New York: Springer, 1980). See also Mary Brown Parlee, "The Premenstrual Syndrome," *Psychological Bulletin* 80 (1973):454-65. It should be noted that the theory of Broverman and others has also been criticized on the grounds that it slurs the boundary between "routine" versus "higher level" thinking tasks. Any task involving language (at which women tend to excel more than men) requires sophisticated grammatical thought, and many of the "routine" tasks of women workers involve social skills that require impulse restraint and careful diplomacy.

[12]John W. Money, "Sex Hormones and Other Variables in Human Eroticism," W. C. Young, ed., *Sex and Internal Secretions*, 3rd ed., 2 (Baltimore: Williams and Watkins, 1961), pp. 1383-1400. See also Money and Ehrhardt, *Man & Woman*, chaps. 1 and 10.

[13]Other effects of steroid use include kidney damage and high blood pressure in men, and menstrual irregularities, genital enlargement and masculinization in women. See "The Drug Busters: The Expanding Pharmacopoeia of Performance-Enhancing Drugs Represents an Insidious Challenge," *MacLean's Magazine* 101, no. 4 (February 1988):123-26.

[14]Joanna Bunker Rohrbaugh, *Women: Psychology's Puzzle* (New York: Basic Books, 1979), p. 46.

[15]George Mandler, "Emotion" in Roger Brown, Edward Galanter, E. H. Hess and George Mandler, eds., *New Directions in Psychology* (New York: Holt, Rinehart, and Winston, 1962), pp. 257-343.

[16]Louise Lander, *Images of Bleeding: Menstruation as Ideology* (New York: Orlando Press, 1988), p. 162.

[17]A good introduction to neuroscience from a Christian perspective is D. Gareth Jones' *Our Fragile Brains* (Downers Grove, Ill.: InterVarsity Press, 1981). Another readable introduction is Richard Restak's *The Brain: The Last Frontier* (New York: Warner, 1979).

[18]A very thorough and readable introduction to research on brain lateralization can be found in Sally Springer and Georg Deutsch, *Left Brain/Right Brain* (San Francisco: W. H. Freeman, 1981). A shorter but equally readable treatment can be found in Diane F. Halpern, *Sex Differences in Cognitive Abilities* (Hillsdale, N.J.: Lawrence Erlbaum, 1986), chap. 4.

[19]Halpern, *Sex Differences*, p. 80.

[20]The visual tasks are similarly structured, with different input to each eye and a test for recall later. For more details, see Halpern, *Sex Differences*, and Springer and Deutsch, *Left Brain/Right Brain*.

[21]For two opposite interpretations of these findings, see Jerre Levy, "Lateral Specialization" and Meredith Kimball, "Women and Science: A Critique of Biological Theories," *International Journal of Women's Studies* 4 (1981):318-38.

[22]Roger Sperry, "Some Effects of Disconnecting the Cerebral Hemispheres," *Science* 217 (1982):1223-26.

[23]See Halpern, *Sex Differences,* chap. 4, for a review of these findings.

Chapter Six: Nature, Culture and Common Grace

¹This research is reported in V. Mary Stewart, "Tests of the 'Carpentered World' Hypothesis by Race and Environment," and "A Cross-Cultural Test of the 'Carpentered World' Hypothesis Using the Ames Distorted Room Illusion," *International Journal of Psychology* 8, no. 1 (1973):12-34 and 9, no. 2 (1974):79-89.

²This work, comparing differences in subsistence, socialization and cognitive styles among the Pygmy and a Bantu group in the Central African Republic, is reported in John W. Berry and others, *On the Edge of the Forest: Cultural Adaptation and Cognitive Development in Central Africa* (Lisse, Netherlands: Swets and Zeitlinger, 1986) and discussed in more detail in chapter seven.

³Even anthropologists committed to a thoroughgoing cultural relativism may find themselves forced to back away from this in the course of actual field-work experience. For an honest and poignant account of such a transition, see Eleanore Smith Bowen, *Return to Laughter* (New York: Doubleday Anchor, 1964).

⁴Herman Bavinck, *Our Reasonable Faith: A Survey of Christian Doctrine,* trans. Henry Zylstra (Grand Rapids: Eerdmans, 1956), pp. 44-45.

⁵Bavinck, *Our Reasonable Faith,* p. 50 (emphases his; also the non-inclusive language.)

⁶For a further treatment of these themes, see Richard J. Mouw, *When the Kings Come Marching In* (Grand Rapids: Eerdmans, 1983); Vincent J. O'Donovan, *Christianity Rediscovered* (Maryknoll, N.Y.: Orbis Books, 1978), and for a more detailed anthropological account, Eugene Nida's *Customs and Cultures: Anthropology for Christian Missions* (New York: Harper and Row, 1954.)

⁷See Rom Harre, *Social Being: A Theory for Social Psychology* (Totowa, N.J.: Rowman and Littlefield, 1980) This is a view for which I have considerable sympathy, since the human concern for "self-image"—or what Harre calls people's concern to advance their "moral careers"—can be seen as yet another crucial aspect of the social image of God in them. Thus, people may argue as to what is "socially acceptable," but with the exception of extreme sociopaths, all are concerned to be "in good standing" with one or more reference groups. As the old proverb recognizes, there is even "honor among thieves."

⁸Sherry B. Ortner, "Is Female to Male as Culture Is to Nature?" in Michelle Zimbalist Rosaldo and Louise Lamphere, eds., *Woman, Culture and Society* (Stanford, Calif.: Stanford University Press, 1974), p. 67.

⁹Rosaldo and Lamphere, *Women, Culture and Society,* p. 3. See also Carol MacCormack and Marilyn Strathern, eds., *Nature, Culture and Gender* (Cambridge University Press, 1980), and Peggy Reeves Sanday, *Female Power and*

Male Dominance: On the Origins of Sexual Inequality (Cambridge University Press, 1981). A minority of anthropologists still argue that at some point in the distant past matriarchal cultures existed, but the evidence cited for this is largely that of mythic legends, since no clear archeological indicators have ever been found. And even if such cultures did exist, the implications are at best mixed. One could argue (as, in fact, the myths of many patriarchal societies do) that although matriarchy existed at the dawn of culture, the men had to take over because rule by women turned out to be so inept or corrupt. See for example Joan Bamberger, "The Myth of Matriarchy: Why Men Rule Primitive Society," in Rosaldo and Lamphere, *Woman, Culture and Society,* pp. 263-80.

[10]See Ortner, "Is Female to Male," p. 72 and also Sherry B. Ortner and Harriet Whitehead, eds., *Sexual Meanings: The Cultural Construction of Gender and Sexuality* (New York: Cambridge University Press, 1981). We should note in passing that the identification of men with culture and women with nature is not restricted to simpler, pre-industrial cultures. For treatments of this same theme in Western thought, see Genevieve Lloyd, *The Man of Reason: "Male" and "Female" in Western Philosophy* (Minneapolis: University of Minnesota Press, 1984) or Evelyn Fox Keller, *Reflections on Gender and Science* (New Haven: Yale University Press, 1985).

Some critics take issue with too easy a dichotomy between nature and culture. This very distinction, they argue, is itself a cultural creation. Many primitive groups do not recognize or even intuit any difference between human culture and the state of nature, but rather see all their experience in terms of a single, seamless whole. Ortner recognizes this; but she also points out that even the most primitive groups practice rituals aimed at creating and sustaining what they believe to be desirable relations between human existence and natural forces. This universality of ritual suggests that all human beings desire in some way to act upon and regulate such forces, rather than simply move with and be moved by them.

This, of course, is consistent with the fact that dominion over the earth is part of the image of God in human beings (even when it is exercised without conceding accountability to God). But it is also noteworthy that in virtually all primitive cultures studied, women are excluded from the most prestigious of these rituals, suggesting that they are considered less able to transcend nature, or even that their presence is somehow an evil that will interfere with such attempts.

[11]See Richard B. Lee, "What Hunters Do for a Living, or: How to Make Out on Scarce Resources," in Richard B. Lee and Irvin DeVore, eds., *Man the Hunter* (Chicago: Aldine, 1968), pp. 30-48 and also Frances Dahlberg, ed., *Woman the Gatherer* (New Haven: Yale University Press, 1981).

[12]Ortner, "Is Female to Male as Nature Is to Culture?" p. 76.

13See chapter four, note 1.

14For a more detailed analysis, see Elisabeth Schüssler-Fiorenza, *In Memory of Her: A Feminist Theological Reconstruction of Christian Origins* (New York: Crossroad, 1985), especially chaps. 3-8.

15This scorn for Christian "weakness" is, of course, most scathingly developed in Frederick Nietzsche's *The Anti-Christ*, written in 1888. It is reprinted in *The Portable Nietzsche*, trans. William Kaufmann (New York: Viking Press, 1954).

16Psychiatrist R. D. Laing, in *The Politics of Experience* (New York: Pantheon, 1967) uses the term *mystification* to describe the process by which professionals adopt privileged dress, rituals, language and know-how as a way of distancing themselves from others and becoming a "guild" that controls who, and how many, may enter the profession. Laing is speaking mainly about the context of doctor/patient relations, but his point is equally applicable to the clergy/laity distinction and especially salient when ordination (and the specialized training that preceeds it) is limited to men.

17See for example James Alsdurf and Phyllis Alsdurf, *Battered into Submission: The Tragedy of Wife Abuse in the Christian Home* (Downers Grove, Ill.: Inter-Varsity Press, 1989); Marie H. Fortune, *Sexual Violence: The Unmentionable Sin* (New York: Pilgrim Press, 1983); Maxine Hancock and Karen Burton Mains, *Child Sexual Abuse: A Hope for Healing* (Wheaton, Ill.: Harold Shaw, 1987); and Lenore E. Walker, *The Battered Woman* (New York: Harper and Row, 1979).

18Historian Margaret Bendroth points out that, among early twentieth-century fundamentalists, evangelistic "workaholism" itself was one way of creating a separate male subculture. Many well-known evangelists took pride in working incessantly—not as teams with their wives (as was more usual in the 19th century), but on their own, actually taking pride in sheltering wives from the rigors of mission work, even though they were rarely home themselves. See her article "Fundamentalism and Femininity: The Reorientation of Women's Role in the 1920's," *Evangelical Studies Bulletin* 5, no.1 (March 1988):1-4.

19Dorothy L. Sayers, "The Human-Not-Quite-Human," in *Are Women Human?* (Downers Grove, Ill.: InterVarsity Press, 1971), p. 47.

Chapter Seven: The Persistence of Patriarchy

1Sociologist Peter Berger would call the church a "mediating structure"—that is, one which necessarily mediates between the isolation of the individual and the faceless, bureaucratized structures of modern, largely urban life. See his *Facing Up to Modernity* (New York: Basic Books, 1976).

2There is, of course, no guarantee that the present lifestyle of hunter-gatherers is virtually the same as it was thousands of years ago. Even so, since fossil evidence is insufficient to reconstruct those earlier lifestyles, the remaining hunter-gatherer groups are our best link to this earliest stage of human culture. See chapter six, note 12, for references on the comparative food contribution of men and women in hunter-gatherer groups.

³See especially Peggy Sanday, "Female Status in the Public Domain," in Michelle Zimbalist Rosaldo and Louise Lamphere, eds., *Woman, Culture, and Society* (Stanford, Calif.: Stanford University Press, 1974), pp. 189-206, and also her *Female Power and Male Dominance: On the Origins of Sexual Inequality* (Cambridge University Press, 1981).

⁴A phrase made famous by Betty Freidan in *The Feminine Mystique* (New York: Norton, 1963).

⁵Michelle Zimbalist Rosaldo, "A Theoretical Overview," in Rosaldo and Lamphere, *Women, Culture, and Society*, p. 23.

⁶Ibid.

⁷Ibid., p. 24.

⁸The following are some basic theoretical references in object-relations theory: Harry Guntrip, *Psychoanalytic Theory, Therapy, and the Self* (New York: Basic Books, 1971); Margaret S. Mahler, Fred Pine, and Anni Bergman, *The Psychological Birth of the Human Infant: Symbiosis and Individuation* (New York: Basic Books, 1975) and D. W. Winnicott, *The Child, the Family, and the Outside World* (Harmondsworth, U.K.: Penguin Books, 1974). An excellent feminist synthesis of object-relations theory and critical theory can be found in Jessica Benjamin, *The Bonds of Love: Psychoanalysis, Feminism, and the Problem of Domination* (New York: Pantheon, 1988).

⁹See in particular Lawrence Kohlberg, "A Cognitive-Developmental Analysis of Children's Sex-Role Concepts and Attitudes," in Eleanor E. Maccoby, *The Development of Sex Differences* (Stanford, Calif.: Stanford University Press, 1966), pp. 82-173, and Joanna Bunker Rohrbaugh, *Women: Psychology's Puzzle* (New York: Basic Books, 1979), chap. 5.

¹⁰Nancy Chodorow, "Family Structure and Feminine Personality," in Rosaldo and Lamphere, *Woman, Culture, and Society*, p. 49. See also Chodorow, *The Reproduction of Mothering: Psychoanalysis and the Sociology of Gender* (Berkeley: University of California Press, 1978) and her later work, *Feminism and Psychoanalytic Theory* (New Haven: Yale University Press, 1984).

¹¹See for example Benjamin, *The Bonds of Love,* and Rosaldo and Lamphere, *Woman, Culture, and Society* for anthropological concurrence.

¹²Sociobiology offers a convenient rationale for the avoidance of women in its theory about the biological immutability of "male bonding." In a thinly Christianized version, neoconservative George Gilder has argued that this is part of the creation order which cannot and should not be changed. See his *Men and Marriage* (Greta, La.: Pelican Press, 1987)..

¹³The term *dread of women,* and a historically precocious understanding of its roots, come from psychoanalyst Karen Horney, one of Freud's disciples who

later broke away from him. See her *Feminine Psychology* (New York: Norton, 1967), a collection of her essays written in the 1920s and 1930s. See also Benjamin, *The Bonds of Love,* chap. 1.

[14]Samuel Osherson, *Finding Our Fathers: How a Man's Life Is Shaped by His Relationship with His Father* (New York: Fawcett, 1986). p. x.

[15]For a more detailed analysis, see *The Forest People,* Colin Turnbull's ethnography of the Mbuti Pygmy and the contrast between their lifestyle and that of the Bantu farmers for whom they work in the hunting off-season (New York: Simon and Schuster, 1965). See also his *Wayward Servants: The Two Worlds of the African Pygmies* (Garden City, N.Y.: Natural History Press, 1965). For a more psychological treatment of this contrast and its application to Western societies, see Mary Stewart Van Leeuwen, "A Cross-Cultural Examination of Psychological Differentiation in Males and Females," *International Journal of Psychology,* vol. 13, no. 2 (1978):87-122.

[16]M. Kithara, "Polygyny: Insufficient Father-Son Contact and Son's Masculine Identity," *Archives of Sexual Behavior,* 1976, vol. 5, pp. 201-209; M. M. West and Melvin J. Konner, "The Role of the Father: An Anthropological Perspective," in Michael E. Lamb, ed., *The Role of the Father in Child Development* (New York: Wiley, 1976), and John W. M. Whiting, R. Kluckhorn and A. Anthony, "The Function of Male Initiation Ceremonies at Puberty," in Eleanor E. Maccoby, T. M. Newcomb and E. L. Hartley, eds., *Readings in Social Psychology,* 3rd ed. (New York: Holt, Rinehart and Winston, 1958), chap. 6.

[17]See John W. Berry, *Human Ecology and Cognitive Style: Comparative Studies in Cultural and Psychological Adaptation* (New York: Wiley, 1976).

[18]Rosaldo and Lamphere, *Woman, Culture, and Society,* Introduction to the volume, p. 14. See also Alice Schlegel, ed., *Sexual Stratification: A Cross-Cultural View* (New York: Columbia University Press, 1977), especially the chapter by Albert Bacdayan on "Mechanistic Cooperation and Sexual Equality."

Chapter Eight: The Case for Co-Parenting

[1]For an especially perceptive and empathetic treatment of these conflicting emotions in both sexes, see Lillian Rubin, *Intimate Strangers: Men and Women Together* (New York: Harper and Row, 1983).

[2]Ibid., pp. 22-23.

[3]Ibid., p. 25.

[4]A sociological analysis of some of these differences can be found in Rebecca E. Klatch, *Women of the New Right* (Philadelphia: Temple University Press, 1987).

[5]James Dobson, *What Wives Wish Their Husbands Knew about Women* (Waco, Tex.: Word Books, 1974).

[6]Billy Graham, "Candid Conversation with the Evangelist," in *Christianity Today* 25, no. 13 (July 17, 1981):18-24.

[7]C. S. Lewis, *Mere Christianity* (New York: MacMillan, 1943), p. 88. For a detailed analysis of Lewis's view of marriage throughout his writings, see Gilbert Meilender, *The Taste for the Other: The Social and Ethical Thought of C. S. Lewis* (Grand Rapids: Eerdmans, 1978), chap. 4.

[8]Carol Gilligan, *In a Different Voice: Psychological Theory and Women's Development* (Cambridge, Mass.: Harvard University Press, 1982), p. 82. See also Gilligan, ed., *Mapping the Moral Domain: A Contribution of Women's Thinking to Psychological Theory and Education* (Cambridge, Mass.: Harvard University Press, 1989). For a good overview of some theological implications, see Barbara Hilkert Andolsen, "Agape in Feminist Ethics," in *Journal of Religious Ethics*, 9, no. 1 (Spring 1981): 69-83.

[9]For a pleasant exception, see Stephen Brown, "No More Ms. Nice Woman," *Today's Christian Woman*, 9, no. 5 (September/October 1987):96.

[10]So new is the idea of (let alone research on) active fathering that one recent volume on the topic was ironically titled *Men's Transition to Parenthood*, Phyllis W. Berman and Frank A. Pedersen, eds. (Hillsdale, N.J.: Lawrence Erlbaum, 1987).

[11]M. Greenberg and N. Morris, "Engrossment: The Newborn's Impact upon the Father," *American Journal of Orthopsychiatry* 44 (1974):520-31; R. D. Parke and S. E. O'Leary, "Father-Mother-Infant Interactions in the Newborn Period: Some Findings, Some Observations, and Some Unresolved Issues," in Klaus Riegel and J. Meacham, eds., *The Developing Individual in a Changing World*, 2, *Social and Environmental Issues* (The Hague, Netherlands: Mouton, 1976).

[12]Or, as the researchers put it, infants were "monotropically matricentric."

[13]M. Kotelchuk, "The Infant's Relationship to the Father," in Michael E. Lamb, ed., *The Role of the Father in Child Development* (New York: Wiley, 1976). The classic (and long-accepted) theory of exclusive mother-child bonding was made by John Bowlby, *Attachment and Loss* (New York: Basic Books, 1969). For further explanation of the laboratory attachment paradigm, see for example Michael Lewis and L. A. Rosenblum, eds., *The Child and Its Family* (New York: Plenum, 1979).

[14]Lamb, *Role of the Father*, chap. 7.

[15]Ibid., especially chaps. 11 and 13.

[16]L. Lein, M. Durham, M. Pratt, M. Schudson, R. Thomas and H. Weiss, *Final Report on Work and Family Life* (Cambridge, Mass.: National Institute of Education Project No. 3-3094, Center for the Study of Public Policy, 1974); M. Meissner, E. Humphreys, C. Meis and J. Scheu, "No Exit for Wives: Sexual Division of Labor and the Cumulation of Household Demands," in *Canadian Review of Sociology and Anthropology* 12 (1975):424-39; Joseph H. Pleck, "Men's New Roles in the Family," in C. Safilios-Rothschild, ed., *Family and Sex Roles* (New York: Wiley, 1976); J. Robinson, *How Americans Use Time:*

A Social-Psychological Analysis (New York: Praeger, 1979), and K. Walker and M. Woods, *Time Use: A Measure of Household Production of Goods and Services* (Washington D.C.: American Home Economics Association, 1976).

[17]Robert B. Zajonc and G. B. Marcus, "Birth Order and Intellectual Development," in *Psychological Review* 82 (1975):74-88; M. Shinn, "Father Absence and Children's Cognitive Development," in *Psychological Bulletin* 85 (1978):295-324.

[18]Lamb, *The Role of the Father*, chap. 9.

[19]E. Mavis Hetherington, "Effects of Father-Absence on Personality Development in Adolescent Daughters," in *Developmental Psychology* 7 (1972):313-26.

[20]Rae Helson, "Women Mathematicians and the Creative Personality," in *Journal of Consulting and Clinical Psychology* 36 (1971):210-20; Margaret Hennig and Anne Jardim, *The Managerial Woman* (New York: Simon and Schuster, 1976).

[21]Shelagh Emmot, *Fathering Style*, unpublished major doctoral paper, 1981, Psychology Department, York University, Toronto, Canada, pp. 98-99.

[22]Phyllis W. Berman and Vickie Goodman, "Age and Sex Differences in Children's Responses to Babies," in *Child Development* 55 (1984):1071-77; Alan Fogel and Gail F. Melson, eds., *Origins of Nurturance: Developmental, Biological, and Cultural Perspectives* (Hillsdale, N.J.: Lawrence Erlbaum, 1986).

[23]Kotelchuk, "The Infant's Relationship to the Father."

Chapter Nine: Marriage, Family and the Kingdom of God

[1]Barbara Ehrenreich, *The Hearts of Men: American Dreams and the Flight from Commitment* (Garden City, N.Y.: Anchor/Doubleday, 1984), p. 42.

[2]For more on the roles played by American women during and after World War 2, see Cynthia Enloe, *Does Khaki Become You?: The Militarization of Women's Lives* (Boston: South End Press, 1983), and also Betty Friedan, *The Feminine Mystique* (New York: W. W. Norton, 1963), especially chaps. 8 and 10. Also very informative is the documentary film (and accompanying discussion guide), *The Life and Times of Rosie the Riveter* (Emeryville, Calif.: Clarity Educational Productions, 1982).

[3]Christopher Lasch, *Haven in a Heartless World: The Family Beseiged* (New York: Basic Books, 1977).

[4]Rus Walton, *One Nation under God* (Old Tappan, N.J.: Fleming H. Revell, 1975), p. 99. This and the following quotations (through note 9) are from James Davison Hunter, *Evangelicalism: The Coming Generation* (Chicago: University of Chicago Press, 1987), pp. 81-82.

[5]Ibid., p. 99.

[6]W. Peter Blitchington, *Sex Roles and the Christian Family* (Wheaton, Ill.: Tyndale House, 1980), p. 16.

[7]Ibid., p. 48.

[8]Kenneth Chafin, *Is There a Family in the House?* (Minneapolis: World Wide Publications, 1978), p. 15.

[9]Edward Hindson, *The Total Family* (Wheaton, Ill.: Tyndale House, 1980), p. 37.

[10]Peter Laslett, *Household and Family in Past Time* (Cambridge, U.K.: Cambridge University Press, 1972).

[11]Hunter, *Evangelicalism,* p. 91. See also Philippe Aries, *Centuries of Childhood* (New York: Vintage Books, 1972).

[12]See for example Robin Norwood, *Letters from Women Who Love Too Much* (New York: Pocket Books, 1988), chaps. 3 and 4, and Maxine Hancock and Karen Burton Mains, *Child Sexual Abuse: A Hope for Healing* (Wheaton, Ill.: Harold Shaw, 1987), chaps. 10 and 11.

[13]The entire rhyme goes as follows:
There was a little girl, who had a little curl,
Right in the middle of her forehead.
And when she was good, she was very, very good.
But when she was bad, she was horrid!

[14]Geoffrey W. Bromiley, *God and Marriage* (Grand Rapids: Eerdmans, 1980), pp. 2-3.

[15]Gretchen Gaebelein Hull, *Equal to Serve: Women and Men in the Church and the Home* (Old Tappan, N.J., Fleming Revell, 1987), p. 80.

[16]Bromiley, *God and Marriage,* pp. 35-36.

[17]Ibid., p. 37.

[18]The response continues: "He has fully paid for all my sins with his precious blood, and has set me free from the tyranny of the devil. He also watches over me in such a way that not a hair can fall from my head without the will of my Father in heaven. In fact, all things must work together for my salvation. Because I belong to him, Christ, by his Holy Spirit, assures me of eternal life and makes me whole-heartedly willing and ready from now on to live for him."

[19]Rodney Clapp, "Is the 'Traditional' Family Biblical?" *Christianity Today* 32, no. 13 (September 16, 1988):24-28. Quoted from p. 26. See also his *First Family, Second Family* (Downers Grove, Ill.: InterVarsity Press, in preparation).

[20]Clapp, "Is the 'Traditional' Family Biblical?" p. 27.

[21]Jeron Ashford Frame, "Letter to the Editor," *Christianity Today* 32, no. 16 (November 4, 1988):6.

[22]Elaine Botha, "Voices from a Troubled Land," *Christianity Today* 30, no. 17 (November 21, 1986):8 (in a special insert on South Africa).

[23]Jessie Bernard, *The Future of Marriage* (New York: World, 1972).

[24]Emile Durkheim, *Suicide,* trans. J. A. Spaulding and George Simpson (Glencoe, Ill.: The Free Press, 1951), p. 271.

[25]Bernard, *The Future of Marriage*, reviews the literature to that date; for an updated review see Harold Feldman and Margaret Feldman, eds., *Current Controversies in Marriage and the Family* (Beverly Hills: Sage, 1985).

[26]Jessie Bernard, "The Paradox of the Happy Marriage," in Vivian Gornick and Barbara K. Moran, eds., *Woman in Sexist Society: Studies in Power and Powerlessness* (New York: Basic Books, 1971), p. 93.

[27]The research on gender-role stereotypes up to 1970 is reviewed in Inge K. Broverman, Susan R. Vogel, Donald M, Broverman, Frank E. Clarkson and Paul S. Rosenkrantz, "Sex-Role Stereotypes: A Current Appraisal," *Journal of Social Issues* 28, no. 2 (1972):59-78. An updated review can be found in D. Ruble and T. S. Ruble, "Sex Stereotypes," in A. G. Miller, ed., *In the Eye of the Beholder: Contemporary Issues in Stereotyping* (New York: Praeger, 1982). Note that the constellation of supposedly ideal "feminine" traits is remarkably similar to white stereotypes about blacks prior to the civil rights era. Sociologist Helen M. Hacker noted this parallel well before the current feminist revival. See her article "Women as a Minority Group," *Social Forces* 30 (1951):60-69 and also Jean Baker Miller, *Towards a New Psychology of Women* (Boston: Beacon Press, 1978).

[28]Joanna Bunker Rohrbaugh, *Women: Psychology's Puzzle* (New York: Basic Books, 1979), chap. 8.

[29]For a historical analysis of the mutually reinforcing nature of Nazi ideology, practice and family life, see Claudia Koonz, *Mothers in the Fatherland: Women, the Family, and Nazi Politics* (New York: St. Martins, 1987). For a similar treatment of the pre-Civil War American South, see Catherine Clinton, *The Plantation Mistress: Women's World in the Old South* (New York: Pantheon, 1982).

[30]Susan Faludi, "Diane Joyce: Tenacious Fighter for Working Rights," *Ms.* 16, no. 7 (January 1988):65.

[31]Rachel Rosenfeld, *Farm Women: Work, Farm, and Family in the United States* (Chapel Hill: University of North Carolina Press, 1985). See also Mary Stewart Van Leeuwen, "Trouble and Hope on the Farm," *Reformed Journal* 38, no. 8 (August 1988):14-19.

Chapter Ten: Gender, Work and Christian Vocation

[1]Carol Sternhell, "Life in the Mainstream," *Ms.* 15, no. 1 (July 1986):48-51, 86-91.

[2]Ibid., p. 50.

[3]Ibid., pp. 50-51. The court finally ruled that Sears was not guilty of sex discrimination in its hiring and promotion of sales personnel. The company had in fact been one of the earliest advocates of affirmative action, and its percentage of commissioned saleswomen was growing steadily. That there was a residual gender gap might be due to many causes, but the jury con-

cluded that systematic discrimination by the company was not one of them.

[4]I would like to say that such research has focussed equally on working-class and professional women; but the priorities of psychologists being what they are, their work has concentrated mostly on women in professional and managerial careers. But even the work done on this limited group will help us to answer the question posed earlier—namely, whether it is mainly women's own personalities or the structure of the workplace that limits their accomplishments in the paid work force.

[5]A historical treatment of the concept of work can be found in Lee Hardy, *The Fabric of Our Lives* (Grand Rapids: Eerdmans, 1990), on which I have drawn generously for this section. A more detailed treatment can be found in Yves Simon, *Work, Society, and Culture* (New York: Fordham University Press, 1971).

[6]Plato, *The Republic*, trans. H. D. P. Lee (London: Penguin, 1955). This edition also divides the text by subject-matter.

[7]Aristotle *Politics* 1.15.1254b13-14.

[8]See for example Georges Duby, *The Knight, the Lady and the Priest: The Making of Modern Marriage in Medieval France*, trans. Barbara Bray (New York: Pantheon, 1983); Margaret Wade Labarge, *A Small Sound of the Trumpet: Women in Medieval Life* (Boston: Beacon Press, 1986), and Ruth A. Tucker and Walter Liefeld, *Daughters of the Church: Women and Ministry from New Testament Times to the Present* (Grand Rapids: Zondervan, 1987).

[9]Hardy, *The Fabric of Our Lives*, chap. 1, p. 26 (of draft manuscript).

[10]Ibid., chap. 2, p. 5.

[11]For a contemporary treatment of this theme in terms of the biblical drama, see Albert M. Wolters, *Creation Regained: Biblical Basics for a Reformational Worldview* (Grand Rapids: Eerdmans, 1985) or Brian J. Walsh and J. Richard Middleton, *The Transforming Vision: Shaping a Christian Worldview* (Downers Grove, Ill.: InterVarsity Press, 1984).

[12]Chapter 2 of Hardy's book documents in detail this ecumenical convergence on the theology of work.

[13]See Tucker and Liefeld, *Daughters of the Church*, chap. 5, or for a more detailed analysis, Roland H. Bainton, *Women of the Reformation*, 3 vols. (Minneapolis: Augsburg, 1971, 1973, 1977).

[14]Martin Luther, *Luther's Commentary on Genesis* (Grand Rapids: Zondervan, 1958), quoted in Tucker and Liefeld, *Daughters of the Church*, p. 174.

[15]See Jane Dempsey Douglass, *Women, Freedom, and Calvin* (Philadelphia: Westminster Press, 1985).

[16]On Menno Simons, see Joyce L. Irwin, *Womanhood in Radical Protestantism* (New York: Mellen, 1979), p. 55. On Bernard Rottman, the Anabaptist defender of polygamy, see John Cairncross, *After Polygamy Was Made a Sin: The Social History of Christian Polygamy* (London: Routledge and Kegan Paul,

1974).

[17]Quoted in Julia O'Faolain and Lauro Martines, *Not in God's Image* (New York: Harper and Row, 1973), pp. 196-97.

[18]Quoted in Tucker and Liefeld, *Daughters of the Church*, p. 173.

[19]Quoted in Irwin, *Womanhood in Radical Protestantism*, p. 55.

[20]For a further discussion of these issues in a Christian and sociological context, see Elaine Storkey, *What's Right with Feminism?* (Grand Rapids: Eerdmans, 1986), and also James Davidson Hunter, *Evangelicalism: The Coming Generation* (University of Chicago Press, 1987).

[21]Margaret Hennig and Anne Jardim, *The Managerial Woman* (New York: Anchor/Doubleday, 1977).

[22]For an in-depth treatment of these factors, including a good historical survey, see Ann Harriman, *Women/Men/Management* (New York: Praeger, 1985).

[23]Reviews of this literature include R. D. Arvey, "Unfair Discrimination in the Employment Interview: Legal and Psychological Aspects," *Psychological Bulletin* 86 (1979):736-65; and B. S. Wallston and V. E. O'Leary, "Sex Makes a Difference: Differential Perceptions of Women and Men," Ladd Wheeler, ed., *Review of Personality and Social Psychology* 2 (Beverly Hills, Calif.: Sage, 1981), pp. 9-41. A good summary and discussion can also be found in Margaret W. Matlin, *The Psychology of Women* (New York: Holt, Rinehart, and Winston, 1987), chaps. 5 and 6.

[24]The accumulated gender literature on self-attributions versus the attributions of others as explanations for success and failure is reviewed by Kay Deaux, "From Individual Differences to Social Categories: Analysis of a Decade's Research on Gender," *American Psychologist* 39 (February 1984):105-116. Summary reviews can also be found in Matlin, *The Psychology of Women*, chaps. 5 and 6, and in Harriman, *Women/Men/Management*, chap. 8.

[25]This literature is reviewed in Ann M. Morrison, Randall P. White and Ellen Van Velsor, *Breaking the Glass Ceiling: Can Women Reach the Top of America's Largest Corporations?* (Reading, Mass.: Addison-Wesley, 1987).

[26]See for example Marilyn Loden, *Feminine Leadership, or, How to Succeed in Business without Being One of the Boys* (New York: Times Books, 1985).

[27]Morrison and others, *Breaking the Glass Ceiling*, p. 68. See also the rest of chap. 3 especially.

[28]Quoted in "Giving Parents More Homework" (no by-line), *Family Policy* (November-December 1988):1-2. Published by the Family Research Council of America, Inc., 601 Pennsylvania Ave., Suite 901, Washington, D.C., 20004.

Chapter Eleven: Sexual Values in a Secular Age
[1]For a historical overview of shifting sexual attitudes and behaviors, see John D'Emilio and Estelle B. Freedman, *Intimate Matters: A History of Sexuality in*

America (New York: Harper and Row, 1988).

[2]My theological consideration of sexuality is largely dependent on Lewis Smedes's *Sex for Christians* (Grand Rapids: Eerdmans, 1976). Because Smedes is a Reformed theologian/ethicist who teaches in an evangelical seminary, he has managed to capture the strengths (and point out the weaknesses) of each tradition's treatment of this topic. In addition, his writing contains a balance between the normative and the pastoral that is often lacking in other Christian writings on sexuality.

[3]Smedes, *Sex for Christians,* p. 26.

[4]Rodney Clapp, "What Hollywood Doesn't Know about Romantic Love," in *Christianity Today* 28, no. 2 (February 3, 1984), p. 33.

[5]Smedes, *Sex for Christians,* p. 28 (my emphasis).

[6]The translation is Phyllis Trible's. See her *God and the Rhetoric of Sexuality* (Philadelphia: Fortress Press, 1977), p. 12.

[7]See Karl Barth, *Church Dogmatics,* 3, part. 1 (Edinburgh: T. & T. Clark, 1961). For a further elaboration see Paul K. Jewett, *Man as Male and Female: A Study in Sexual Relationships from a Theological Point of View* (Grand Rapids: Eerdmans, 1975).

[8]Smedes, *Sex for Christians,* p. 31.

[9]Ibid., pp. 32-33.

[10]C. S. Lewis, *Mere Christianity* (New York: MacMillan, 1952), p. 81. See also *The Four Loves* (New York: Harcourt Brace Jovanovich, 1960).

[11]Smedes, *Sex for Christians* p. 37.

[12]See Lawrence Foster, *Religion and Sexuality: The Shakers, the Mormons, and the Oneida Community* (Urbana: University of Illinois Press, 1981).

[13]Compare the lines of the hymn: "Heaven above is softer blue, earth around is sweeter green. Something lives in every hue Christless eyes have never seen. Birds with gladder songs o'erflow, flowers with deeper beauty shine Since I know, as now I know, I am His and He is mine" (George Wade Robinson, 1938-1977).

[14]For a psychological treatment of this human tendency toward self-deception, see David G. Myers, *The Inflated Self: Human Illusion and the Biblical Call to Hope* (New York: Seabury, 1980).

[15]See for example Letha D. Scanzoni and Virginia R. Mollenkott, *Is the Homosexual My Neighbor?* (New York: Harper and Row, 1980).

[16]Smedes, *Sex for Christians,* pp. 50-51.

[17]Ibid., p. 50.

[18]Since the literature on anomalous sexuality is so complex, it would be irresponsible to make a definitive statement as to a single cause for homosexuality or any other unusual sexual preference. Most likely a number of factors are involved, in varying combinations in various individuals. For a balanced orientation to the literature from an evangelical perspective, see

Stanton L. Jones and Don E. Workman, "Homosexuality: The Behavioral Sciences and the Church," *Journal of Psychology and Theology* 17, no. 3 (Fall 1989):213-225. For a more detailed psychological treatment, see for example Louis Diamant, ed., *Male and Female Homosexuality* (New York: Hemisphere, 1987) or Judd Marmor, ed., *Homosexual Behavior: A Modern Re-appraisal* (New York: Basic Books, 1980).

[19]See the so-called Big Book of the Twelve-Step movement, Alcoholics Anonymous (New York: A. A. World Services, 1978).

[20]On sexual addiction, see especially Patrick Carnes, *Out of the Shadows: Understanding Sexual Addiction* (Minneapolis: CompCare Publishers, 1983). On relationship addictions, see for example Robin Norwood, *Women Who Love Too Much* (Los Angeles: Jeremy Tarcher, 1985). For a more general treatment, see for example Anne Wilson Schaef, *When Society Becomes an Addict* (San Francisco: Harper and Row, 1987). It is noteworthy that even persons from the political left who formerly tended to glorify drug taking as a civil liberty, then to attribute responsibility for any resulting addiction to the pathology of the surrounding society, have begun to join and publicly advocate Twelve-Step movements for recovery. See for example Lilly Collett (pseudonym), "Step By Step: Working to Overcome a Childhood Shadowed by Alcoholism," *Mother Jones* 13, no. 4 (July/August 1988):42-48. See also the responses in 13, no. 8 (October 1988):4, and Roger Wilkins's column "Facing the Holiday Blues" in 13, no. 10 (December 1988):64.

[21]See John Money and Anke A. Ehrhardt, *Man & Woman, Boy & Girl* (Baltimore: Johns Hopkins University Press, 1972), chaps. 4-5. See also John Money, *Gay, Straight, and In Between* (New York: Oxford University Press, 1988).

[22]Elizabeth Moberley, *Psychogenesis: The Early Development of Gender Identity* (London: Routledge and Kegan Paul, 1983).

[23]See Jones and Workman, "Homosexuality," for pertinent references.

[24]C. S. Lewis, *Mere Christianity*, pp. 178-79. For more detailed theological treatment of homosexuality in a compassionate pastoral context, see David Atkinson, *Homosexuals in the Christian Fellowship* (Grand Rapids: Eerdmans, 1979), or John Stott, *Involvement: Social and Sexual Relationships in the Modern World* (Old Tappan, N.J.: Fleming Revell, 1984), chap. 8. See also Smedes, *Sex for Christians*, chap. 3.

[25]Richard J. Mouw, "The Call to Holy Worldliness," *The Reformed Journal* 39, no. 1 (January 1989):8-14. (Quotation from p. 10.) See also "The Life of Bondage in the Light of Grace: An Interview with Richard Mouw," *Christianity Today* 32, no. 18 (December 9, 1988):41-44.

[26]Jones and Workman, "Homosexuality."

[27]See Jessie Bernard, *The Future of Marriage* (New York: World Publishers, 1972).

Chapter Twelve: All Things Made New

[1]Council on Biblical Manhood and Womanhood (P.O. Box 1173, Wheaton, Ill.), "The Danvers Statement," *Christianity Today* 33, no. 1 (January 13, 1989):40-41. A counter to this document, couched in terms of mutual submission rather than male headship, can be found in the statement "Men, Women, and Biblical Equality," issued in 1989 by Christians for Biblical Equality (2830 Lower 138th St., Rosemount, Minn. 55068).

[2]"Danvers Statement," p. 41.

[3]Quoted in *Christianity Today* 33, no. 1 (January 13, 1989):58, in the "North American Scene: Trends" department.

[4]"Danvers Statement," p. 41.

[5]See note 3.

[6]For a helpful historical survey of these debates, see Willard M. Swartley, *Slavery, Sabbath, War, and Women: Case Issues in Biblical Interpretation* (Scottsdale, Pa.: Herald Press, 1983).

[7]There are parallels here to recent feminist theories of cooperative, non-zero-sum work endeavors. See for example Jean Baker Miller, *Towards a New Psychology of Women* (Boston: Beacon Press, 1978) and Anne Wilson Schaef, *Women's Reality: An Emerging Female System in a White Male Society* (San Francisco: Harper and Row, 1981).

[8]Don Williams, *The Apostle Paul and Women in the Church* (Van Nuys, Calif.: BIM Publishing Co., 1977), p. 70.

[9]Swartley, *Slavery, Sabbath, War, and Women*, p. 21.

[10]Andrew Walls, "Culture and Conversion," public lecture delivered at Calvin College, March 1989.

[11]Swartley, *Slavery, Sabbath, War, and Women*, pp. 188-89.

[12]Albert Taylor Bledsoe, "Liberty and Slavery, or Slavery in the Light of Moral and Political Philosophy," E. W. Elliott, ed., *Cotton Is King* (New York: Negro Universities Press, 1969; originally published 1860), pp. 379-80. Quoted in Swartley, *Slavery, Sabbath, War, and Women*, p. 49.

[13]Ibid.

[14]Charles Hodge, "The Biblical Argument on Slavery," in Elliott, *Cotton Is King*, p. 863. Quoted in Swartley, *Slavery*, p. 49.

[15]Cornelius Plantinga, "Partnership in the Gospel: Some Observations," lecture given at the Partnership in the Gospel Conference of the Committee for Women in the Christian Reformed Church, Grand Rapids, Michigan, November 1988, pp. 18-19.

[16]See for example the Report of the Committee on Headship, *Acts of Synod of the Christian Reformed Church* (Grand Rapids: Christian Reformed Church Publications, 1984).

[17]Janette Hassey, *No Time for Silence: Evangelical Women in Public Ministry around the Turn of the Century* (Grand Rapids: Zondervan, 1986), p. 123. Two

more personal accounts of the declining acceptance of women's ministries, as well as the inconsistencies between subordinationists' theology and actual practice, can be found in Gretchen Gaebelein Hull, *Equal to Serve: Women and Men in the Church and Home* (Old Tappan, N.J.: Fleming H. Revell, 1987) and Faith Martin, *Call Me Blessed: The Emerging Christian Woman* (Grand Rapids: Eerdmans, 1988). The arguments of these older women are given even more force by the fact that both spent many years sincerely believing and trying to live up to the theology of male headship practiced in their churches, only concluding after years of observation and Bible study that both subordinationist exegesis and practice were inconsistent.

[18]For example, Francis Schaeffer, *Genesis in Space and Time* (Downers Grove, Ill.: InterVarsity Press, 1972), pp. 93-94. On violent tendencies of men see Perry Treadwell, "Biologic Influences on Masculinity."

[19]"Danvers Statement," p. 41.

[20]Swartley, *Slavery*, pp. 185-186.

[21]Hull, *Equal to Serve*, p. 240.

[22]Ibid., p. 241.

Index